THE

SIXTH AND SEVENTH

BOOKS OF MOSES

MOSES' MAGICAL SPIRIT-ART

KNOWN AS THE

WONDERFUL ARTS

OF THE OLD WISE HEBREWS, TAKEN FROM THE MOSAIC BOOKS
OF THE CABALA AND THE TALMUD. FOR THE
GOOD OF MANKIND.

———————

*Translated from the German, Word for Word, according to Old
Writings.*

———————

WITH NUMEROUS ENGRAVINGS.

———————

The 6th and 7th Books of Moses

ISBN 978-1-58509-508-7

© 1999

THE BOOK TREE

All Rights Reserved

INTRODUCTION

It is hard to determine when these magical books were first written, but we do know that they were translated from the ancient Hebrew.

The *Sixth Book of Moses* is also known as *Moses' Magical Spirit-Art,* and is composed of a number of "Secret Seals" used in magical rituals. Each seal is presented and described, followed by a conjuration meant to be used with it. The conjuration is a verbal spell summoning entities or energies beyond our reality that may in fact respond and help to achieve the goal of the summoner.

The *Seventh Book of Moses* consists of a number of magical tables, each of which is meant to perform a certain function. Instructions such as carrying the table with you or bringing it to a certain area is supposed to bring results like wealth, love, or good luck. Also tacked on to the *Seventh Book* is a larger section called "The Magic of the Israelites." This contains a wealth of information, including many scriptural instances of magic being performed in the Bible.

Following this section is "Volume Two: Formulas of the Magical Kabala", with additional seals and magical instructions. This section takes up more than half the book and reveals secret Kabalistic wisdom, the application of charms and remedies, hidden wisdom of the Psalms, astrological influences upon man, and magical cures of the old Hebrews.

Although this book has been attributed to Moses and is a rather old work, it's not likely that Moses wrote it. Even so, it is a powerful book of magical spells that should not be taken lightly. Use of this book should be done with caution and respect for what it contains. Its claim is that, if used properly, the book will bring good fortune to those who proceed with good intentions.

Paul Tice

Preface.

THE first edition of this volume has been commended and criticised by the public. It was admitted to be a valuable compendium of the curiosities of literature generally, and especially of that pertaining to magic, but that it was at the same time calculated to foster superstition, and thereby promote evil—a repetition of the charge made against the honorable HORST, the publisher of a magical library.

In our enlightened age, the unprejudiced will observe in the publication of such a work, only what the author claims, namely, a contribution in reference to the aforesaid literature and culture of no trifling merit; but in regard to the believer also, the issue of a cheap edition will be more serviceable than the formerly expensive productions on sorcery, which were only circulated in abstract forms and sold at extortionate rates. What other practical value the above named edition may possess is not the question. Let us not, therefore, underrate this branch of popular literature; the authors wrote in accordance with a system which was, or at least, seemed clear to them, and illustrious persons, in all ages and climes have not considered the labor requisite to fathom the mysteries of magic as labor expended in vain, and although they condemned the form, they could not deny the possibility or even fact that gifted men, of inherent worth, could accomplish such wonderful things.

In regard to the present edition it can only be said, that the so-called Sixth and Seventh Books of Moses, which have for several centuries attracted the popular faith, is reality in accordance with an old manuscript (the most legible among many), and given word for word, divested only of orthographical errors which the best interest of literature demand—with unerring fidelity. The publisher guarantees that not one syllable has been added.

THE

Sixth Book of Moses.

MOSES' MAGICAL SPIRIT-ART.

Translated from the Ancient Hebrew.

MAGIA ALBA ET NIGRA UNIVERSALIS SEU NECROMANTIA ;

That is, that which embraces the whole of the White and Black Art, (Black Magic,) or the Necromancy of all Ministering Angels and Spirits; how to cite and desire the IX. Chori of the good angels and spirits, Saturn, Jupiter, Mars, Sun, Venus, Mercury, and Moon.

The most serviceable angels are the following:

SALATHEEL, MICHAEL, RAPHAEL, URIEL,

together with the Necromancy of the black magic of the best Ministering Spirits in the Chymia et Alchymia of Moses and Aaron.

That which was hidden from David, the father of Solomon, by the High Priest

SADOCK,

as the highest mystery, but which was finally found in the year CCCXXX., among others, by the first Christian Emperor Constantine the Great, and sent to Pope Sylvester at Rome, after its translation under Julius II. Pontifice max. Typis manabilis sub pœna excommunicationis de numquam publica imprimendis sent to the Emperor Charles V., and highly recommended in the year MDXX., approved by Julii II. P. M. Cme. duos libros quos Mosis condidit arter antistis summus sedalitate SADOCK. Libri hi colorum sacra sunt vota sequenter spiritus omnipotens qui uigil illa facit at est sumis pia necessaria. Fides.

Instruction.

These two Books were revealed by God, the Almighty, to his faithful servant Moses, on Mount Sinai, intervale lucis, and in this manner they also came into the hands of Aaron, Caleb, Joshua, and finally to David and his son Solomon and their high priest Sadock. Therefore, they are Bibliis arcanum arcanorum, which means, Mystery of all Mysteries.

The Conversation of God.

Adonai, Sother, Emanuel, Ehic, Tetragramaton, Ayscher, Jehova, Zebaoth, the Lord of Hosts, of Heaven and Earth; that which appertains to the Sixth and Seventh Book of Moses, as follows:

Adonai, E El, Zeboath, Jebaouha, Jehovah, E El, Chad, Tetragramaton Chaddai, Channaniah, al Elyon, Chaye, Ayscher, Adoyah Zawah, Tetragramaton, Awiel, Adoyah, Chay, Yechal, Kanus, Emmet, thus spake the Lord of Hosts to me Moses.

Eheye, Ayscher, Jehel, Yazliah, Elion. Sum qui sum ab æterno in æternum, thou my servant Moses, open thou thine ears, hear the voice of thy God. Through me Jehovah, Aglai, the God of heaven and earth, thy race shall be multiplied and shall shine as the stars of heaven. In addition to this I will also give thee might, power and wisdom, to rule over the spirits of heaven and hell.

Over the ministering angels and spirits of the fourth element as well as of the seven planets. Hear also the voice of thy God wherewith I give thee the seven seals and twelve tables. Schem, Schel, Hamforach, that the angels and spirits may always yield obedient service to thee, when thou callest upon them and citest them by these seven seals and twelve tables of my omnipotence; and hereunto thou shalt also have herewith a knowledge of the highest mysteries.

Therefore, thou, my faithful friend, dear Moses, take thou the power and high might of thy God.

Aclon, Ysheye, Channanyah, Yeschayah, E El, Elijon, Rachmiel, Ariel, Eheye, Ayscher, Eheye, Elyon. Through my Seals and Tables.

THE FIRST MYSTERY.

Sigillum Chori Servilium Archangelorum of the Ministering Archangel.

CONJURATION.

I, N. N., a servant of God, desire, call upon the OCH, and conjure thee through water † fire, air and earth, and everything that lives and moves therein, and by the most holy names of God, Agios, Tehirios, Perailitus, Alpha et Omega, Beginning and End, God and Man-Sabaoth, Adanai, Agla, Tetragramaton, Emanuel, Abua, Ceus, Elioa, Torna, Deus Salvator, Aramma, Messias, Clerob, Michael, Abreil, Achleof, Gachenas et Peraim, Eei Patris et Peraim Eei fiiii, et Peraim Dei spiritus Teti, and the words by which Solomon and Manasses, Cripinus and Agrippa conjured the spirits, and by whatever else thou mayest be conquered, that you will yield obedience to me, N. N. the same as Isaac did to Abraham, and appear before me. N. N. this instant, in the beautiful, mild, human form of a youth, and bring what I desire. (This the conjuror must name.)

Fig. 2

The Seal.

(Fig. 2.)

The most useful ministering arch angels of this seal are the following with their Hebrew verbis revelatis Citatiori divinitus coactivis: Uriel, Arael, Zacharael, Gabriel, Raphael, Theoska, Zywolech, Hemohon, Yhahel, Tuwahel, Donahan, Sywaro, Samohayl, Zowanus, Ruweno. Ymoeloh, Hahowel, Tywael.

THE MYSTERY OF ALL MYSTERIES.

The particularly great secret and special use of this seal is also ex Bible, arcan. Thoro. I. If this Seal is buried in the earth, where treasures exist, they will come to the surface of themselves, without any presence in plane lunio.

THE SECOND MYSTERY OF THE SEAL.

The Name is True.

Seal of the Choir of Hosts seu Dominatorium of the Ministering Angels

CONJURATION.

I, N. N., a servant of God, desire, call upon and conjure thee, Spirit Phuel, by the Holy Messengers and all the Disciples of the Lord, by the four Holy Evangelists and the three Holy Men of God and by the most terrible and most holy words Abriel, Fibriel, Zada, Zaday, Zarabo, Laragola, Lavaterium, Laroyol, Zay, Zagin, Labir, Lya, Adeo, Deus, Alon, Abay, Alos, Pieus, Ehos, Mibi, Uini, Mora, Zorad, and by those holy words, that thou come and appear before me, N. N., in a beautiful human form, and bring me what I desire. (This the conjuror must name.)

The Seal.

(Fig. 3.)

This Seal from the Choir of the Dominationen, or Hosts, the following are the most useful: Aha, Roah, Habu, Aromicha, Lemar, Patteny, Hamaya, Azoth, Hayozer, Karohel, Wezynna, Patecha, Tehom.

The special secret of this Seal is the following ex Thoro Bibliis arcanorum, Sacra Script.

If a man carries this Seal with him, it will bring him great fortune and blessing; it is therefore called the truest and highest Seal of Fortune.

THE MYSTERY OF THE THIRD SEAL.

Seal of the Ministering Throne Angels ex Thoro III. Bibliis Arcanorum.

CONJURATION.

I, N. N., a servant of God, desire, call upon thee, and conjure thee Tehor, by all the Holy Angels and Arch Angels, by the holy Michael, the holy Gabriel, Raphael, Uriel, Thronus, Dominationes principalis, virtutes, Cherubim et Seraphim, and with unceasing voice I cry, Holy, Holy, Holy, is the Lord God of Sabaoth, and by the most terrible words: Soab, Sother, Emmanuel, Hdon, Amathon, Mathay, Adonai, Eel, Eli, Eloy, Zoag, Dios, Anath, Tafa, Uabo, Tetragramaton, Aglay, Josua, Jonas, Calpie, Calphas. Appear before me, N. N., in a mild and human form, and do what I desire. (This the conjuror must name.)

The Seal.

(Fig. 4.)

The ministering Throne Angels of this Seal are the following; Tehom Aaseha, Amarzyom, Schawayt, Chuscha, Zawar, Yahel. La hehor. Adoyahel, Schimuel Achusaton, Schaddyl, Chamyel, Parymel, Chayo. The special secret of this Throne is also ex Thoro III. Bibliis arcanorum script. Carrying this Seal with you will cause you to be very agreeable and much beloved, and will also defeat all your enemies.

THE FOURTH SEAL OF THE MINISTERING

Cherubim and Seraphim with their Characteristics.

CONJURATION.

I, N. N., a servant of God, call upon thee, desire and conjure thee, O Spirit Anoch, by the wisdom of Solomon, by the obedience of Isaac, by the blessing of Abraham, by the piety of Jacob and Noe, who did not sin before God, by the serpents of Moses, and by the twelve tribes, and by the most terrible words: Dallia, Dollia, Dollion, Corfuselas, Jazy, Agzy,

Ahub, Tilli, Stago, Adoth, Suna, Eoluth, Alos, Jaoth, Dilu, and by all the words through which thou canst be compelled to appear before me in a beautiful, human form, and give what I desire. (This the conjuror must name.)

The Seal

(Fig. 5.)

The most obliging ministering Cherubim and Seraphim of this Seal, are the following with their Hebrew calling: Anoch, Sewachar, Chaylon, Esor, Yaron, Oseny, Yagelor, Ehym, Maakyel, Echad, Yalyon, Yagar, Ragat, Ymmat, Chabalym, Schadym.

The special secret of this Seal is the following Thora IVta. Biblii arcan. To carry this Seal upon the body will save a person from all misery, and give the greatest fortune and long life.

The Fifth Seal.

Seal of the Angels of Power.

CONJURATION.

I, N. N., a servant of God, call upon thee, desire and conjure thee, Spirit Scheol, through the most holy appearance in the flesh of Jesus Christ, by his most holy birth and circumcision, by his sweating of blood in the Garden, by the lashes he bore, by his bitter sufferings and death, by his Resurrection, Ascension and the sending of the Holy Spirit as a comforter, and by the most dreadful words: Dai, Deorum, Ellas, genio Sophiel, Zophiel, Canoel, Elmiach, Richol, Hoamiach, Jerazol, Vohal,

Daniel, Hasios, Tomaiach, Sannul, Damamiach, Sanul, Damabiath, and by those words through which thou canst be conquered, that thou appear before me in a beautiful, human form, and fulfil what I desire. (This must be named by the conjuror.)

The Fifth Seal.

(Fig. 6.)

The most serviceable Power-Angels with their verbis heraicis sitatiores divinis ex Thora Vta. ser. are the following :·

Schoel, Hael, Sephiroth, Thamy, Schamayl, Yeehah, Holyl, Yomelo, Hadlam, Mazbaz, Elohaym.

The special secret of this Seal is the following ex Thoro V. D. B. A. If this Seal be laid upon the sick in full, true faith, it will restore him, if, N. B., he has not lived the full number of his days. Therefore, it is called the Seal of Power.

THE SIXTH MYSTERY.

The Seal of the Power-Angels seu Potestatum ex Thoro VI. Biblis arcanorum, over the Angels and Spirits of all the Elements.

CONJURATION.

I, N. N., a servant of God, desire, call upon and conjure thee, Spirit Alymon, by the most dreadful words, Sather, Ehomo, Geno, Poro, Jehovah, Elohim, Volnah, Denach, Alonlam, Ophiel, Zophiel, Sophiel, Hariel, Eloha, Alesimus, Dileth, Melohim, and by all the holiest words through which thou canst be conquered, that thou appear before me in a mild, beautiful human form, and fulfil what I command thee, so surely as God will come to judge the living and dead. Fiat, Fiat, Fiat.

Fig 5

The Seal.

(Fig. 7.)

The most obedient Angels of Power, seu Potestates, with their Citati-oriis Divinlis verbis hebraicis, are the following four elements: Schunmyel, Alymon, Mupíel, Symnay, Semanglaf, Taftyah, Melech, Seolam, Waed, Sezah, Safyn, Kyptip, Taftyarohel, Aeburatiel, Anyam, Bymnam. This is the mystery or Seal of the Might-Angels. The peculiar Arcanum of this Seal of the Mighty is the following: ex Thoro VIta Arcanorum sacra scriptura. If a man wears this Seal in bed, he will learn what he desires to know through dreams and visions.

THE SEVENTH SECRET SEAL.

Of the Most Obedient Angels, Cœli Cœlorum Legionum over the Angels of the Seven Planets and Spirits.

CONJURATION.

I, N. N., a servant of God, call upon, desire and conjure thee, Ahael, Banech, by the most holy words Agios, (Tetr.,) Eschiros, Adonai, Alpha et Omega, Raphael, Michael, Uriel, Schmaradiel, Zaday, and by all the known names of Almighty God, by whatsoever thou, Ahael, canst be compelled, that thou appear before me, in a human form, and fulfil what I desire. Fiat, Fiat, Fiat. (This must be named by the conjuror.)

The Seal.

(Fig. 8.)

The most obedient Angels and Spirits of this Seal of the Seven Plane'
are the following: Ahaeb, Baneh, Yeschnath, Hoschiah, Betodah, Le)
kof, Yamdus, Zarenar, Sahon.

This Seal, when laid upon the treasure earth, or when placed within
the works of a mine, will reveal all the precious contents of the mine. A:
the VII. Arcanorum

END OF THE SIXTH BOOK OF MOSES.

THE

Seventh Book of Moses

Fig. 9

RAB CALEB. DOCTOR. ORIENTAL.

TRANSLATED BY

RABBI CHALEB.

From the Weimar Bible

The First Table of the Spirits of the Air.
(See Fig. 10.)

Jehovah Father	Deus Schadday
Deus Adonay Elohe I cite Thee through Jehovah	Eead I conjure thee through Adonay

To carry upon the person the First Table of the Spirits of the Air who are as quick to help as thought, will relieve the wearer from all necessity.

The Second Table of the Spirits of Fire.
(See Fig. 11.)

Aha I conjure Thee (Tetr,) Aha by
Eheye * by Ihros, Eheye, by Agla
Aysch, Jehovah,
conjure I Thee,
that thou appear unto me.

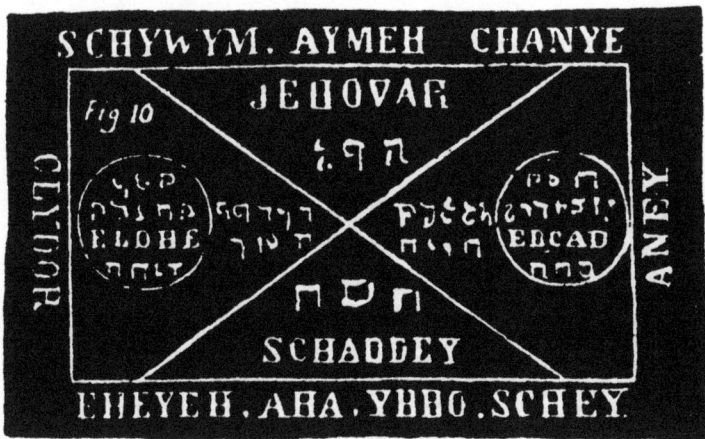

Fig 10

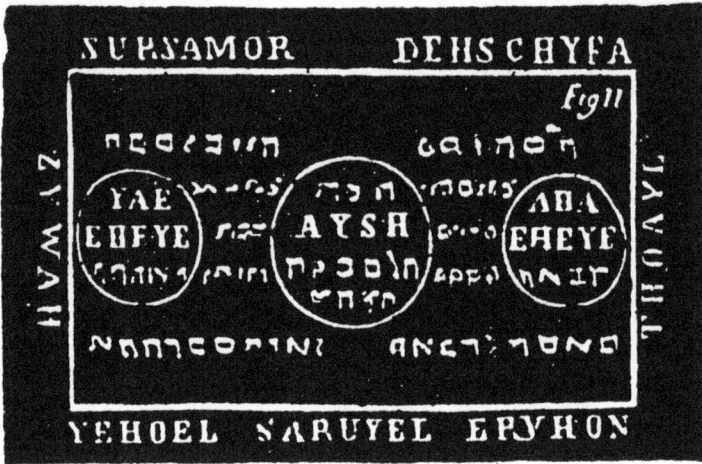

The Third Table of the Spirits of the Water.
(See Fig. 12.)

I call upon and command Thee Chananya by God Tetragramaton Eloh

I conjure Thee Yeschaijah by Alpha et Omega

and thou art compelled through Adonai.

The Third Table brings great fortune by water, and its spirits will amply supply the treasures of the deep.

The Fourth Table of the Spirits of the Earth.

(See Fig. 13.)

I, N. N., command Thee, Awijel, by Otheos as also by Elmez through Agios.	I, N. N., a servant of God, conjure Thee, Ahenatos Elijon, as also Adon was cited and called Zebaoth.

This Fourth Table will give the treasures of the earth, if it be laid in the earth. Its spirits will give the treasures of earth at all times.

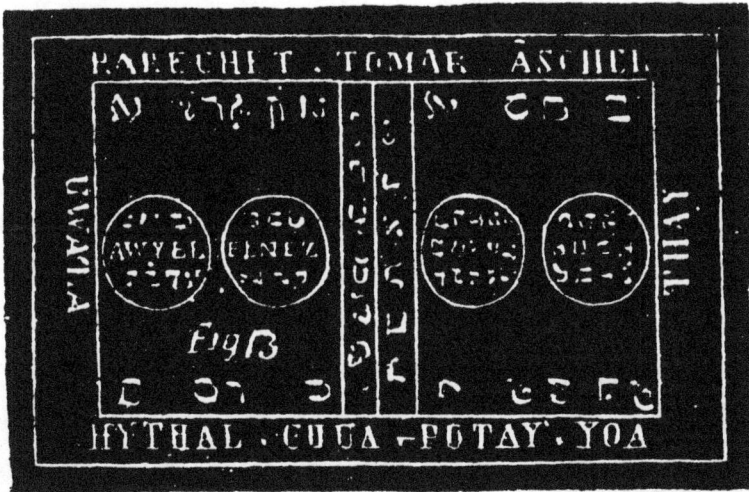

Fig 13.

The Fifth Table of Saturn.

(See Fig. 14.)

I, N. N., order, command and conjure Thee Sazlij, by Agios, Scdul, by Sother, Veduij, by Sabaot, Sove, Amonzion * Adoij by Heloim, Jaho, by the Veritas Jehovah * Kawa, Alha, natos that ye must appear before me in a human form, so truly as Daniel overcame and conquered Baal. F. f. f.

The Spirits of the Fifth Table of Saturn will serve in everything according to wish; their Table will bring good luck in play.

The Sixth Table of Jupiter.

(See Fig. 15.)

I conjure thee, Spirit Ofel, by Alpha et Omega, Lezo and Yschirios * Ohin Ission * Niva, by Tetragramaton, Zeno, by Peraclitus * Ohel, by Orlenius, Lima, by Agla, * that ye will obey and appear before me and fulfil my desire, thus in and through the name Elion, which Moses named. F. f. f.

The Sixth Table of Jupiter assists in overcoming suits at law, dispute, and at play, and their spirits are at all times ready to render assistance.

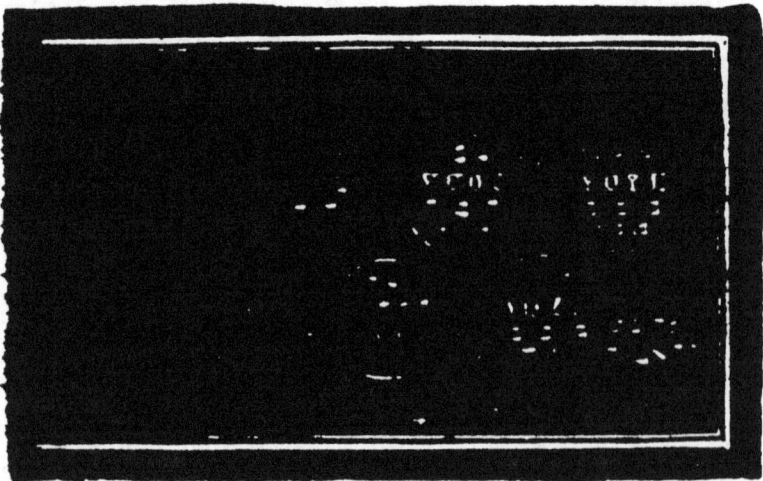

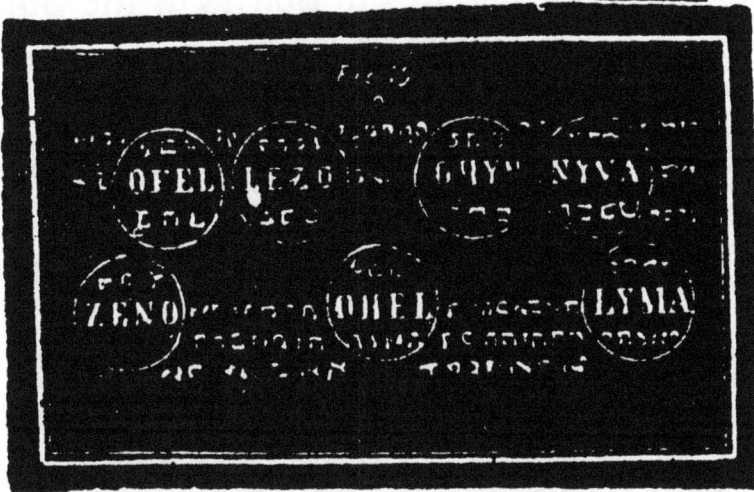

The Seventh Table of the Spirits of Mars.

(See Fig. 16.)

I; N. N., cite Thee, Spirit Emol, by Deus Sachnaton * Luil, by Acumea * Luiji, by Ambriel * Tijlaij, by Ehos * by Jeha, by Zora * Ageh, by Awoth * that you appear before me in a beautiful, human form, and accomplish my desire, thus truly in and through the anepobeijaron, which Aaron heard and which was prepared for him. F. f. f.

The Seventh Seal of Mars brings good fortune in case of quarrels. The Spirits of Mars will help you.

The Eighth Table of the Spirits of the Sun.

(See Fig. 17.)

I, N. N., conjure Thee, Wrjch by Dalia † Jka, by Doluth, * Auet, by Dilu * Veal by Λιub † Meho, by Igfa * Ymij by Eloïj * that Ye appear before Liy s) true Zebaoth, who was named by Moses, and all the rivers in Egypt were turned into blood.

The Eighth Table of the Spirits of the Sun will help to attain places of honor, wealth, and they also give gold and treasure.

The Ninth Table of the Spirits of Venus.

(See Fig. 18.)

Reta, Kijmah, Yamb, Yheloruvesopijhacl, I call upon thee, Spirit Awel, through God Tetragramaton, Uhal, by Pomamiach † that you will obey my commands and fulfil my desires: Thus truly in and through the name of Esercheije, which Moses named, and upon which followed hail, the like of which was not known since the beginning of the world, f. f. f.

The Ninth Table of the Spirits of Venus makes one beloved in all respects and makes known secrets through dreams. Its spirits also assist liberally in all kinds of business.

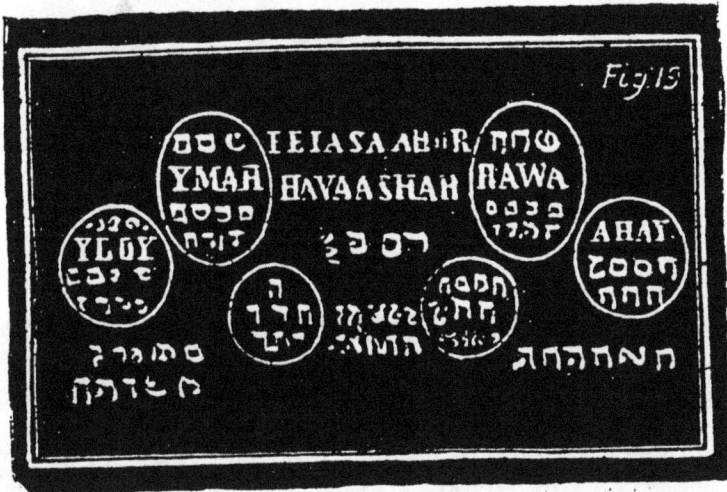

Fig 18

The Tenth Table of the Spirits of Mercury.

(See Fig. 19.)

Petasa, Ahor, Havaashar. N. N. cite Thee Spirit Yloij * through God, God Adonaij † Ymah, through God Tetragrammaton † Rawa, through God Emanuel * Ahaij, through Athanatos † that Thou appear before as truly in and through the name of Adonai, which Moses mentioned, and there appeared grasshoppers.

Fiat, fiat, fiat.

The Tenth Table of the Spirits of Mercury give wealth in chemistry. These spirits contribute treasures of the mine.

Fig. 20

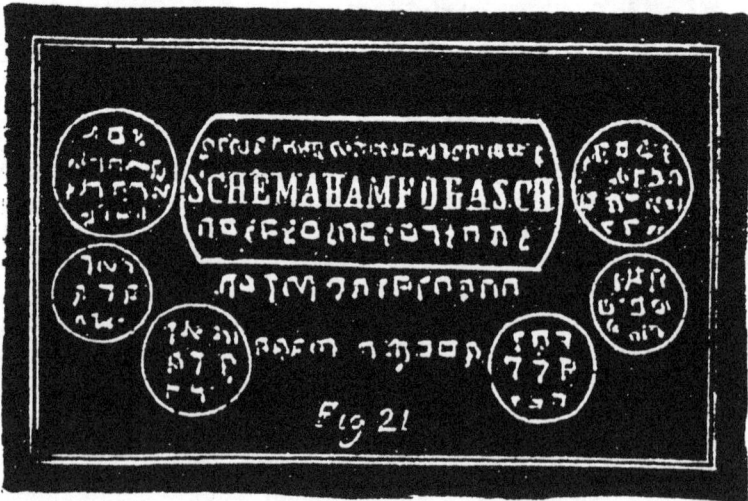

Fig 21

The Eleventh Table of Spirits,

(See Fig. 20.)

I, N. N., cite thee, Spirit Yhaij, by El, Yvaij, by Elohim, Ileh,
by Elho * Kijlij, by Zebaoth, Taijn Iseij, by Tetragramaton, Jeha,
by Zadaij * Ahel, by Agla, that you will obey my orders, as truly
in and through the name Sehemesumatie, upon which Joshua
called, and the sun stood still in its course. Fiat, f. f. f.

The Eleventh Table (See Fig. 20) gives luck and fortune; its Spirits
give the treasures of the sea.

The Twelfth Table of Schemhamforasch,

On all Spirits of the Magia Alba et Nigra.

(See Fig. 21.)

I, N. N., cite and conjure thee, Spirit of Schemhamforasch, by
all the seventy-two holy names of God, that Thou appear before
me and fulfil my desire, as truly in and through the name Emanuel,
which the three youths Sadrach, Mijsach, and Abed-negro sung in
the fiery furnace from which they were released. F. f. f.

This Twelfth Table, laid upon the Table or Seal of the Spirits, will
compel them to appear immediately, and to serve in all things.

The General Citation.

NECROMANTIA, SEU MAGIA ALBA ET NIGRA TRANSLATED EX THORA
XXTA BIBL. ARCAN.

Aba, Jehovah, Agla, Aschaij, Chad, Yah, Saddaij, Vedreh, Aschre,
Noosedu, Zawa, Agla. Here utter the names of the Angels of the Seal
or Table, and their proper names.

Eheije, Aijscher, Eneije, Weatta, Eloheij, Harenij, Yechuateche, Hag-
edola, Merof, Zaroteij, Agla, Pedenij, Zije, Kotecha, Barach, Amijm,
Gedolijm, Verachena, Aleij, Weijazijloti, Mijkol, Zara, Umikol, Ra,
Schadaij, Jehovah, Adonai, Zeboath, Zah, Elohim, Yeasch, Jepfila, Valj,
Bearechet, Vaij, Yomar, Ahaha, Elohim, Ascher, Hithalleij, Chuabotheij,
Lepha, Vaij, Yehuel.

Here stop for a short time in prayer to God. Surrender yourself into
the will of Almighty God; He will conduct your undertaking to your
best interest. Hereupon take again the Seal or the Table written on
parchment, in your hand, and begin anew the citation above. Should
your desire still remain unfulfilled, continue as follows:

Hamneijs, Hakha, Elohim, Horro, Heotij, Meo, Dij, Adhaijijon, Hasse,
Hamalach, Haggo, Elohij, Mijcol, Rhab, Yeba, Rech, Elhaneah, Tijmneik,
Fj, Rebe, Hem, Sohemne, Schembotaij, Veischak, Vegid, Gulaooc,
Kered, Haarez, Jeha. Since the effects and appearances will now fol-
low, your wishes are fulfilled, otherwise repeat the Citation toties quoties.

The Magical Operation is made within this Circle.

(See Fig. 22.)

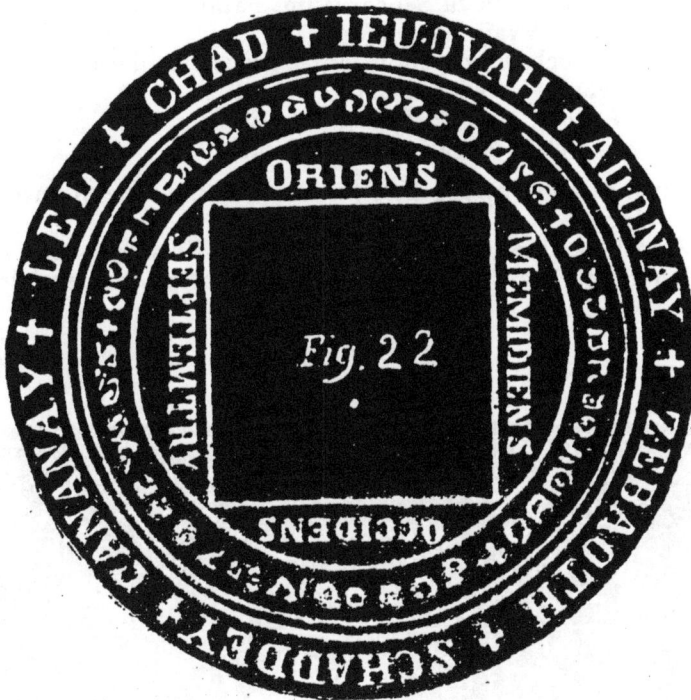

Fig. 22

The Ministering Formulas or Mysteries

ARE THE FOLLOWING:

Astarte, Salamonis familiarum III. Eegum.
Spirit of Water; Spirit of Air; Spirit of Earth.
Astoreth in Palestina familiari.
Schaddaij, Driffon, Agrippa, Magaripp.
Azijelzm, Sinna, familiarus, IV. Buch Regum.
Schijwin * Aimeh, Chanije, Cijbor.
Bealherith ijud Judicum IX. XIII.
Adola, Eloheij, Umijchob Channanijah.
Adramelech zu Sepharvaijm, Familiaris.
Yhaij, Vvaij, Yles, Kijgij.
Nisroch, Regis Serucheril Assijris familiaris.
Jehuel, Sarwiel, Urikon, Thoijil.
Asijma, virorum Emach familiaris.
Barechel, Jomar, Ascher, Uwula.

These must be cited by the Twelfth Table at the time of an Eclipse by the Sun or Moon.

This Moloch familiarum or Ammonitarium Ministering Spirits the following Generation-Seal for all services caracteristico obedientiale.

(See Fig. 23.)

This Seal, at the time of Citation, must be written on parchment and be held in the right hand. But it must not be read.

END OF THE SEVENTH BOOK OF MOSES.

PART I.

THE MAGIC OF THE ISRAELITES.

THE complete and reliable history of the human and divine—the divine revelations, and the influence of godly or pious men are found in the Scriptural monuments of the old Hebrews in the Holy Scriptures.

The Bible is justly styled the Holy Scripture, because it contains the knowledge of the saints, while at the same time, it unites and harmonizes word and deed, doctrine and action. It points out the true relation of man to the Omnipotent—it affords the most direct reference to the great truths of the spiritual and intellectual; it treats of the origin of the universe and its laws, through which all things have to be brought to light—of the anterior and posterior history of mankind—of his future destiny and how to attain it; of the living and visible agents which God employs in the great work of redemption, and, finally, of the most exalted of all beings—of the world's Saviour, who was an univ rsal expression in his own person, and who exhibited all divine power and action in one person, while all his forerunners were endowed only with single powers and perfections; who revealed to fallen man the highest and purest ends of his life and the means of his purification and restoration.

We find among oriental nations every grade of Magic—the steps necessary to solve the mysteries of somnambulism and second-sight, and the infinitely multiplied operations by which unusual occurrences are produced; in like manner we also find these things among the Israelites, but differing totally in character. In the former instance, it was the individual and his presence; in the latter, it was not the individual upon which magic depended, but upon mankind in general, and upon the great future. There, the light of man was made to shine by skilful actions, produced by the lowest arts; here, shone a pure, unclouded, quiet life, vitalized by the warm breath of the Almighty, a light shining into the future, and upon this light depended all life and action. To the Israelite seer not only the fate of single individuals stand revealed, but the fate of nations, yea, of mankind, which in the end must be reconciled to God by the unfolding of magical art, as often happened under the old dispensation, by instinctive somnambulistic influences. If we examine the history of the old covenant we shall find that this remarkable people stood solitary and alone like a pillar of fire amid heathen darkness.

Although we find, among other nations, worthy men, who seek after the divine light, surrounded by darkness and uncertainty, here are men of God, bearing the impress of true faith, who give undoubted evidence of higher powers, by visible acts and signs which everywhere separate life from death, and truth from error, and while the ancient remnants of other nations show only theory without application, here we find a connected chain of acts and events—in fact, a divine and lifelike drama. Of all these things the various books of the Holy Scriptures speak with confidence, so that the history of no other people, interwoven with fables, can be compared with them. According to this, the Bible contains the light which illuminates every dark phase in life; it is the ground-work of all human actions, the guiding-star of the earthly to the eternal—of the intellectual to the divine, the aim and end of all knowledge. It is the first of three great lights, guiding and governing our faith, and bears no relation to the other two great lights of the angle which shall make these actions lawful, or the circle which sensualizes the fixed limits of the condition of mankind. The Bible is also more instructive and richer in reference to our subject than all other books taken together. We will, therefore, cite a few principal points, as well of the phenomena as of the mode of action and theory relating to magnetism, and then call attention especially to the healing of the sick according to scriptural teachings. We will give an account of the dreams, a great many of which are recorded in the Bible.

The dreams recorded in the Bible are many and remarkable. The voice with which God spoke to the prophets and the men consecrated to Him, were generally heard in dreams.

The visions of the ancients, according to the testimony of Moses, were nearly always dreams. Numbers xii. 6: "And he said: Hear now my words: If there be a prophet among you, I, the Lord, will make myself known unto him in a vision, and will speak unto him in a dream." Job xxxiii. 15: "In a dream, in a vision of the night, when deep sleep falleth upon men, in slumberings upon the bed; then he openeth the ears of men, and sealeth their instruction." 1 Kings iii. 5: "In Gibeon the Lord appeared to Solomon in a dream by night: and God said, Ask what I shall give thee. And Solomon said, Thou hast showed unto thy servant David my father great mercy, according as he walked before thee in truth, and in righteousness, and in uprightness of heart with thee; and thou hast kept for him this great kindness, etc., give therefore thy servant an understanding heart to judge thy people, that I may discern between good and bad: for who is able to judge this thy so great a people?" Genesis xx. 3: "But God came to Abimelech in a dream by night, and said to him, Behold, thou art but a dead man, for the woman thou hast taken; for she is a man's wife; and God said unto him in a dream, Yea, I know that thou didst this in the integrity of thy heart; for I also withheld thee from sinning against me." Genesis xxxi. 23: "And God came to Laban the Syrian in a dream by night, and said unto him, Take heed that thou speak not to Jacob either good or bad." The dreams of Joseph concerning his brethren are also remarkable. Genesis xxxvii. 5: "And Joseph dreamed a dream, and he told it to his brethren: and they hated him yet the more: and he said unto them, Hear, I pray you, this dream, which I have dreamed: For behold, we were binding sheaves in the field, and lo, my sheaf arose, and also stood upright: and behold, your sheaves stood round about, and made obeisance to my sheaf. And his brethren said to him, Shalt thou indeed reign over us? or shalt thou indeed have dominion over us?" And he had still another dream, and he told it to his brethren and said: Behold, I have dreamed a dream more: and behold, the sun and the moon and the stars made obeisance to me. And his father rebuked him, and said unto him, What is this dream that thou hast dreamed? Shall I and thy mother and thy brethren indeed come to bow down ourselves to thee on the earth?"

Sacred history proves that after Joseph was sold by his brethren to the Egyptian traders that he actually became their king in the court of Pharaoh. The power of Joseph to interpret dreams is further shown by the interpretation of the dreams of the butler and baker while in prison, Genesis i. 40; so, also, of the dreams of king Pharaoh, of the seven fat and lean kine which came out of the water, and of the seven rank and good ears of corn and the seven thin and blasted ears, Genesis xli. 1. In the New Testament many dreams are mentioned through which God designed to speak to his followers. In this manner Joseph, the husband of Mary, was told by an angel (Matthew i. 20), that she should conceive of the Holy Ghost and bear a son, who would become the Saviour of the world; and then again, that he should take the child and flee into Egypt to escape the murderous intent of Herod; and after the death of Herod, that he should again return to Nazareth (Matthew ii. 13–19). In like manner, the three wise men of the East were warned in a dream, that they should not return to Herod, but depart to their own country another way. The Apostles frequently had visions in the night; for example, Paul was commanded to go to Macedonia (Acts x. 9). And in the same book of the New Testament (xviii. 9), we read: "Then spake the Lord to Paul in the night by a vision. Be not afraid, but speak, and hold not thy peace." Many similar passages might be quoted, e. g., xxiii. 11; xxvii. 23, etc., etc.

Let us begin with the history of the creation, as recorded by Moses. "In the beginning God created heaven and earth."

Herein lies the great first cause. God is an uncreated being—heaven and earth are the first things created; the antithesis: that which was made of God. In reference to a second antithesis, Moses speaks of light and darkness: "And darkness was upon the face of the earth, and God said, Let there be light, and there was light." Here, too, the question is about light as a creation, which, however, had for its opposite darkness; therefore did the old Egytians regard darkness as the beginning of all things. Even according to the writings of Moses, this was the Egyptian doctrine, for he says, "Darkness was upon the face of the deep." But as the Egyptian doctrine in its first inception may be regarded as good authority, their error originated in this, that they accepted the darkness before the light; as also a like error of the Persians, inasmuch that they accepted the light before the darkness as being created, the one before the other. The light stands beside darkness as its natural opposite, created and present, as Moses plainly says: "And God divided the light from the darkness, and God called the light day, and the darkness he called night." The Bible also points out another antithesis in the first germs and figures of the earth, namely, water and spirit—the water as matter, as the germ of the figurative, and the spirit, the Elohim, as the fruitful, active principle. "And the spirit of God moved upon the face of the waters." One-sided views led the earlier philosophers into numerous error: In this manner Thales brought everything out of the water and overlooked the spiritual active whole, in all of which he was imitated by subsequent champions of Materialism. The other one-sided view is, to hold everything as spiritual and regard matter only as an inert abstraction (caput mortuum), which was the case from the earliest period of time among Spiritualists and the advocates of Spiritualism. Moses, therefore, shows his superiority over all the disciples of Egyptian temple-wisdom, as well as of the more modern sects, inasmuch that he was enlightened by divine wisdom, and represented this subject, not in a partial manner, but in its true bearing and significance; he ascribed to matter its true worth and placed the spiritual beside it. Moreover, Moses has given the narrative of the creation in beautiful and captivating language, as for example, in regard to the waters—the difference between the wet and the dry, and how the dry land came forth from the water; how the grass and herbs, which bore seeds, and fruitful trees grew upon the earth; how the mighty deep was filled with living and moving animals, and the birds that fly in the firmament of heaven; how the earth finally brought forth living animals, each after its own kind, and last of all, how God made man " in his own image," to whom he gave " dominion over the fishes of the sea, over the fowls of the air, over the cattle, and over every creeping thing that creeps upon the earth."

The Mosaic Eden was the habitation of the originally purely created beings, within whose boundaries grew the tree of knowledge of good and evil. The figure of the serpent shows the nature of the fall of man. We spoke, in another part of this work, of the original purity and wisdom of godly men. Here is the place to record additional Bible principles. To this end we avail ourselves of a mystical, interesting manuscript from which we extract what follows: (MAGIKON; or, the Secret System of an Association of Unknown Philosophers, etc., v. 27–31. Frankfort and Leipzig, 1784. A rare Book, whose Teachings, in many Respects, agree with the Indian Brahmin Doctrine).

In view of his divine origin, as an unconditional emanation from God, Adam was not only the noblest being, which, as an expression of divine power, had the preference of all others, for he never owed his existence to a mother; he was a heavenly Adam, brought into being by God himself and was not born into the world in the ordinary manner. He also enjoyed, in consequence of his nature, every prerogative of a pure spirit, surrounded by an invulnerable veil. But this was not the sensual body of the present time, which is only an evidence of his degradation—a coarse mantle—by which he sought to protect himself against the raging elements. His garments were holy, simple, indestructible, and of an indissoluble character. To this condition of perfect glory, in which he enjoyed the purest happiness, he was destined in order to reveal the power of the Almighty, and to rule the visible and invisible. Being in possession of all the prerogatives and insignia of a king, he could also use every means to fulfil his high destiny. As the champion of unity, he was secure from the attacks of all inward and outward enemies, because the veil by which he was covered (the germs of which are still within us), rendered him invulnerable. One advantage that the original pure man possessed was, that no natural poison, nor all the powers of the elements could harm him. Christ promised invulnerability to his apostles and all his followers, through the regeneration of man. In this condition man also bears a fiery, double-edged, all-penetrating sword, a living word, which combines in itself all power, and through which "everything is possible to him." Of this sword Moses says, Genesis iii. 24: "So he drove out the man, and he placed at the east end of the garden of Eden Cherubims, and a flaming sword which turned every way, to keep the tree of life." In Revelations i. 16, we read: "And out of his mouth went a two-edged sword," etc. By this sword we are to understand the living word, which was originally inherent in man, and which can only be restored to him by his return to a pure state, and by being cleansed from the blot of sensualism. It is the word of which we read in Hebrews iv. 12: "For the word of God is quick and powerful, and sharper than a two-edged sword, piercing even to the dividing asunder of soul and spirit."

Most extraordinary is the powerful, all-conquering Honover (word of power), of Zoroaster, which fully corresponds with the foregoing, by which Ormuzd overcame Ahriman and all evil. "In this condition of kingly honor and power," we read further, "man, as the most lifelike image of his father, (whose viceregent he was on earth), could have enjoyed the purest happiness had he properly guarded his Eden, but he committed a breach of trust. Instead of ruling over the things of sense and striving for a higher spiritual state, to which he was ordained, he imbibed the unhappy idea of exchanging the great cardinal points of light with truth, that is, he confounded light with truth, and in this confusion he lost both and robbed himself. Because he lost sight of the boundary of the kingdom over which he was placed as a watchman, and confined himself to only a portion of it, namely, the sensual, the glitter of which blinded him so greatly as to make him forget all else; because he flattered himself that he could find the light in another place than the first great fountain, he fastened his voluptuous eye on a false existence, became enamored of sensualism and became sensual himself. Through this adultery he sank into darkness and confusion, the result of which was, that he was transplanted from the light of day into the night of innumerable small twinkling stars, and now he experienced a sensual nakedness of which he was ashamed. The abuse of the knowledge of the connection between the spiritual and the bodily, according to which man endeavors to make the spiritual sensual and the sensual spiritual, is true adultery, of whom, he who is moved by the female sex is simply a consequence and an imitator. Through sin man lost not only his original habitation, and became an exile into the religious state of the fathers and mothers, having to go in the way of the flesh, but he also lost the fiery sword, and with it everything else that had made him all-seeing and unconquerable. His holy garments now became as the skin of animals, and this mortal, perishable covering afforded him no protection against the elements. With the wasted half of his body, the spiritual also added to the confusion, and discordant sounds were heard in the dark places of his spiritual domain.

Although man had sunk deep in sin, the hope of a full restoration was given to him on condition of a perfect reconciliation. Without such reconciliation, however, he sinks deeper and deeper, and his return be-comes still more precarious. In order to be reconciled he must become self-abased, and resist the false allurements which only serve to steep him in the mire of the elements, and he must seek, by prayer, to obtain the more exalted blessings of benevolent influences, without which he cannot draw a pure breath. In this reconciliation he must gradually overcome everything, and put away everything from him that will cloud his inner nature and separate him from the great source of his being; because he can never enjoy peace within himself and with nature around him until he has thus overcome everything opposed to his own nature, and gained the victory over all his enemies. But this can only be done when he re-turns the same road upon which he had wandered away. He must wean himself by degrees from the sensual by a heroic life, and like a weary, footsore wanderer, who has many steep mountains to scale, con-tinue to mount upward, until he reaches the goal, which is lost in the clouds. Overcoming one obstacle after another, he must dispel the dark vapors that intervene between himself and the true sun, so that in the end the pure rays of light may reach him without interruption. The follow-ing is a genuine scriptural doctrine according to the Indian creed, differ-ing, however, in character:

"The Almighty has provided means to aid man in the work of recon-ciliation. God has appointed higher agents to lead him back to Him from the error of his ways. But he can only be fully restored through the Saviour of the world, who finished and perfected all that these agents had accomplished only in part at different times. Through Him all power became animated and exalted; through Him he approaches the first and only true light, a knowledge of all things, and especially, a knowledge of himself. If the man is willing to accept this offered help, he will surely arrive at the desired goal, and he will be so firmly established in faith, that no future doubts can ever cause him to waver. If he elevates his will, so as to bring it in unison with the divine will, he may spiritualize his being already in this world, so that the higher spiritual kingdom may become visible to his eyes, and feel God nearer to him than he ever thought it possible; that all things may become possible to him, because he adds all power to his own, and in this union and har-mony, with a fulness of a higher vitality, the divine agents, Moses, Elias, yea, even Christ himself, may become visible to him, when, living amid thought, he requires books no longer. In short, man can attain to such a degree of perfection, even in this life, that death will have nothing more to do than to disrobe him of his coarse covering in order to reveal his spiritual temple, because he then lives and moves within the eternal. Only when he arrives at the end of this vale of darkness, will he receive, at each stage of his journey, more extended life, greater inward power, purer air, and a wider range of vision. His spiritual being will taste nobler fruits, and at the end of his race nothing can separate him from the exalted harmonies of those spheres, of which mortal sense can draw but a faint picture. Without distinction of sex, he will begin to live the life of angels, and will possess all their powers, of which he had but a faint sign here; he will then again enjoy the incense of the eternal temple, the source of all power, from which he was exiled, and Christ will be his great High Priest (Hebrews vii. 17, 24, 25). Man will not only enjoy his own gifts, but he will have a part in the gifts of the elect, who constitute the council of the wise; that holy sovereign will be more exalted there than he could be here; there will be no rising or setting of the light of the stars; no changes of day and night, and no multiplicity of languages; every being will in that moment be enabled to read the name of that holy book, out of which flows life for every creature (Hebrews xii. 22, 23). And here, too, the views of Zoroaster are in accord with the foregoing, for he also speaks of a heavenly meeting, and the participation of every follower of Ormuzd in the sacrifices and prayers of all, etc.

In placing this prominent treatise so plainly before the reader I felt no hesitation, because it was so clear and true, and because it seemed so proper for this work here, and to show why only pure and truly Christian men can perform great wonders and see visions of which the worldly-minded have not even a conception. I will now relate a few instances of magnetic appearances and occurrences, many of which are recorded in the Bible.

The first and most striking one we find in connection with Adam. Moses writes (Genesis ii. 21) as follows: "And the Lord caused a deep sleep to fall upon Adam, and he slept." And now, the question arises, What kind of a sleep was this? The answer is, it was a deep sleep. It was either the sleep of death, or a state of lethargy, or a trance (raptus divinus), or, was it merely an ordinary sleep? The first appears improbable, and had this been the case, we know, that in the release of the body from its earthly bonds, and shortly before death, the clearest instances of second sight have occurred; but the question is not of a mortal illness, but of a deep sleep. If it was a trance, then that inward second-sight may be regarded the more probable. The seventy-two translators of the Bible actually regard this sleep as a trance, and Tertullian says, in direct reference to it, "The power of the prophecies of the Holy Ghost fell upon him." (Accidit super-illum spiritus sancti vis operatrix prophetiæ.)

Another remarkable vision is that which Noah had of the ark long before the deluge occurred. Again, the call of Abraham, in which he was commanded to leave his fatherland and move toward Haran in Canaan. Abraham had many visions, or was the conversation of the Lord with him, recorded in the Bible really only than a figurative expression of intuition? Through these visions or conversations, as you will, he was taught that he would be greatly blessed, and that he should be the father of a great nation, etc. As he came into the sacred grove of Moria, the Lord again appeared unto Abraham and said: "This land will I give unto thy seed."

The innocent life of the shepherds, and their frequent abode in sacred groves, very naturally brought such intuition to the very highest point of perfection, and this was especially the case, when their minds were occupied with God and godly things. And this is particularly shown in the history of the shepherd-life of the pious Israelites, not only by the ancient fathers, but subsequently, in the time of the kings and judges. Isaac and Jacob had visions similar to those of Abraham. We notice especially the vision of Jacob while journeying into Mesopotamia, in which he saw a ladder reaching from earth to heaven. It is written (Genesis xxviii. 10): "And Jacob went out from Beersheba, and went toward Haran. And he lighted upon a certain place, and tarried there all night, because the sun was set: and he took of the stones of that place, and put them for his pillows, and lay down in that place to sleep. And he dreamed, and behold, a ladder set up on the earth, and the top of it reached to heaven: and behold, the angels of God ascending and descending on it. And behold, the Lord stood above it, and said, I am the Lord, etc. The land whereon thou liest, to thee will I give it, and to thy seed, etc. And in thee and in thy seed shall all the families of the earth be blessed. And Jacob awake out of his sleep, and he said, Surely the Lord is in this place; and I knew it not. This is none other but the house of God, and this is the gate of heaven." How truly was Jacob's dreamed fulfilled! The promised land became the possession of the Jews; through his seed, namely, through Christ the Saviour, who is the heavenly ladder upon which the angels of God ascended and descended, all the nations of the earth have been or will be blessed.

We find another remarkable instance of the magnetic influence in changing the nature and complexion of living objects, in the history of Jacob. It is as follows: Jacob agreed with Laban that he would still guard his sheep, provided, that Laban would give him as a reward for his service, all spotted lambs and goats that should in the future be added to his flocks. Laban consented to this proposal, and Jacob became immensely rich. It is worth the trouble to insert the passage relating to this transaction, as an application of the mysterious doctrine of magnetism.

When Jacob would no longer watch over the sheep and desired to go away with his wives and children, Laban said unto him, Genesis xxx. 27–43: "I pray thee, if I have found favor in thine eyes, tarry: for I have learned by experience that the Lord hath blessed me for thy sake. And he said Appoint me thy wages, and I will give it. And he said unto him, Thou knowest how I have served thee and how thy cattle was with me. For it was little which thou hadst before I came, and it is now increased unto a multitude: and the Lord hath blessed thee since my coming: and now, when shall I provide for mine own house also? And he said, What shall I give thee? And Jacob said, Thou shalt not give me anything: if thou wilt do this thing for me, I will again feed and keep thy flock: I will pass through all thy flock to-day, removing from thence all the speckled and spotted cattle, and all the brown cattle among the sheep, and the spotted and speckled among the goats: and of such shall be my hire. So shall my righteousness answer for me in time to come, when it shall come for my hire before thy face: every one that is not speckled and spotted among the goats, and brown among the sheep, that shall be counted stolen with me. And Laban said, Behold, I would it might be according to thy word. And he removed that day the he-goats that were ring-streaked and speckled, and all the she-goats that were speckled and spotted and every one that had some white in it, and all the brown among the sheep, and gave them into the hands of his sons. And he set three days' journey betwixt himself and Jacob: and Jacob fed the rest of

Laban's flocks. And Jacob took him rods of green poplar, and of the hazel and chestnut-tree: and pilled white streaks in them, and made the white appear which was in the rods. And he set the rods which he had pilled before the flocks in the gutters in the watering-troughs when the flocks came to drink, that they should conceive when they came to drink. And the flocks conceived before the rods, and brought forth cattle ring-streaked, speckled, and spotted. And Jacob did separate the lambs, and set the faces of the flocks toward the ring-streaked, and all the brown in the flock of Laban; and he put his own flocks by themselves, and put them not unto Laban's cattle. And it came to pass whensoever the stronger cattle did conceive, that Jacob laid the rods before the eyes of the cattle in the gutters, that they might conceive among the rods. But when the cattle were feeble, he put them not in; so the feeble were Laban's and the stronger Jacob's. And the man increased exceedingly, and had much cattle, and maidservants, and menservants, and camels, and asses."

This proves clearly that the sheep and the goats could be made to bring forth their young changed in color and appearance corresponding with the pilled rods which were placed before them by Jacob as they drank from the water. In these days, the theory that the features of the offspring of a human mother can be affected by an object upon which the mother gazes, is pronounced absurd; and yet this theory, in the very nature of things, is as fully established as the fact that the mental qualities of many children differ totally from those of their parents. The fact that the sheep and the goats, upon seeing the objects which Jacob so skilfully placed before them, brought forth their young differing in appearance from themselves, has a very deep significance. Either Jacob knew what the result of this stratagem would be from experience, or it was revealed to him in a dream, for we read, Genesis xxxi. 10: "And it came to pass at the time the cattle conceived, that I lifted up mine eyes, and saw in a dream, and behold, the rams which leaped upon the cattle were ring-streaked, speckled, and grizzled." With the water which they drank, and in which at the same time they saw their own reflection, they transmitted the image of the speckled rods to their young.

We have not the space here to enter into a more extended argument to prove the truth of this phenomenon, but the fact that the female progenitor, both human and animal, is capable at the period of gestation to transmit to her offspring the image and likeness of surrounding objects, has a surer foundation than is commonly believed to be possible. The great army of Materialists, who represent the spirit of the scriptures and of life as an ordinary earthly matter, so as to make it appear that nothing is hidden in the sanctuary that they cannot comprehend by their intellect, will never be converted, and those who rely upon the benign influences of a higher light in the temple, which will exist beyond the life of this world, will never need conversion.

Moses himself, the great man of God, had many remarkable visions. These visions consisted in part of dreams and partly in ecstasies, and for this reason was he educated in all the mysteries of the Egyptians and in all their magical arts, in which he excelled all others. On account of his extraordinary piety and wisdom he has made the savior of his people from the thrulldom of Pharaoh. His visions were of a diversified character. His ability to lead and govern the people was the direct result of a deep intuition. If we regard this ability as mere inward sight, then we must admit that it was a purely magical gift; if as the result of direct command of the voice of God (for according to the scriptures God often spoke personally with Moses), we find in it a confirmation of the truth, that a pious mind, open to divine influences, can also perform divine acts.

The first important vision of Moses occurred at Mount Horeb, while he was yet engaged in watching over the flocks of Jethro, his father-in-law (Exodus iii. 2): "And the angel of the Lord appeared unto him in a flame of fire out of the midst of a burning bush: and Moses said, I will now turn aside, and see this great sight, why the bush is not burned. And when the Lord saw that he turned aside to see, God called unto him out of the burning bush, and said, Draw not nigh hither: put off thy shoes from off thy feet; for the place whereon thou standest is holy ground."

Moses, the prophetic seer, acquainted with the weakness of his brethren, full of religious zeal, and gifted with a glowing phantasia, came to the lodge of his father-in-law in Midian, where he had time and opportunity, as a shepherd, to store his mind with religious contemplations, so that in a state of ecstatic second-sight, he could review the ways and means by which he might become the leader and shepherd of his people. The centrum of his mind was open to the higher influences of God, who appeared unto him as a light in the burning bush which was not consumed, and with whom, with veiled countenance, he conversed familiarly. We find in Moses the emotions of an inward psychological struggle with hopes and fears, with extreme weakness and supernatural strength of will; of submission, reverence and obedience; of confidence, and finally of an enthusiasm, that, regarding all earthly obstacles as nought, he overcame all things. While he was thus equipped with godlike powers, he subdued the elements of nature and compelled them to testify to the greatness and glory of God by the marvelous wonders which he performed. In such ecstasies Moses could tarry long on the mountains and separate himself from the people on the journey in the wilderness, and would yet be venerated as a man of wonders. The visions of Moses embrace the present and the future. He not only delivered the commands of God from the mountain, but he also foresaw the offerings that were brought to the golden calf; he foresaw that he could prepare the children of Israel for the pure worship of God, and guard them against error and idolatry only by isolating them in the wilderness from the heathen nations around them. In addition to the above indications we need only call attention to the special visions of Moses, his gifts, his ability to transfer the power of divination to others, and class them among magnetic occurrences; we may omit the different kinds of sacrifices, the consecration and blessing with water, oil and blood, and laying on of hands, etc., as well as the stringent prohibitions against taking any part in sorcery, false divination, conjuring and inquiring of the dead.

Among a few instances, resembling magnetism, we mention particularly the rod with which Moses performed his wonders before Pharaoh, and the stretching out of his hands by which he divided the waters of the sea (Exodus xiv. 16): "But lift thou up thy rod and stretch out thy hand over the sea, and divide it; and as Moses stretched out his hand over the sea, the waters were divided. And when the Egyptians pursued them, Moses stretched forth his hand over the sea, and the sea returned to his strength when the morning appeared; and the Egyptians fled against it, and the Lord overthrew the Egyptians in the midst of the sea, so there remained not so much as one of them." The stretching out of the hand of Moses and the wonders he performed with his rod are of great significance. With his rod he smote the rock in Rephidim, and the water gushed forth to quench the thirst of the murmuring people (Exodus xvii. 5): "And the Lord said unto Moses, go on before the people, and take with thee of the elders of Israel; and thy rod, wherewith thou smotest the river take in thy hand and go; and thou shalt smite the rock, and there shall water come out of it, that the people may drink." And when Amalek came and fought against Israel, Moses said unto Joshua (Exodus xvii. 9—11): "Choose us out men, and go out, fight with Amalek; to-morrow I will stand on the top of the hill with the rod of God in my hand. And it came to pass, when Moses held up his hand, that Israel prevailed; and when he let down his hand, Amalek prevailed."

The gift of prophecy seems also to have been given to the pious elders of Israel through their intercourse with Moses, for it is written (Numbers xi. 23—29): "And the Lord said unto Moses, Is the Lord's hand waxed short? thou shalt see now whether my word shall come to pass unto thee or not. And Moses went out and told the people the words of the Lord, and gathered together the seventy men of the elders of the people, and set them around about the tabernacle. And the Lord came down in a cloud, and spake unto him and took of the spirit that was upon him, and gave it unto the seventy elders: and it came to pass, that, when the spirit rested upon them, they prophesied, and did not cease. But there remained two of the men in the camp, the name of the one was Eldad, and the name of the other Medad: and the spirit rested upon them: and they were of them that were written, but went not out into the tabernacle: and they prophesied in the camp. And Joshua the son of Nun, the servant of Moses, one of his young men, answered and said, My lord Moses, forbid them. And Moses said unto him, Enviest thou for my sake? would God that all the Lord's people were prophets, and that the Lord would put his spirit upon them!

The various conditions of clairvoyance are clearly described by Moses. Miriam and Aaron spoke against Moses because of the Ethiopian whom he had married, and they said (Numbers xii. 2–8): "Hath the Lord indeed spoken only by Moses? Hath he not also spoken by us? And the Lord heard it. And the Lord came down in a pillar of the cloud and called Aaron and Miriam: and they both came forth. And he said, Hear now my words: If there be a prophet among you, I the Lord will make myself known unto him in a vision and will speak unto him in a dream. My servant Moses is not so, who is faithful in all my house. With him will I speak mouth to mouth, even apparently and not in dark speeches, and the similitude of the Lord shall he behold." And so it was also among the Israelites and other nations, and is now in our magnetic appearances and revelations by visions, and especially in dreams and dark words and figures, which is frequently the case in the lower condition of somnolency; but in the highest grades of clairvoyance, when the mind is pure as in the case of Moses, it is to behold in the true form.

The personal conversations of God with Moses, and his power of beholding the Almighty in his true similitude are figurative expressions, and must not be taken in a literal sense. For the Lord speaks through revelation and by means of the light, and not by word of mouth, neither can God be seen by mortal eyes, for He says in another place, " No man can behold me and live." This language is the expression or impression of the divine word, and a light from the very purest source ; it is the spiritual gift and revelation of the Deity to man, which must be taken according to the various grades of intelligence of beings, as in nature, according to the kind of light produced by different actions, whether the effect be produced upon near or distant, thick or thin, hard or soft objects, etc.

This language was understood by prophets and consecrated men in all ages, and these could not communicate the light they had received in any other language than those which were spoken in their day, although, that which came over them was much more simple, comprehensive and spiritual than any spoken communication could have been. The language of God is the influence of a higher light through which the spirit which he pervades becomes electrified. God acts as a centrum only on the centrum of things, that is, on the inner or spiritual, and the outward manifestations follow ex post. It is not less significant that the bite of the fiery serpents was healed by gazing upon the brazen serpent. "And the soul of the people was much discouraged because of the way, and spake against God and against Moses. And the Lord sent fiery serpents among the people, and they bit the people ; and much people of Israel died. Therefore the people came to Moses and said, We have sinned, for we have spoken against the Lord and against thee : pray unto the Lord that he take away the serpents from us. And Moses prayed for the people. And the Lord said unto Moses, make thee a fiery serpent and set it upon a pole ; and it shall come to pass that every one that is bitten, when he looketh upon it, shall live." (Numbers xxi. 4–9.)

The visions and prophecies of Balaam, son of Beor, to whom Balak sent Messengers, that he might curse Israel, are also of a remarkable character. (Numbers xxii. 23, 24) : "If Balak would give me his house full of silver and gold, I cannot go beyond the word of the Lord, my God, to do less or more." So spake Balaam to Balak, who tried to bribe him to do evil.

In Numbers xxiv. 4, 15, 16, 17, 19, we have an account of the visions of the heathen seer, in which was announced the advent of Christ : "And the spirit of the Lord came upon him and he took up his parable and said : And the man whose eyes are open hath said : He hath said, which heard the words of God, and knew the knowledge of the Most High, which saw the visions of the Almighty, falling into a trance, but having his eyes open, I shall see him, but not now ; I shall behold him, but not nigh ; there shall come a Star out of Jacob and a Sceptre shall rise out of Israel. Out of Jacob shall come he that shall have dominion." The history of Balaam proves that the power to perform wonders was not possessed by holy seers alone. Balak, king of the Moabites, being afraid of the Israelites, desired to form a league with the Midianites. But since neither the Moabites nor the Midianites felt like engaging in hostilities with the Israelites, they resorted to magic, and since they had no magician among themselves, they sent for Balaam, who was celebrated for his powers of charming and divining. The messengers came to Balaam with costly presents in their hands (for he took money for his serv·ices as soothsayer), and demanded that he should curse this strange people. Balaam invited them to tarry over night ; in the morning he arose and made known to the messengers that God neither permitted him to curse the Israelites, nor allowed him to accompany them to their coun-try, for "that people was favored of God." Balak thinking he had not offered enough, sent more costly presents by the hands of his nobles, in order to induce Balaam to visit him and curse Israel. Balaam, a mixture of faith and fickleness, of truth and avarice, of true prophecy and magic, said to the servants of Balak : "If Balak would give me his house full of silver and gold, I cannot go beyond the word of the Lord my God, to do less or more." And yet, after he had spoken with the Lord during the night, he arose in the morning, saddled his ass, and prepared to go with the Moabite princes, and afterward told the enemies of Israel how they could lead them into idolatry.

Here follows the history of Balaam's perfect somnambulism. Being a visionary, he was divided within himself, because he tried to serve God and Mammon. His conscience upbraided him. "And God's anger was kindled against him because he went : and the angel of the Lord stood in his way for an adversary against him." Now he changed his inward per-ception from the angel and transferred it to the ass, which now also be·held the angel standing in the way, and therefore began a rational con-versation with its rider. The ass, with characteristic obduracy, preferred the fields to the uneven paths in the vineyards, and when force was em-ployed to turn her in the way, she thrust herself against the wall, and crushed Balaam's foot against the wall, for which he smote her with his staff; and since there was no path to turn aside either to the right or to the left, the ass fell down under Balaam, and he smote her again. Finally the ass spoke to Balaam and pointed out to him his unreasonable conduct, and when he came unto himself he again saw the angel instead of the ass ; but his conscience smote him ; he confessed his sin and promised to go back again. But the angel permitted him to proceed upon condition that he should speak only what the Lord had commanded him to say, which condition he fulfilled in spite of every temptation that Balak could offer ; and he went not at other times to seek for enchantments, but he set his face toward the wilderness." Instead of cursing the Israelites he blessed them, and afterward actually prophesied concerning the Star of Jacob. (Numbers xxiv.)

This spurious prophet had no truly divine inspirations, but he prophesied in the same manner as do our mesmeric clairvoyants. For, first, he always went into retirement, when he was about to prophesy, to avoid outward disturbance, which no true prophet ever did. Second, His in-ward perceptions were opened by closing his outward senses. "So sayeth the hearer of the word, whose eyes will be opened when he bows down

It is evident that the angel with the drawn sword was a vision, and the fact that the ass speaking did not appear strange to him, proves clearly that he could not have been awake. According to the Arabic, Balaam was called "the man with the closed eye," and this induces Tholuck to compare his condition to a state of magnetic ecstasy. Third, Balaam was so incapable of distinguishing between the real object and the apparent subject, that the ass, gifted with speech, made no impression upon him, so that, after he had regained his senses, he saw the angel standing before him and bowed himself before him. Fourth, Balaam made use of certain external means to throw himself into an ecstatic state, which true prophets never did. He was led from place to place in order to obtain visions, differing in their nature, so as to make them conform with the pleasure of Balak. He even employed magic, for it is written: "And when Balaam saw that it pleased the Lord to bless Israel, he went not, as at other times, to seek for enchantments, but he set his face toward the wilderness." Fifth, finally, Balaam's ecstasies were unstable and uncertain, and his figures and expressions were symbolical, for we read, for example: "He couched, he lay down as a lion, and as a great lion." This false prophet then returned to his dwelling, but appears again later in the camp of the Midianites, where he finally perished by the sword at the hands of those whom Moses sent out to fight.

In the days of the judges and kings, dreams and prophetic visions signified the same thing. In I Samuel xxviii. 6, we read: "In olden times in Israel, when men inquired of the Lord, they said: Come let us go to the seer, for they were called seers who are now called prophets."

In Numbers xxvii. 18–21, when Moses asked the Lord to give him a worthy follower, it is written: "And the Lord said unto Moses, Take Joshua, a man in whom is the spirit, and lay thine hand upon him, etc., and thou shalt put some of thine honor upon him, etc. And he shall stand before Eleazar the priest, who shall ask counsel for him after the judgment of Urim before the Lord," etc. I have already quoted passages from the Bible to show that dreams and prophetic visions were regarded as the same thing; and indeed, so important were dreams, that a dreamer was placed in the same category with a prophet. "And when Saul saw the host of the Philistines, he was afraid, and his heart greatly trembled. And when Saul inquired of the Lord, the Lord answered him not, neither by dreams, nor by Urim, nor by prophets." (I Samuel xxviii. 6.) We read in Deuteronomy xiii. 1–4: "If there arise among you a prophet, or a dreamer of dreams, and giveth thee a sign or wonder, and the sign or wonder come to pass, whereof he spake unto thee, saying Let us go, after other gods, which thou hast not known, and let us serve them: Thou shalt not hearken unto the words of that prophet, or that dreamer of dreams: for the Lord your God proveth you, to know whether ye love the Lord your God with all your heart and with all your soul." From this we learn that persons who were not prophets, and who were not of a pure heart, also had prophetic visions.

It would be tedious as well as superfluous to recite all the visions of the prophets. In the meantime we will not pass over the most remarkable in silence. In I Samuel xvi., we find the history of Saul, who, after the spirit of God had departed from him, became gloomy and ill, and whose condition could only be ameliorated by the sweet sounds of music. "But the spirit of the Lord departed from Saul, and an evil spirit from the Lord troubled him. And Saul's servants said unto him, Behold now, an evil spirit from God troubleth thee. Let our lord now command thy servants, which are before thee, to seek out a man, who is a cunning player on the harp: and it shall come to pass when the evil spirit of God is upon thee, that he shall play with his hand, and thou shalt be well: and Saul sent to Jesse, saying, Let David, I pray thee, stand before me, etc. And it came to pass, when the evil spirit from God was upon Saul, that David took a harp, and played with his hand: so Saul was refreshed, and was well, and the evil spirit departed from him." When Saul saw the Philistine host his heart failed him, and he inquired of the Lord, but the Lord answered him not, "neither by dreams, nor by Urim nor by prophets. If there arise among you prophets, or a dreamer of dreams, and giveth a sign, etc. Saul was a seeker after signs and wonders, for he at one time inquired of Samuel about his missing asses; at another time he inquired of the witch of Endor, and at another time he depended upon deceptive dreams. The witch said to Saul: "Wherefore dost thou ask of me, seeing that the Lord is departed from thee, and thy kingdom is gone out of thy hand."

In the books of Samuel, who was a clairvoyant in his youth, we find many prophetic visions recorded. The most remarkable of these visions were those of Samuel and David. Even Saul attempted to prophesy until the spirit of the Lord departed from him. The history of the aged king David, who could no more obtain warmth of body, even though he was covered with clothing, we have already related. A young virgin was procured, who slept in the king's arms and cherished him, and so he obtained heat. (1 Kings i. 1.)

Among all the prophets of the old dispensation there was none more exalted than Elias, whose very name was a synonyme for a higher grade of being. We find in him an example of great significance in magnetic transactions. He imparted the most important doctrines of life, and he gave life to such as had apparently died, a history of which is here inserted verbatim: "And it came to pass after these things, that the son of the woman, the mistress of the house, fell sick, and his sickness was so sore, that there was no breath left in him. And she said unto Elias, What have I to do with thee, O thou man of God? art thou come unto me to call my sin to remembrance, and to slay my son? And he said unto her, Give me thy son. And he took him out of her bosom, and carried him up into a loft, where he abode, and laid him upon his own bed. And he cried unto the Lord, and said, O Lord, my God, hast thou also brought evil upon the widow with whom I sojourn, by slaying her son? And he stretched himself upon the child three times, and cried unto the Lord, and said, O Lord my God, I pray thee, let this child's soul come into him again. And the Lord heard the voice of Elias; and the soul of the child came into him again, and he revived. And Elias took the child, and brought him down out of the chamber into the house, and delivered him to his mother." (1 Kings xvii. 17-24.)

Of a similar kind a still more remarkable instance of the striking and powerful magnetic influence is given in the history of the Shunammite's son who was restored to life by the prophet Elisha. (2 Kings iv. 18-37.)

"And when the child was grown, it fell on a day, that he went out to his father, to the reapers. And he said unto his father, My head, my head! And he said to a lad, Carry him to his mother. And when he had taken him, and brought him to his mother, he sat on her knees till noon, and then died. And she went up, and laid him on the bed of the man of God, and shut the door and went out. And she called unto her husband and said, Send me, I pray thee, one of the young men, and one of the asses, that I may run to the man of God, and come again. And he said, Wherefore wilt thou go to him to-day? it is neither new moon, nor Sabbath. And she said It shall be well. Then she saddled an ass, and said to her servant, Drive, and go forward; slack not thy riding for me, except I bid thee. So she went, and came unto the man of God to mount Carmel. And it came to pass, when the man of God saw her afar off, that he said to Gehazi his servant, Behold, yonder that Shunammite: Run now, I pray thee, to meet her, and say unto her, Is it well with thee? is it well with thy husband? is it well with the child? And she answered, It is well. And when she came to the man of God to the hill, she caught him by the feet: but Gehazi came near to thrust her away. And the man of God said, Let her alone; for her soul is vexed within her: and the Lord hath hid it from me, and hath not told me. Then she said, Did I desire a son of my lord? did I not say, Do not deceive me? Then he said to Gehazi, Gird up thy loins, and take thy staff in thy hand, and go thy way: if thou meet any man, salute him not; and if any salute thee, answer him not again: and lay my staff upon the face of the child. And the mother of the child said, As the Lord liveth, I will not leave thee. And he arose, and followed her. And Gehazi passed on before them, and laid the staff upon the face of the child; but there was neither voice nor hearing. Wherefore, he went again to meet him, and told him, saying, The child is not awaked. And when Elisha had come into the house, behold the child was dead, and laid upon his bed. He went in therefore, and shut the door upon them twain, and prayed unto the Lord. And he went up, and lay upon the child, and put his mouth upon his mouth, and his eyes upon his eyes, and his hands upon his hands: and he stretched himself upon the child, and the flesh of the child waxed warm. Then he returned, and walked in the house to and fro; and went up, and stretched himself upon him: and the child sneezed seven times, and the child opened his eyes. And he called Gehazi, and said, Call this Shunammite. So he called her. And when she was come in unto him, he said, take up thy son."

What may we learn from this? First, that one must be a man of God as Elisha was. Second, Elisha must have been well acquainted with the transferring of this power by means of a conductor, or he would not have sent his servant before him with the staff, by simply laying the same upon the face of the dead child, and thereby restore him to life. Third, the command that he gave unto his servant, to salute no one by the way, has a deep significance. He was to give his undivided attention to the business of raising the dead unto life, and not to be led away by any other consideration or occasion whatever. A proof that is highly necessary and important that a magnetic physician should be free from all diversions in order to concentrate all his energies upon the one object,—the patient.

Fourth, the very management in this case, is incomparable.   Fifth, it is a proof that perseverance and continuance is a chief requisite in a mag netic operation: you cannot fell a tree with one stroke, so Elisha, after the first effort, arose and walked to and fro in the house, and only upon the second effort did the dead lad begin to breathe.   By the conduct of Elisha (and Saul), we may learn, that the inner sense may also be de veloped by music, as for instance, when Elisha was called upon to proph esy to the kings of Israel and Judah, against the Moabites, he said: "But now, bring me a minstrel."   And as the minstrel played the hand of the Lord came upon him, and he prophesied.   (2 Kings iii. 15.)   That they knew the method of healing by laying on of hands, and that they prac ticed it, is proven in the passage (2 Kings v. 11.)   Naaman, the Syrian captain, expected Elisha to move his hand over the leprous part, and thus put away his leprosy.

We often read that the remains of saints worked marvelous wonders and healed the sick long after their decease.   This was the case with Elisha, for we read (2 Kings xiii. 20): "And Elisha died, and they buried him.   And the bands of the Moabites invaded the land at the coming in of the year.   And it came to pass as they were burying a man, that behold they spied a band of men; and they cast the man into the sepulchre of Elisha: and when the man was let down, and touched the bones of Elisha, he revived and stood upon his feet."   If it might prob ably appear, that in the earliest ages men were chiefly given to prophecy and inner perceptions, in our day and among us the female more fre quently possesses these gifts: still, there are numerous instances of prophetic women recorded in the Bible also, as, for example, the woman of Endor, who possessed the spirit of divination and to whom Saul went to inquire of.   Huldah, the Prophetess, (2 Kings xxii. 14), and Deborah, the wife of Lapidoth, etc.

Let us once more take a retrospective glance upon the people of Israel, according to the history of the Old Testament, and upon the ancient days of the Orientals, and compare the magic among them to that of later years and we shall find many and essential differences.   In the first place, I have remarked before, how that the people of Israel stood single and alone before all the heathen nations, and how the magic among them assumed an essential and diversified form.   For although the Jews re mained so long in Egypt, they brought very little Egyptian magic with them on their return; that is, of the genuine theurgical magic art, which is the result of natural powers and of human inventions.   These magi cal ecstasies and wonder workings were more of the nature of divine in spiration, while the black art, practiced by natural means, which was to produce supernatural effects, was met with severe punishment as an un holy work of sorcery and witchcraft.   We find quite the contrary in heathendom, since here the true knowledge of the divine was either lack ing altogether, or it was adulterated by traditions and darkened by mys teries.   As for instance, in Egypt Athor, according to the Theogony of Hesiod, the darkness of night was worshipped as the great unknown, through profound silence; but to the Israelites the light appeared in the unity of God, whom they worshipped with loud hymns.   In the entire old world of Heathendom the power of the principle of nature governed, and brought down the spiritual vibration to the level of the terrestrial or earthly. The true magic of the divine was hid from that erring people, being covered with a veil through which but few glimpses of light penetrated. The light shown in the darkness, but the darkness comprehended it not. Hamberger says: "Heathendom was capable only to take up single rays, as it were, in an oblique direction, but the elect of God, as the posterity of Shem, in whom mankind was to be exhibited as such, and to whom all the rest of mankind, as the mere common people (Gojim) were retained, they could rejoice not only in a circuitous, but in a central influence on the part of the Lord. "Thou art a holy people unto the Lord, says God. (Deut. vii. 6.) The Lord thy God hath chosen thee to be a special people to Himself, above all people that are upon the face of the earth."

Israel was appointed thereto, not so much to conceive and grasp the outward glory of God, the ideal world, but much more His inner being, to be led deeper and deeper into the sanctuary of divine personality. This, however, cannot be done at once; and if Israel is not the only pardoned and favored, but if through him all the nations of the earth shall be blessed, this could only be accomplished gradually, and by degrees. Madam Schlegel says: "A longing or love is the root and beginning of every higher and divine knowledge. Perseverance in searching, in faith, and in the contest of life, only prefigure the middle of the way; the termination must always remain something that is hoped for. The necessary epoch for preparation to this gradual process may not be overturned nor set aside by the noblest strivings of man. The character and the history itself of the Hebrew nations are greatly misunderstood, for the very reason, that these things are not duly observed. The whole existence of this people was built only upon hope, and the highest centre of their inner life was placed at a great distance in the future. Upon this also rests the chief difference in the method of the holy deliverance of the Hebrews. as is exhibited by other old Asiatic nations. In the old records of these nations their glance in the proper historic parts is directed more toward the glorious past, with a regretful feeling in consequence of that which man has since lost. Out of all the fulness of these touching, holy remembrances, and out of the oldest joint proverbs, Moses, in his most direct and fixed revelations for the Hebrew children according to the wisest law of economy, brought out but very little, and only what seemed the mos indispensable and necessary for his people and the object of God with the same. And as all the writings of the first lawgiver, who for this sole object led and brought out his favorite people from Egyptian servitude in a spiritual sense and according to the whole mode of thought, until up to the time of the prophet king and singer of psalms to the last voice of warning and promise that died away in the wilderness—the outward contents and the inward understanding are, according to prophetic writings: so may the people themselves be called a prophetic people in the highest sense of the word, and is such really, taken historically, in the whole course of the world and in their wonderful destinies they were and are such.

Molitor says further: —"The leading of the Israelites furnishes the most apparent proof of the divine nature of religion. Among all nations there are oracles, and in all important affairs and transactions inquiry is made of them, and nothing is undertaken in life unless the favorable judgment of the gods is first obtained. Meantime these oracles do not appear to be positive leaders of the people. They simply reply to inquiries made. Not in a single heathen religion, therefore, do we observe a really positive, sensitive and divine guidance. But man stands here, solely in his own power. The case is entirely different with the people of Israel, who are nothing, and have nothing of themselves, but whose whole existence and guidance is singly the work of Divinity. Where is there a nation to be found that had such an ethical guidance? Where do you find a people who have made humility and obedience and a childlike surrender to God, their first and chief duty, and accepted chastisement as a token of love, and were brought to their destination through adversity and humiliation? True, there are guidances and trials also in Heathendom, but they are trials only in the vigorous subduing of evil, and the courageous bearing of great burdens. Nowhere, therefore, do we find merit or praise for baseness or lowness. When, for instance, it was said of Moses: "He was an humble man," it was a compliment which was never bestowed upon a heathen hero." (Kabbalah, Part III., page 116.)

The Hebrew prophets and the heathen seers present an essential difference. Even if the ground-work of natural magical visions appear here as elsewhere; if imagination and sympathy—if the outer influences of nature often produced like affects, and if the Israelites had learned and brought with them many and various Egyptian secrets, as for instance, Samuel's School of Prophets in the Old Testament gives ample proof, as also the holy inspired dance, the prophetic signing, etc., has in it something contagious, insomuch that prophetic students were seized and overcome, as was also Saul, who fell in with them and prophesied, so that the proverb, "How came Saul among the Prophets?" still shows something very curious and surprising; yet, in view of the motive and effect, great differences are found, so that they well deserve to be held to view in this place. They are as follows:

1. The Magician, the Indian Brahmin, the mystical Priest, etc., brings himself into an ecstatic condition, and into supposed union with God, by self-elected methods; Moses and the true prophets of Israel receive an unexpected call to serve Him.

2. The Magician elevates himself by his own innate strength to a higher state and condition than the world by whom he is surrounded; he isolates himself intentionally and his isolation becomes imperative, and through it follow the various castes and grades in life, as, for example, the Indian and Egyptian castes, which produces a special influence upon the diversified conditions of earthly life and intellect; Moses and the prophets are more casual, and in the passive dread of deep solitude, they suddenly hear the call and follow in humility, with veiled countenances. The liberation of his people is not effected by a strong will, and he claims no preference; he does not separate the different castes, but he separates the organic unity of the people from heathen blindness, which he dedicates to God; he is himself the expounder of the faith of God's overruling

providence; of the hope in future punishment; of the love of God, and of order and justice among men.

3. Contempt of the world and pride in his own worthiness and knowledge characterize the magical seer. A wise use of life, obedience in serving God and a constant recollection of his sinful weakness, incites the prophet to implore divine help, to pray for a knowledge of the truth, to fulfil not his own, but a higher will. To the Brahmin, for example, the earth is a hell, a place of torment; to the prophet it is a school, through which, in the performance of duty, the peace of true happiness may be found.

4. The magician is a lawgiver, the prophets are obedient disciples, who preach and explain the revelations of God.

5. There we have the means of falling into a state of ecstasy, self-denial and unnatural mortification of the body. Here the world is adapted to the most judicious enjoyment of life. The prophet does not require extraordinary means to fall into a state of ecstasy; he utters the immediate word of God without preparation and without mortifying the body, presents it, and lives among his kind.

6. The index of prophecy itself, in the highest ecstasies of the magicians, is a kind of light lustre; when they are steeped therein, the world with its signatures, and perhaps too, the inner condition of the spirit may become plainly visible, like unto the clairvoyants of our day; but their lips are sealed in this ecstatic state of happiness and in the dazzling lustre of a pathological self-illumination. Therefore, the numerous antagonistic figures of truth and deception, of sensational emotions and phantasmagoria in broken and jarring forms, of convulsions and contortions of the body and the soul, which we find among our mesmeric subjects. Their visions are, like those of certain somnambulists, not reliable, and cannot, in their proper surroundings, be understood without a previous explanation. With the prophets, the visions according to form, are the illumination of a mildly divine light, reflected from the mirror of a pure mind, which retains a perfect personality, and causes a feeling of dependence on God and the outer world. The index of their visions relates to the general concerns of life in respect to religion and citizenship; the prophet speaks and his words are true doctrines, uttered clearly for the benefit of all men and ages, and comprehended by all. He seeks happiness yet finds it not in penance, but in his calling, in spreading abroad the word of God, not in secret contemplations, but by imparting it to his fellow-beings through active coöperation. The true prophet, therefore, is not lost in inward contemplations, neither does he forget himself in the world, but he continues in living relation with God and his neighbor, in word and in deed. Finally,

7. Since the motives and proceedings differ essentially among inspired races, so their aims and results also differ. The Indian magician mourns on account of the gradual lowering of the spiritual from its original lustre, following the rapidly succeeding eras of the world into perishing nature and into the kingdom of death, and deprecates the misery connected therewith, namely, discontent, the confusion and laceration of the spirit, all of which we may find among the different heathen nations. On the other hand, how greatly has universal brotherhood and companionship

increased, step by step, through the agency of the true prophet, and how has the spiritual been glorified! The spirit that waved over the Jewish religion in the west spread its peaceful influences farther and wider, and while in the former instance everything is lost in weakness and darkness, in the latter mountains are removed by active faith, and trees are planted by mutual help and counsel, whose fruit will only ripen for enjoyment in another world, toward which we should turn our faces and our exertions.

The aim of the magician's life is to secure a pleasurable inward contemplation; the true prophet lives by faith and not by sight.

Historians and philosophers of modern times have declared that the ecstatic visions of the prophets of Israel and those of the apostles were identical with magnetic appearances. In order to form a clearer judgment of the circumstances given above, we will add the following:

True prophets receive an extraordinary call from God, and are urged by the Holy Spirit to proclaim the will and counsel of God. They are called seers, men of God, servants and messengers of the Lord, angels and watchmen. The marks of the true prophets of the Old Testament were: 1st. That their prophecies agreed with the doctrines of Moses and the patriarchs (Deuteronomy xiii. 1). 2d. Their prophecies were fulfilled (Deuteronomy xviii. 21; Jeremiah xxviii. 9). 3d. That they performed miracles, but only when a special covenant was made, or when a special reformation was to be undertaken. 4th. That they agreed with other prophets (Isaiah viii. 2; Jeremiah xxvi. 18). 5th. That they led a blameless life (Jeremiah xxvii. 4; Micah ii. 11). That they exhibited a holy zeal in the work of God (Jeremiah xxvi. 13); and 6th, That they possessed great elocutionary powers (Jeremiah xxiii. 28, 29). Their office consisted in this, 1st, That they instructed the people, when the priests, whose duty it was, became indifferent. 2d. That they restored the slack and decayed worship of God (2 Kings xvii. 18; Ezekiel iii. 17). 3d. That they foretold future events, and to this end asked counsel of God (1 Kings xiv. 2, 3; Ezekiel xxii. 5–8). 4th. That they prayed for the people and in this manner averted impending judgments (Genesis xx. 7; 2 Kings xix. 2); and 5th, That they composed the will of God (1 Chronicles xxix. 9).

The same may be said of the apostles and the preachers of the living word. They were called ministers because Christ had himself chosen them and sent them to the ends of the earth to proclaim the atonement and gather His elect. They did not force themselves in to his service, but Christ called them in a direct manner, and taught them personally to proclaim the advent of the Messiah, and with these credentials, to perform wonders through the divine word. This new doctrine originated expressly from the prophets of the old covenant: repent and believe in the gospel of the atonement, and prove thereby that ye love God above all things and your neighbor as yourselves. Their lives proved that they were true followers in the footsteps of their Lord and Master, in word and deed, in works and in suffering.

If we select these characters by which to form our judgment, it will not be difficult to distinguish between magnetic sight and prophetic inspiration, not to regard the former too highly, and not to underrate the latter. For if their superficial appearance at first sight seems the same, their di ference will soon become apparent when we examine them in a threefold point of view, namely, of cause, content or form and intention.

According to the cause, the palpable difference consists in this, that magical and magnetic second-sight is mainly the work of man, which grows out of a diseased physical soil, no matter whether it is developed by the arts of the physician or whether it is unfolded by chance. An abnormal condition of health always precedes it, and the somnolent state of the outward senses is the first condition of it. If in one person this mesmeric disposition is greater than in another, then the physiological foundation is in his own body, and if occasional circumstances promote second-sight in others, then such causes belong to the kingdom of nature, which binds the clairvoyant in strong bonds and which remains his determinate state even should he reach the highest degree.

Prophetic inspiration is not a procreation of nature or of man but it is an emanation of the Holy Spirit and a divine decree. The divine call comes unexpectedly, and the physical condition has no connection with it whatever. The physical powers can never become the determinate powers, but they remain dependent upon the spirit, which makes it a means to spiritual aims. A mesmeric life with changed functions of the senses and a physical crisis does not take place here.

Secondly, according to form, magnetic second-sight depends directly upon the health and on the life of the seer, or rather, it predominates in the relative modes of earthly life. The clairvoyant directs his attention at will to self-selected objects, at least in a majority of instances, or he interprets his own visions, conducts his own affairs or those immediately surrounding him, or he suffers himself to be outwardly determined without active and persistent independence, and without activity for the common good. Purely human nature, affectation and inclination are never wanting in the magic circle of the seer, and the operation of his will and his faith produces no supernatural or permanent effect, either upon himself or upon others.

The true prophet, according to form, has no diversity of visions, but an unchanging index of scriptural work—the annunciation of Him, who is the Beginning and the End, and by whom all things were created. A prophet is not only a seer, but he is the organ of the divine will. Instruction in the true knowledge of God, and spreading abroad his kingdom, which is truth and love, is his only and constant occupation, therefore he fights against error and wickedness, in order to overcome the world. That which is worldly or changeable—bigotry or sensuality, health, riches and honor in the world, and dominion over his fellow-men, is not his affair. He does not preach a present, but a future state of happiness, genuine peace in God, and the hope of eternal life in His presence, not from personal impulse or selfishness, or from human considerations, but as a willing instrument of perpetual enlightenment, inspired by God himself—a worthy example in work and walk; as an obedient servant and a mediator between God and man, between time and eternity, between heaven and earth. Through prayer, and in word and deed, the prophet continues in a living relation with God and his fellow-beings.

True prophets do not isolate themselves, neither do they sink into the absorbing depths of their own visions, feelings and relations. Their prophecies do not refer to personalities, but to the fate of nations and the world, therefore, are they able in their works to exhibit supernatural powers, strengthened by the omnipotent power of their faith and will, and this power they exercise over their own bodies as well as over the bodies of others and over all nature in its wide and temporal boundaries. The sudden conversions and changes of opinion, the instantaneous healing of severe and lingering diseases, the warnings against threatening dangers, and help for the needy from a distance, giving consolation and strength in trouble and suffering, etc., are proofs of their divine powers.

As we have already stated, the aim of the true prophets was, the revelation of the divine word to man; the spread of the kingdom of God on earth; the ennobling and well-being of the human race. Impelled by the spirit of God, upon whose assistance they relied, their efforts were directed to nothing less than to spread the light of truth and to infuse courage into their fellow-beings, to fight against evil; to awaken mutual attention and assistance, and to extend peace and happiness among men. Self-aggrandizement and the personal advantage of these organs of the Deity were not thought of. The foundation of all their works was faith in the power of God, and they fulfilled the whole sum of the commandments through love, the noblest of all virtues, " but the fruit of the spirit is love" (Galatians v. 22); " And God gives wisdom to them that love Him," (Ecclesiasticus i. 10); "And His banner over me was love." (Song of Solomon ii. 4.)

To these obvious variations the children of Israel bear special witness. 1st. That the causes of inward visions were actually objective, and that there is something outside of human intelligence that governs and controls the world of man, and that too, independently of the inner centrum of the mind, while the peripheral sense of day and nature are either inactive, or while they are in a very subordinate condition. 2d. That there is a still more exalted spiritual region which takes a positive hold upon the reason and offers revelations which are not of a natural order, and which cannot exist in these lower regions, and which are not merely phantasies, illusions or hallucinations of an abnormal condition of the brain. "The hand of the Lord was upon them." 3d. The ignoring, or rather, the denial of sophistical rationalism, especially by the Israelites, is also represented superficially, just as the pantheistical philosophy of nature is, which distils everything into a common mass, and which represents the prophets and the saints only as somnambulistic sects, upon a somewhat higher plane than is ascribed to them in the partial Tellurian dark ages. 4th. Notwithstanding that this class of visions has an outward resemblance to the magical and magnetic, as well according to the anthropological expression as to the symbolical representations, as we have already seen, and it should remind us of magnetic relations. Inasmuch as prophetic revelation agrees with the purest forms of second-sight, and whereas dream-visions and fortune-telling originate from circumstances and conditions, so we may find many preparations and arrangements in the old covenant, the same as we have learned to know them among the rest of the magicians of the Orient. We often find among the prophets also, that they secluded themselves in solitary places, and that they fasted and gave themselves up to quiet contemplation.

They, like the clairvoyants, speak of an inward higher light, of a light that enlightens them, and they admit this higher illumination to be the spirit of the Eternal, whose hand came upon them and transfigured them, and they walked, as the Psalmist says, in the light of His countenance, "For in Thy light, we shall see light; the Lord my God will enlighten my darkness. Thou art the living fountain and in thy light we see the light." (36, 10, 18, 29.)

The prophets describe the divine higher light as an instantaneous view, presented very frequently in the most familiar symbols, of which the vision of Daniel, by the side of the great river Hiddekel, is one of the most remarkable, and which will serve as an illustration (Daniel x. 2–21): "In those days I Daniel was mourning three full weeks. I ate no pleasant bread, neither came flesh nor wine in my mouth, neither did I anoint myself at all, till three whole weeks were fulfilled. Then I lifted up mine eyes, and looked, and behold a certain man clothed in linen, whose loins were girded with fine gold of Uphaz: His body also was like the beryl, and his face as the appearance of lightning, and his eyes as lamps of fire, and his arms and his feet like in color to polished brass, and the voice of his words like the voice of a multitude. And I Daniel alone saw the vision: for the men that were with me saw not the vision; but a great quaking fell upon them, so that they fled to hide themselves. Therefore I was left alone, and saw this great vision, and there remained no strength in me: Yet I heard the voice of his words: and when I heard the voice of his words, then was I in a deep sleep on my face, and my face toward the ground. And behold, a hand touched me, which set me upon my knees and upon the palms of my hands. And he said unto me, O Daniel, a man greatly beloved, understand the words that I speak unto thee, and stand upright: for unto thee am I now sent. And when he had spoken this word unto me, I stood trembling. Then said he unto me, Fear not, Daniel: for from the first day that thou didst set thine heart to understand, and to chasten thyself before thy God, thy words were heard, and I am come for thy words. And when he had spoken such words unto me, I set my face toward the ground, and I became dumb. And behold, one like the similitude of the sons of men touched my lips: then I opened my mouth, and spake, and said unto him that stood before me, O my lord, by the vision my sorrows are turned upon me, and I have retained no strength, for how can the servant of this my lord talk with this my lord? for as for me, straightway there remained no strength in me, neither is there breath left in me. Then there came again and touched me one like the appearance of a man, and he strengthened me, and said, O man greatly beloved, Fear not; peace be unto thee, be strong, yea, be strong. And when he had spoken unto me, I was strengthened, and said, Let my lord speak; for thou hast strengthened me. Then said he, Knowest thou wherefore I came unto thee? but I will show thee that which is noted in the scripture of truth, etc." The following passage from Passavant will serve as an illustration of this vision:

"Such a condition, and so penetrating an illumination of the spirit can find its agreement only in the original relation of the creature to the Creator. The created spirit does not generally exist for itself, nor by itself, but only in reference to absolute being. The more perfect the creature, the more inward and free is the communion between the creature and the Creator—the more is man a free agent and a co-worker with God. That which holds good in human nature and in all spiritual power in perception and accomplishment, holds good also especially in the region, in which the human spirit, free from earthly nature and of the bonds of time and place, is more active. As we have, therefore, assumed, that the highest magical operation is, where the human spirit becomes the divine organ, so we are justified in assuming, that the highest magical knowledge must be a divinely illuminated power of second-sight, a spiritual beholding, which is moved and led by the divine spirit. So far now, as we must regard the most inward communion of the creature with the Creator as the final destiny of created spirits, so may we regard the holy power of prophecy as an anticipation of a higher and more perfect condition, in which man knows as he is known (1 Corinthians xiii. 9), where his spiritual freedom shall have attained a knowledge in which he can no longer be circumscribed by earthly laws. But since man must elevate himself to that which is good as well as receive good, so this law of the free and created spirit will repeat itself, because man can raise himself, in different degrees to a higher order in this world, and become enlightened in the same degree. If taken in this connection, the power of the divine seer is not to be regarded separately from other spiritual powers by which he can overcome anything foreign to his nature, but rather as a fixed form, a normal and regenerated soul-power. The spirit of man, the image of God, may become the mirror in which the divine type is reflected just in proportion to the purity of this image." (Passavant's Magnetic Life. Second edition, p. 167.)

Further it will only be necessary to remark, in a general way, that God has made use only of the nobleness of the spirit of Israel for the education and redemption of the human family, and that this people, which had become attached to heathen idolatry, and were disobedient and refractory, could only be brought slowly to their true destiny in the severe school of adversity and by heavy chastisements. The way from Ur in Chaldea to Canaan, which was taken by the patriarch Abraham, how far it stretched through its lengths and breadths across to Egypt, and from thence through the wilderness to the promised land of which they were to take possession! Yea, the children of Israel were compelled to wander hither and thither in the wilderness during a period of forty years on account of their vacillation between the service of God and heathen idolatry; were sent in captivity to Babylon; the holy city had to be destroyed, and finally, they were compelled to endure the very fulness of woe and persecution, and all because of their vacillating between the service of the true God and of heathen idolatry. If Israel then is, as it is represented, the favored people of God, then it can be nothing less than the pearl of perfection, and consequently the mirror of perverseness, which always strives after outward forms and ceremonies, and seeks happiness in nature and the dissipations of the present, a happiness which cannot be found on earth. The divine word of revelation alone can disclose the happiness of the peace and blessedness of Paradise, and in order to become partakers thereof, the spirit of man must become inured to two great qualifications, namely, natural obedience to the law and a more than natural hope of reaching his final destiny beyond the life of earth. In order to teach the children of Israel humble obedience to the laws, they were exposed to the severest trials and subjected to the meanest slavery.

To this people and to no other, the commandments were communicated in thunder tones by divinely appointed leaders, in order that it might heed with the inner depths of the mind and not merely superficially with the outward senses. Sacrifices and feasts were not to serve as temporal occasions of rejoicing, but they were to serve as a typical covering through which might be seen the true light of the coming Messiah, as the flower-bud turns toward the approaching light of the sun. The Mercy-seat, the Cherubim, the Holy of Holies, the Pillar of Fire, and Solomon's Temple, are all symbolical manifestations originating in magical visions and point to the coming of Christ. That the entire Mosaic regulation was symbolical and hieroglyphical is admitted by every expert, and the following words express this fact clearly: "and look that thou make them after their pattern, which was showed thee in the mount." Moses, the man of God, therefore, constitutes in the history of the children of Israel the second period of the beginning of religious development. The forms and ceremonies of the law were only now strictly enforced in order to impress men with the importance of the revealed word. But how long a period intervened between the wanderings and sufferings of the Israelites, the wonders by which they were surrounded, the death of the firstborn in Egypt, the lightnings which flashed from the heights of Mount Sinai, and the time of King David, with whom commenced the third period. "He was ruddy, and withal of a beautiful countenance, and goodly to look to," (1 Samuel xvi. 12,) and he, the shepherd of his father's sheep was chosen by the Lord to be king over His people. His obedience toward God, and his unwavering faith not only caused it to be said of him, "that he was a man after God's own heart," but as the root of Judah, born in Bethlehem, he also became the type of Christ. He was both king and prophet, and had to bear many troubles and trials. As a servant of God he sought to lead the children of Israel to God at Jerusalem, the mountain of peace, where finally, the mild, illuminating light of the divine Prince of Peace appeared to the world out of the dark, transitory night, on the cross.

"Now I say, that the heir, as long as he is a child, differeth nothing from the servant, though he be Lord of all; but is under tutors and governors until the time appointed by the father. Even so we, when we were children, were in bondage under the elements of the World." (Gal. iv. 1–3.)

"But when the fulness of time was come, God sent forth his Son, made of a woman, made under the law, to redeem them that were under the law, that we might receive the adoption of sons." (Galatians iv. 4, 5.)

The coming of Christ on earth was not an accidental occurrence as other natural events were. His coming was a revelation ordained by God from the foundation of the world. I have already shown in my anthropological views, that Christ, if he actually was the Son of God, would necessarily have to appear at a fixed time and place, and that his appearance would constitute the beginning of the second period of human power, and that this event would take place on the western coast of Asia.

THE NEW COVENANT.

Having brought forward many of the most extraordinary events of the old covenant which have reference to magic and magnetism, it seems important in more than one sense, also to speak of the new covenant, in order to extract from it that which concerns us so directly, because in the new covenant the magical healing of diseases was effected in so many instances without visible means, as well by Christ himself as by the apostles, from which it would appear that all these miracles and healings were the result of nothing else than magic or magnetism. There are a few extremes here which have been maintained by both the advocates and opponents of these miracles, which we will notice more particularly in this place. In concluding this section we will glance at the existence and signification of Christianity in a general sense, as well as the relation which it bears to magic.

The men of God under the old covenant, who performed such great wonders, and accomplished such wonderful works, were always rather more on the side of humanity than that of the divine, that is, they always evinced only single powers and perfections. The universal expression of full perfection became an absolute reality only through Christ. He it was who first unbarred the new door—severed the chains of slavery, and pointed out the true image of perfection and wisdom in all their fulness to man. Christ again restored to humanity the assurance of immortality. He elevated the spiritual being to a temple of holy fire, and made it a living altar and incense to an eternal peace.

" Since the first man Adam " we read in the Magikon, " is the first fountain of evil, so none of his posterity could be the Saviour, because weakness could not rule over strength ; to be a Saviour it required a being that was more than man. Since God alone is superior to man, this agent, or Saviour, could be nothing less than the essential idea of divine powers. In order to awaken a consciousness in the soul of man of what God really was, he had to bear the Divine character in himself. Even the various judgments of men regarding Christ, show conclusively that all power, all gifts and perfections were united in him."

There are beings for whom the Redeemer has already come, others for whom he comes now, and still others for whom he is yet to come. Since his advent all things have become simplified, and he will simplify himself more and more until everything earthly will vanish. A great sabbath of universal love and peace, as it was in the creation, will signalize the end. He entered the Holy of Holies as the true High Priest, and restored to the elect, through his spirit, not only the lost words of the old book, but gave them a new one, richer in content for the healing of all evil, and for making them invulnerable. In addition he gave to them the holy incense of prayer, and showed them, that without it they would be unable, except through Him alone, to obtain every principle of life. He performed on earth what is found above. He was constantly active, as the highest embodiment of wisdom, in spiritual and temporal arts of charity, and united both in one. But this could only be when He himself was joined in this unity on earth in which he was joined from all eternity. In the end he crowned his work by conferring a spirit which created a knowledge and vitality that were never experienced before. He chose an object of sense as a channel through which to communicate the highest powers of life. Even man may transfer his weak powers in any object: how much more must the mysteries (baptism by water, the communion through bread and wine), instituted by Himself, have possessed a power which man could never possess. The action of the Holy Communion is at the same time corporeal, spiritual and divine, and all things therein contained must become spirit and life, because He himself, who instituted it, was the spirit and the life.

Each true Christian is a living expression of this doctrine and an image of its author. He possesses fervor enough to absorb everything that is diseased and dissolute, and his life is a daily offering in humility and holy fear before God, for the mysteries of God are only revealed to those who fear Him. The true Christian relies upon the commandments of the author of his name. Only such a man can enter into the counsel of peace. If the highest human wisdom continues to be a tottering and perishable structure, a single ray of the sun of the world will make him purer and wiser than all the wise of this earth. Since there are mysteries in every religion, so there are certain things of indescribable power and of the highest weight in Christianity which cannot be explained. So long as these were known only to the true possessors as a sanctuary, Christianity was at rest. But after the great of earth began to set their feet within this sanctuary and desired to see with unprepared eyes; so soon as it was converted into a political machine, divisions and uncertainties ensued. Upon this came the High Priests who separated themselves farther and farther from original purity, and in this way a misshapen mixture of a true monstrosity resulted. Sophists, who flourished like weeds, multiplied these evils by their subtleties, separating that which was united, and covering with darkness and death what was formerly light and life. If even a few traces of purity, zeal and power could be seen here and there, they could accomplish nothing, because the horrors of desolation had already become too general and were preferred by too many. These corruptions were the cause, in later times, that the structure of Christianity was sapped in its very foundations. Only one step from Deism to utter ruin. Out of Deism grew a still worse brood of materialists, who declared that all connection of humanity with higher powers to be idle imagination, and who did not even believe in their own existence. It was very seldom that the generations of the earliest times sinned through great enterprises; those of later periods, on the contrary, sinned through nullity. But there is a truth whose sanctity cannot be shaken, and which will remain firm as long as the world exists.

But if man, through his reconciliation and return to God, and through a true Christian life, receives the powers which the Saviour promised to his followers, namely, "To expel serpents, to heal the sick, and to cast out devils," and this to the same extent that he did himself, (John xiv. 12) and if such a Christian man can in deed and in truth perform greater wonders than one who lives in a state of sin (and we find this to be the case not only with the apostles, but with all godly men of every age), then we must accord to man what is human. I have already spoken of the Christian method of healing, and inasmuch as I refer back to it in this place, the fact will not admit of a doubt, that the healing of Christ as well as by the apostles really had reference to magic and magnetism. They never obtained the means to heal diseases from the apothecary, neither did they possess any secret remedies or magical essences; they possessed an inherent power to heal diseases, and by words they cast out devils, restored the dead to life, healed, through prayer and the laying on of hands, the lame and paralytic, and caused the blind to see and the dumb to speak. To prove this, not however to represent them solely as magnetic cures, but to examine them as 'umanly divine wonders, I will mention a few cures performed by Christ and his apostles as they stand recorded by the Evangelists and the Acts of the Apostles :—

"When he was come down from the mountain, great multitudes followed him. And, behold, there came a leper and worshipped him, saying, Lord, if thou wilt, thou canst make me clean. And Jesus put forth his hand, and touched him, saying, I will; be thou clean. And immediately his leprosy was cleansed." (Matt. viii. 1-3.)

"And when Jesus was entered into Capernaum, there came unto him a centurion, beseeching him to heal his servant. And Jesus saith unto him, I will come and heal him. The centurion answered and said, Lord, I am not worthy that thou shouldest come under my roof: but speak the word only and my servant shall be healed. When Jesus heard it, he marveled, and said to them that followed: Verily I say unto you, I have not found so great faith, no, not in Israel. Go thy way; and as thou hast believed, so be it unto thee. And his servant was healed in the selfsame hour." (Matt. viii. 5-13.)

"And when Jesus had come into Peter's house, he saw his wife's mother laid, and sick of a fever. And he touched her hand, and the fever left her: and she arose and ministered unto him." (Matt. viii. 14, 15.)

"When the even was come, they brought unto him many that were possessed with devils: and he cast out the spirits with his word, and healed all that were sick." (Matt. viii. 16; Mark i. 32.)

"And, behold, they brought to him a man sick of the palsy, lying on a bed and Jesus seeing their faith said unto the sick of the palsy: Son, be of good cheer; thy sins be forgiven thee." (Matt. ix. 2; Mark ii. 3.)

"And, behold, a woman, which was diseased with an issue of blood twelve years, came behind him, and touched the hem of his garment: For she said within herself, If I may but touch his garment, I shall be whole. But Jesus turned him about, and when he saw her, he said, Daughter, be of good comfort; thy faith has made thee whole. And the woman was made whole from that hour." (Matt. ix. 20-22.)

"And when Jesus came into the ruler's house, and saw the minstrels and the people making a noise, he said unto them, Give place; for the maid is not dead, but sleepeth. And they laughed him to scorn. But when the people were put forth he went in, and took her by the hand, and the maid arose."

"And when Jesus departed from thence, two blind men followed him, etc. And when he was come into the house, the blind men came unto him: And Jesus saith unto them, Believe ye that I am able to do this? They said unto him, Yea, Lord. Then touched he their eyes, saying According to your faith be it unto you. And their eyes were opened. (Matt. ix. 27–30.)

The man with the withered hand he healed through the words: "Stretch forth thine hand: and it was restored whole like the other." (Matt. xii. 10–13.)

"And when the men of that place had knowledge of him, they sent out into all that country round about, and brought unto him all that were diseased; and besought him that they might only touch the hem of his garment: and as many as touched were made perfectly whole." (Matt. xiv. 35, 36.)

The daughter of the woman of Canaan, who was grievously vexed with a devil was restored through the faith of the woman. (Matt. xv. 22–28.)

"And great multitudes came unto him, having with them those that were lame, blind, dumb, maimed, and many others, and cast them down at Jesus' feet; and he healed them." (Matt. xv. 30; Luke vii. 22.)

The lunatic who ofttimes fell into the fire and into the water could not be healed by the disciples. But when Jesus rebuked the devil he departed out of him and the child was cured from that very hour. Jesus said unto his disciples: "Because of your unbelief, ye could not cure him. For verily I say unto you, if ye have faith as a grain of mustard seed, ye shall say unto this mountain, Remove hence to yonder place; and it shall remove; Howbeit this kind goeth not out but by fasting and prayer." (Matt. xvii. 14–21.)

Two blind men on the road to Jericho cried unto the Son of David for help: "Then touched he their eyes, saying: according to your faith be it unto you. And their eyes were opened." (Matt. ix. 27–36.)

He healed the lame and the blind in the temple at Jerusalem, who came to him to be healed. (Matt. xxi. 14.)

He healed the man in the synagogue who had a spirit of an unclean devil, whom he rebuked, saying, "Hold thy peace, and come out of him." (Luke iv. 33.)

"Now when the sun was setting, all they that had any sick with divers diseases brought them unto him; and he laid his hands on every one of them and healed them." (Luke iv. 40.)

"Now when he came nigh to the gate of the city (Nain), behold, there was a dead man carried out, the only son of his mother. And when the Lord saw her, he had compassion on her, and said unto her, Weep not. And he came and touched the bier. And he said: Young man, I say unto thee, Arise. And he that was dead sat up and began to speak. And he delivered him to his mother." (Luke vii. 12–15.)

Mary called Magdalene, out of whom went seven devils, the wife of

Chuza and many others possessed of evil spirits were healed and freed. (Luke viii. 2, 3.)

The man possessed of a legion of devils which were driven into a herd of swine. (Luke viii. 27–33.)

"And behold, there was a woman which had a spirit of infirmity eighteen years, and was bowed together, and could in nowise lift up herself. And when Jesus saw her, he called her to him and said unto her Woman, thou art loosed from thine infirmity. And he laid his hands o her, and immediately she was made straight, and glorified God." (Luke xiii. 11–13.)

He healed the king's son at Capernaum who was at the point of deat! through the faith of the lad's father. (John iv. 47.)

The man who had an infirmity thirty and eight years, whom no one would carry into the pool at the sheep market, whose waters when troubled by the angel healed all diseases, he cured by the words: "Rise, take up thy bed and walk." (John v. 2–8.)

The man that was born blind he healed with ground clay and spittle. "He spat on the ground and made clay of the spittle, and he anointed the eyes of the blind man with the clay, and said unto him, Go, wash in the pool of Siloam. He went his way therefore, and washed, and came seeing." (John ix. 1–7.)

St. Mark relates a still more remarkable cure effected by Christ on a blind man: "And he cometh to Bethsaida, and they bring a blind man unto him, and besought him to touch him. And he took the blind man by the hand, and led him out of the town; and when he had spit on his eyes and put his hands upon him, he asked him if he saw aught? And he looked up and said, I see men as trees, walking. After that he put his hands again upon his eyes, and made him look up; and he was restored and saw every man clearly." (Mark viii. 22–25.)

He raised Lazarus from the dead through a fervent prayer to the Father. "Then when Jesus came, he found that he had lain in the grave four days already. It was a cave and a stone lay upon it. Jesus said, Take ye away the stone. Martha, the sister of him that was dead, saith unto him, Lord, by this time he stinketh; for he hath been dead four days. Jesus saith unto her, Said I not unto thee, that if thou wouldst believe, thou shouldst see the glory of God? Then they took away the stone from the place where the dead was laid. And Jesus lifted up his eyes and said, Father, I thank thee that thou hast heard me. And when he thus had spoken, he cried with a loud voice, Lazarus, come forth? And he that was dead came forth, bound hand and foot with grave-clothes; and his face was bound about with a napkin. Jesus saith unto them, Loose him and let him go." (John xi. 17, 38–44.)

These are incidental healings performed by our Saviour and recorded by the Evangelists. There are other legendary narratives of wonders performed by Christ which are not recorded by the Evangelists, of which I will mention only one. It may be found in the History of Jesus, by Eusebius (chap. xii., p. 16), from which Bushing extracted his "Weekly Intelligence for Inquiries into History, Magic and Learning of the Middle Ages" (vol. II., p. 64, Dec., 1817. Breslau)." It is also printed in Kosegarten's Legends. As an extraordinary instance of the vocation and power of Christ and his divine mission and love to man will not prove uninteresting to the friends of Christianity, we will give the contents of several letters written by Abgarus, King of Edessa, who lived cotemporary with Jesus.

The extraordinary mission of Christ and the fame of the wonders which he wrought were noised abroad to the most distant lands, especially his divine power to heal all kinds of diseases. These rumors also attracted the attention of Abgarus, who was the victim of a severe sickness. On this account he wrote the following letter to Jesus:

**Abgarus, King of Edessa, to Jesus, the compassionate Saviour, who appeared in the flesh, in the neighborhood of Jerusalem, All Hail!

" I have heard of Thy exalted virtues and of the wonderful cures performed by Thee without the use of medicine or herbs. The report sayeth, that Thou causest the blind to see, the lame to walk, and thou cleansest the leprous. Thou castest out unclean spirits, and those that are plagued with grievous diseases Thou healest, and Thou bringest the dead back to life. As I heard these reports concerning Thee, I formed two opinions: either that Thou art God, descended from the heights of Heaven, or that Thou art the Son of God, from whom all these wonderful works proceed. Therefore I write this unto Thee, fervently praying that Thou wouldst undertake the trouble to heal me from the heavy sickness by which I am punished. I am told that the Jews threaten Thee with great evil, and resist Thee in anger. It is true, I have but a small city, but it is well appointed and fortified and celebrated, so that it will afford us everything needful."

Thus wrote Abgarus to Christ. Enlightened by divine light, this short letter contains what is of true worth, being full of power and virtue. The following answer was sent by Jesus to Abgarus the King, by the hands of Ananias, who was selected as a messenger:

" Abgarus! Blessed art thou, who hast not seen, yet believed on me. It is written that those which see me believe not on me, that those who see me not may believe on me and be saved. As thou writest to me, I must of necessity fulfil those things for which I was sent into the world; after I have accomplished all these things I shall again be taken up to him who sent me. As soon as I shall have ascended, I will send to you one of my disciples, who will heal you of your painful disease, so that your life and the lives of yours may be preserved."

After the ascension of Christ into heaven, Judas, who was also called Thaddeus, one of the seventy disciples, was sent to Abgarus, who tarried over night on his journey at the house of Tobias, the son of Tobit. Abgarus heard that the disciple whom Jesus had promised to send to him, had arrived, for Tobias had told Abgarus that he had entertained a mighty man of Jerusalem, who healed many diseases in the name of Jesus. " Bring him in to me," said Abgarus. Tobias went immediately to Thaddeus and said : " Abgarus the king sends me to you, and desires that I should lead you to him, in order that you may remove the disease by which he is tormented." " Let us go," answered Thaddeus. " For on his account was I sent here." On the morning of the next day, Tobias took Thaddeus with him and they went to Abgarus. Upon his arrival the lords of the castle stood ready to defend Abgarus, but when the disciple entered Abgarus observed a bright light in his countenance. As Abgarus saw this he humbly worshipped Thaddeus. The astonishment of all present was most complete, for they could not see the strange appearance which Abgarus saw. "Thou art indeed the disciple of Jesus, the Son of God, who promised me in his letter when he said: 'I will send you one of my disciples, who will heal your infirmity, and give you your life and the lives of those belonging to you!'" Hereupon Thaddeus replied: "I have been sent to you because of your trust in Jesus who sent me." And further: "If the faith you have in him increases more and more, then the desire of your heart will be fulfilled according to your faith." Abgarus answered: "I have faith in him to this extent, that if the Roman power did not hinder me, I would annihilate the Jews who crucified Him, with my hosts." Thaddeus said, "The Lord our God, Jesus Christ, fulfilled the will of his Father, and when his will was accomplished, he was taken up to his Father." Then said Abgarus, "I believe in Him and in his Father." Thaddeus answered: "Therefore I lay my hands upon thee in the name of Jesus," and as he did so, Abgarus was made whole from that very hour.

To this belongs the tradition which relates to the sending of the picture of Christ to Abgarus. According to some authors, principally the Damascenes, Abgarus sent a painter to Jerusalem to paint a likeness of Jesus; but the painter was not able to finish a portrait of him because of the splendor of his countenance. Then the Lord stamped his likeness on his mantle through divine power, and in this manner satisfied the desire of Abgarus. According to others, Jesus impressed his features on a linen kerchief and sent it to Abgarus. Be this matter of finishing and sending of this picture as it may, the Damascenes show through later circumstances that such a picture was at Edessa at some time or other, otherwise we should be compelled to reckon the narrative describing the siege of the city of Abgarus by the Persian king Kosroes as among discoveries that cannot be authenticated. According to this legend the walls of Edessa, built of the wood of the olive tree, were surrounded by Kosroes with a funeral-pile of poplar wood, in order to burn them. The then reigning king of Edessa, who is not named, had recourse to the linen shroud upon which were impressed the features of Christ and which was sent to Abgarus. Hereupon (divina vi.) a terrible whirlwind arose which blew the flames away from the city, igniting the funeral-pile of poplar wood, by which all in its immediate vicinity were consumed.

That the promises respecting Christ, namely, that he would heal the sick, were fulfilled, is proven by the additional wonders which were wrought by the apostles, who healed diseases in the same manner that their Master did:—

"And a certain man lame from his mother's womb was carried, whom they laid daily at the gate of the temple which is called Beautiful, to ask alms of them that entered into the temple, who, seeing Peter and John about to go into the temple, asked an alms. And Peter, fastening his eyes upon him with John, said, Look on us. And he gave heed unto them, expecting to receive something from them. Then Peter said, Silver and gold have I none; but such as I have give I thee: In the name of Jesus Christ of Nazareth rise up and walk. And he took him by the right hand and lifted him up, and immediately his feet and anklebones received strength, and he, leaping up, stood and walked, and entered with them into the temple, walking and leaping, and praising God. (Acts iii. 2–8.)

"And believers were the more added to the Lord, multitudes both of men and women, inasmuch as they brought forth the sick into the streets, and laid them on beds and couches, that at the least the shadow of Peter passing by might overshadow some of them. There came also a multitude out of the cities round about unto Jerusalem, bringing sick folks, and them which were vexed with unclean spirits: and they were healed every one." (Acts v. 14–16.)

The history of Simon, the sorcerer, who, on account of his knavery could not perform these wonders, and who attempted to buy the gift to work these wonders from the apostles with money, is especially remarkable. This wonderful story is also applicable to the Simons of our day. "But there was a certain man called Simon, which beforetime in the same city used sorcery (magic), who was converted under the preaching of Philip and was baptized. And the apostles gave unto the new converts the holy spirit. Then they laid their hands on them, and they received the Holy Ghost. And when Simon saw that through laying on of the apostles' hands the Holy Ghost was given, he offered them money, saying, Give me also this power, that on whomsoever I lay hands, he may receive the Holy Ghost. But Peter said unto him, Thy money perish with thee, because thou hast thought that the gift of God may be purchased with money. Thou hast neither part nor lot in this matter: for thy heart is not right in the sight of God. Repent therefore of this thy wickedness, and pray God, if perhaps the thought of thy heart may be forgiven thee. For I perceive that thou art in the gall of bitterness and in the bond of iniquity." (Acts viii. 9–23.) See also the history of Eneas, who had kept his bed for eight years and was sick of the palsy. (Acts ix. 33, 34, 36–41.)

Of the same kind are also the wonderful works of Paul, who challenges our wonder on account of his strength of spirit and his power in all things. "And there sat a certain man at Lystra, impotent in his feet, being a cripple from his mother's womb, who never had walked; the same heard Paul speak, who steadfastly beholding him and perceiving that he had faith to be healed, said with a loud voice, Stand upright on thy feet. And he leaped and walked. (Acts xiv. 8–10.)

"And God wrought special miracles by the hands of Paul, so that from his body were brought unto the sick handkerchiefs or aprons, and the diseases departed from them, and the evil spirits went out of them." (Acts xix. 11, 12.)

The young man named Eutychus who fell from the third story and was taken up dead, and was restored by Paul in the following manner: "And Paul went down, and fell on him, and embracing him said, Trouble not yourselves, for his life is in him. When he therefore was come up again, and had broken bread and eaten, and talked a long while, even till break of day so he departed. And they brought the young man alive, and were not a little comforted." (Acts xx. 8–12.) "And it came to pass that the father of Publius lay sick of a fever and of a flux: to whom Paul entered in and prayed, and laid his hands on him and healed him. So when this was done, others also, who had diseases in the island, came, and were healed." (Acts xxviii. 8, 9.)

Having already spoken about the import of Christian healing and given more or less of a historical character, I will submit the matter to each reader to form his own conclusions to their special peculiarities, in order that he may select that which is most instructive. One thing must not be omitted, in conclusion, and that is, we must first become Christians before we can perform cures by Christian methods. Very few are really Christians who call themselves such; they are only Christians in name and appearance.

The art of healing, according to scriptural principles, deserves special mention in this place, in more than one respect, not only because something truly magical takes place therein, but because scriptural healing is often regarded as the only true one. The principles of this art of healing have been fully established according to certain declarations and doctrines of the Bible. (See Leviticus xxvi. 14; Deuteronomy xxviii. 15–22, etc.; Exodus xiv. 26; also, Ecclesiasticus xxxviii. 9; Psalms cvii. 17–20.)

In this manner, therefore, there exists a higher medical science than the ordinary one, and other pious persons than physicians can heal diseases. "The believing physician," says Marcarius, "is like unto God, but the medical body belongs to the heathen and to the unbeliever." But according to the wise saying of Sirach, the physician is entitled to honor, for he says: "Honor a physician with the honor due unto him for the use ye may have of him, for the Lord hath created him, and he shall receive honor of the king. The skill of the physician shall lift up his head, and in the sight of great men he shall be in admiration." But he too believes that the physician is made only for the sinner: "He that sinneth before his Maker, let him fall into the hands of the physician." (Sirach xxxviii. 15.)

In the New Testament also diseases generally are ascribed to sin. Jesus said to the paralytic when he healed him: "Thy sins are forgiven thee," and he was made whole. And when he healed the man at the pool of Bethesda, who had an infirmity thirty-eight years, when he met him afterward in the temple, he said to him: "Behold, thou art made whole; sin no more, lest a greater evil befall thee." (John v. 14.) The apostles too, and all the saints, insisted upon first curing the patient morally, for a true restoration of the diseased body and spirit can only be effected by a return to God. It is truly remarkable that the wise men of the East, Zoroaster, and all the advocates of the doctrines of emission (system of emanation), the Kabbalists, as well as all later Theosophists, all of whom possesses extraordinary power to heal diseases, defended this doctrine. By some of these, diseases are charged directly to sin, while others attribute them to evil spirits, with whom man becomes associated through sin. That evil spirits are the cause of diseases, destroying and vitiating the healthy sap of the system, no one with less spiritual views than the Theosophists possessed will deny; these are the true bands which Satan has bound. (Luke xiii. 16.)

The originally pure doctrine of Christianity, however, was prepared in early times by the advocates of the system of emanations, which was much more destructive through misrepresentations by model Christians than was intended. Saturninus, Basilides and Karpokrates stood at the head of those according to whose theory everything proceeded from the Æon (heavenly powers). Christ himself was to them an Æon of the first rank, who, by a rigid restraint from sensualism subdued demons (evil spirits), and he who lives as Christ did can subdue them likewise. "Out of Æon, the chief outlet," says Basilides, "heaven was brought into existence." According to Valentine, one of the most celebrated teachers of that day, the Æons were divided into classes, even into male and female classes. Thus, the chief female Æon was the Holy Spirit. By laying on of consecrated hands the subject was made the recipient of this Æon and was sent out to heal demoniac diseases. Notwithstanding that this digression created a variety of ideas, differing from the original doctrine, the effort to heal diseases according to scriptural principles continued for a great length of time a ruling struggle for moral improvement and perfection. If a being is in earnest to live in unconditional obedience toward God, and becomes coverted to God through living, active faith, then God becomes his physician, and he no longer requires the services of an earthly doctor. As soon as the soul is in a perfectly healthy condition, it is stated, so soon will this health be communicated to the body, or rather, the sufferings of the body cannot be regarded as disease—these sufferings cannot affect the soul which has been elevated to heaven. But if a man is not capable of such a self-cure, then let him turn to the physician, for "God created him, and he hath given men skill, that he might be honored in his marvelous works." (Sirach xxviii. 6.) The particular manner in which the physician is to heal according to scriptural principles, is apparent in the foregoing. He must in the first place, become a truly Christian physician, that is a physician priest. He is able to help the sick only through his own health, especially the health of his own soul, and then only when he himself is pure. He must heal the inner man (the soul), for without rest in the soul (inward peace) there can be no real cure of the body; it is therefore indispensable that a true physician must also be a true priest.

The question, whether a scriptural physician is above the necessity of using medicines, or whether he may at times avail himself of their use in healing diseases, can also be easily answered scripturally, and it stands in the same relations as does the question whether a magnetic physician requires any medicines? Generally he must possess the power as a scriptural, and more especially as a Christian physician to heal diseases through prayer and the Divine word, and without medicines; and only in certain cases and when he himself does not possess this power in a sufficient measure, can he avail himself of the use of medicine. They are not made in vain. "For medicine comes from the Most High. The Lord hath created medicines out of the earth, and he is wise that will not abhor them. With such doth he heal men and taketh away their pains." (Sirach xxxviii. 4, 7.) Medicines are good, but they are seldom sufficient. "Go up into Gilead and take balm," says Jeremiah, "in vain shalt thou use many medicines, for thou shalt not be cured." (Jeremiah xlvi. 11.) There are in the meantime also examples in the Bible where, in rare instances, recourse was had to physical remedies. Moses, by casting wood into the waters of Marah, made them sweet. (Exodus xv. 25.) His cure for leprosy by washing, purifying, etc., was truly remarkable. Elias threw salt into the bitter spring, and it became wholesome ever afterward. He also cast meal into the pot, wherein was death, and the vegetables became harmless. Isaiah laid figs on the glands of King Hezekiah and healed him. Tobias cured his blind father with fishgall, a cure that was shown him by an angel. And even Jesus anointed the eyes of the blind man with spittle and clay, and told him to wash in the pool of Siloam, etc. As for the rest, according to the Bible, only outward remedies were used in healing, and these of the simplest and most unstudied kinds. Internal remedies were not used. The means of cure consisted in spiritual purification, in conversion from sin, in prayer to the Father of Life—the physician of the believer. So we read in James v. 13–16: "Is any among you afflicted? let him pray. Is any merry? let him sing psalms. Is any sick among you? let him call for the elders of the church, and let them pray over him, anointing him with oil in the name of the Lord. And the prayer of faith shall save the sick, and the Lord shall raise him up; and if he have committed sins they shall be forgiven him. Confess your faults one to another, and pray for one another, that ye may be healed. The effectual fervent prayer of the righteous man availeth much. In St. Mark vi. 12, we read: "And they went out and preached that all men should repent. And they cast out devils and anointed with oil many that were sick and healed them."

But the scriptural physician does not always heal, and the disease is not always an evil. If temporal enjoyment and earthly felicity were the destiny and end of man, for which the great majority are striving, then should we be justified in regarding sickness as a great misfortune and a heavy punishment, which many will not admit of having deserved. But this planet is not a place of undisturbed peace—not the abode of beings who shall rejoice in a final happiness. Light and shade, day and night, rest and activity, love and hate, peace and war, joy and sorrow, fortune and misfortune, health and sickness, life and death, are the constant changes of this world, and they are not due to accident, but are arranged with caution by a higher hand, to serve as a touchstone, that we may through affliction and suffering, by overcoming evil and purifying ourselves from sensualism, prepare for a better existence. The main object is the health of the soul and the spirit; the health of the body is a secondary matter If the soul is in a state of health the body will become healthy as a consequence. "His flesh shall be fresher than a child's; he shall return to the days of his youth." (Job xxxiii. 25.) If such a strong soul should not become well he will not feel bodily suffering, because he already enjoys a foretaste of the blessedness of the other world. True happiness and perfect rest cannot be found on earth; therefore we should not wonder, but neither should we weep, because of the evanescence of quiet, unmixed pleasure—of purest love, because it is so soon overcast by dark clouds and driven away by fierce storms—neither should we mourn because true happiness can only be found in another world, because true health exist only in the souls of those who are truly united with God, and because help, consolation, and blessing come only from the Father in heaven.

END VOL. I.

VOLUME II.

OF THE

SIXTH AND SEVENTH

BOOKS OF MOSES

FORMULAS

OF THE

MAGICAL KABALA;

OR, THE

MAGICAL ART

OF THE

SIXTH AND SEVENTH BOOKS OF MOSES

TOGETHER WITH

AN EXTRACT

FROM THE GENUINE AND TRUE

Clavicula of Solomon the King of Israel.

NOTE,

FOR THE

FRIENDS OF THE MAGICAL KABALA.

The Citation-Formulas contained in this book must only be pronounced in the Hebrew language, and in no other. In any other language they have no power whatever, and the Master can never be sure of his cause. For all these words and forms were thus pronounced by the Great Spirit. and have power only in the Hebrew Language.

Extract from the Magical Kabala

OF THE

SIXTH AND SEVENTH BOOKS OF MOSES.

BREASTPLATE

OF

MOSES.

These Hebrew words are pronounced as follows:

Jehova, aser Eheje Cether Eleion Eheje.

The Most High, whom no eye hath seen, nor tongue spoke; the Spirit, which did great acts and performed great wonders.

This Breastplate and Helmet pronounced mean Holiness.

HELMET

OF

MOSES

AND

AARON.

Hiebel mare actites barne donene ariaerch.

These are the names which the old Egyptians used instead of the unutterable name of Asser Criel, and are called "The Fire of God," and
"Strong Rock of Faith." Whoever wears them on his person, on a gold
plate, will not die a sudden death.

BREASTPLATE  **OF AARON.**

Sad Jai amara elon hejiana vananel phenaton ebcoel merai.
Tnat is, a Prince of Miens, the other leads to Jehova. Through this
God spake to Moses.

MAGICAL LAW  **OF MOSES.**

Aila himel adonaij amara Zebaoth cadas yeseraije haralius.
These words are terrible, and will assemble devils or spirits, or they
will cause the dead to appear.

ON THE  **HOLINESS.**

Eliaon joena ebreel eloijela aijel agoni sochadon.
These words are great and mighty. They are names of the Creator
and the characters on the Ark of the Covenant.

CONJURATION

OF

ELEAZAR,

THE SON

OF

AARON.

Uniel dilatan Sadai paneim usamigeras saliphos sasna panoi soim Jalaph.

These names, if any one desires to accomplish anything through the four elements or any other things connected therewith, will prove effective. but they cannot be translated into English.

DISMISSION OF ELEAZAR,

AARON'S SON.

Leay yli Ziarite zelohabe et negoramy Zien latebm dama mecha ia meti ozira.

Through this dismission all things dissolve into nothing.

CITATION OF GERMUTHSAI,

OR,

LEVIATHAN.

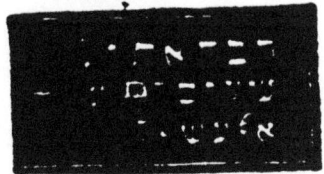

Lagumen Emanuel therefori mechelag laigel yazi Zazael.

With these names Eleazar bound and unbound the spirits of the air

DISMISSION OF LEVIATHAN.

Malooh, Sadaij, cubor Uzuzabiah menkie lejabel maniah ijejavai.

That is: Strong, mighty spirit of heat, go back into thine works, in the name of Jehova.

BALAAM'S SORCERY.

Meloch, bel abAim tiphret hod jesath.

This brings vengeance upon enemies, and must not be disregarded, because it contains the names of the Seven Tables of the Ark of the Covenant.

EGYPT.

Tanabtain ainaten pagnij aijolo asnia hichaifale matae habonr hijcero.

With these words Moses spake to the sorcerers in Egypt. They signify: "the Lord appeared to his servant in the fire, to seal the earth in its four quarters, and the nether earth.

CONJURATION OF THE LAWS OF

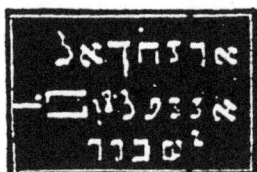

MOSES.

Aijcon dunsanas pethanir thrijgnir ijon cijna nater lavis pistoin.

If you wish to pronounce these words you must fast three days, and you can perform wonders therewith. They cannot be translated on account of the Hebrew characters.

GENERAL CITATION OF MOSES ON

ALL SPIRITS.

Elion goeua adonaij cadas ebreel, eloil ela agiel, aijoni sachadon, essuselas Elohim, deliion jau elijula, delia jari Zazael Paliemao Umiel, onala dilatum Sadati, alma Jod Jael Thama.

This citation is great and mighty; they are the names of the Creator, and the names of the two Cherubim on the Mercy-seat, Zarall and Jael.

DISMISSION OF MOSES.

Waszedim bachanda hezanhad Jehov Elohim asser ehoie Zalim.

GENERAL CITATION OF MOSES ON ALL SPIRITS.

Ahezeraije comitejon Sede leji thomos Sasmagata bij ul ij:os Joua Eloij Zawaijm.

These are the high and powerful utterances which Moses employed in the awakening of the Leviathan, in order to compel him to serve his Lord. The first cannot be uttered and was used by the first inhabitants of earth as a mighty Lord. The whole is good, but not every one can obtain it in perfection without severe discipline.

CHARACTERS

on the left side of the Ark of the Covenant of the Most High.

CHARACTERS ON THE RIGHT SIDE.

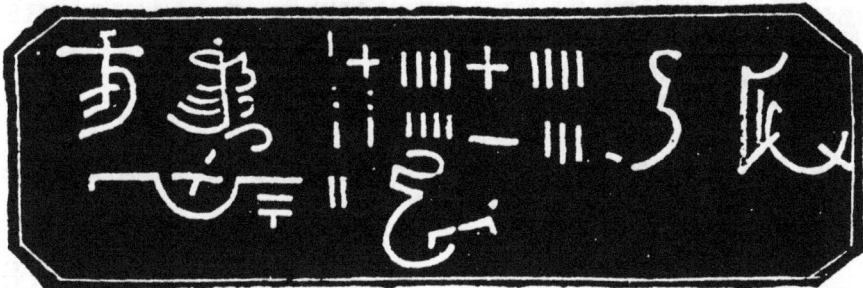

Hear, oh, Israel, the Lord our God is God alone.

CONJURED SPIRIT APPEARS IN A PILLAR OF FIRE.

affabij Zien, Jeramije Latabi damajesano noij lijoij Leaij glij ijre Eijloij liecle loate Eli Eli mecharamethij rijbisas sa fu azira reacha.

The Citation names the twelve evil spirits of man, through the help of the Father, or the Hebrew Eli; it is terrible.

THE SPIRIT APPEARS IN A PILLAR OF CLOUD.

Kahau conor anuhec Zelohae zole hebei ede nego raneij hahabe gizaon

Appendix to the General Citation of Moses on all Spirits.

We, N. N., in this circle, conjure and cite this spirit Fatenovenia, with all his adherents, to appear here in this spot, to fulfil our desires, in the name of the three holy Angels, Schomajen Sheziem, Roknion Averam, Kandile, Brachat Chaijdalic, Ladabas, Labul, Raragil, Bencul, in the name of God. Amen!

THREE NEW SIGNS WITH FROGS, LICE AND PESTILENCE.

Ablan, ageistan, Zoratan, Juran, nondieras portaephias pognij aizamai.

THREE NEW SIGNS AT CATTLE, PESTILENCE, BLACK SMALLPOX AND HAIL.

Ararita Zaijn thanain, miorato raepi sathonik pethanit castas lucias calbera natur sigaim.

GRASSHOPPERS AND DARKNESS.

Hassaday hayloes, Lucasim elayh jacihaga, yoinino, sepactitas barne lud casty!

THE SPIRIT APPEARS IN THE BURNING BUSH.

Baba cuci hiebu ziadhi elenehet na vena vie achya salna.
The spirit which appears here is God himself.

MOSES CHANGES THE STAFF
INTO A SERPENT.

Micrata raepi Sathonik pethanisch, pistan ijttinge hijgatign ijghizian tem
garonusnia castas Lacias astas ijecon cijna caltera Caphas.

MOSES CHANGES WATER INTO
BLOOD.

Aben agla manadel slop siehas malim hajath hajadosch ijonem, cedas
ebreel amphia, demisrael muelle leagijns amaniha.

Principal Citation on all Ministering Spirits of the Air and of Earth, the
like of which Manasses and Solomon used as the true
Key of Salomonis Regis Israel.

EXTRACT

FROM THE

TRUE CLAVICULA OF SOLOMON AND OF THE GIRDLE OF AARON,

bequeathed as a testament to all the wise Magicians, which all the old
Fathers possessed and employed, to have and fulfil all things through the
illustrious power of the mighty God Jehovah, as He, the great Monarch,
gave to His creatures, who worship him day and night with reverence
and in fear, who call loudly upon his name in secret, and sigh to him as
their origin, as of him and from him existing reasonable beings, as on the
point of being environed with the pains of the elements, who strive after
the highest being to and with God. To these He has given this, who will
not forget him in the pleasures of this world, who, still bearing suffering
without forgetting the reality, nor the perishing lustre of the world.

You must stand upon a prominent rock, hold a palm-twig in your right
hand, and wear a wreath of laurel around the temple. Then turn toward the East and say:

Alija Laija Laumin Otheon!

upon this a halo of light will surround you, and when you become sensi-
ble of this light, then fall upon your knees and worship. Then say in an
audible voice, slowly and distinctly:

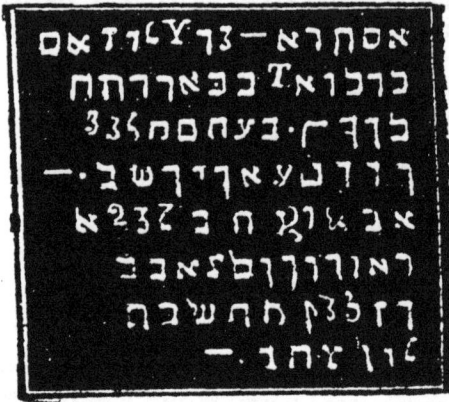

Etiam yoena adonai cadus ebreel eloyela agiel, ayom sachadon ossuselas eloym de liomar elynla lelia yazi zazall Unnel ovela dilatam Saday alma panaim alym canal densy usami yasas calipi calfas sasna saffa sadoja aglata pantomel amriel azien phanaton sarze penerion ya Emanuel Jod jalaph amphia than domirael alowin.

CHARACTERS.

B A m n lazies ala phonfin agaloyes pyol paerteon theserym.

basimel Jael barionia.

apiolet cenet.

FINIS.

BIBLIA,

ARCANA MAGICA ALEXANDER,

ACCORDING TO THE

Tradition of the Sixth and Seventh Books of Moses,

BESIDES

MAGICAL LAWS.

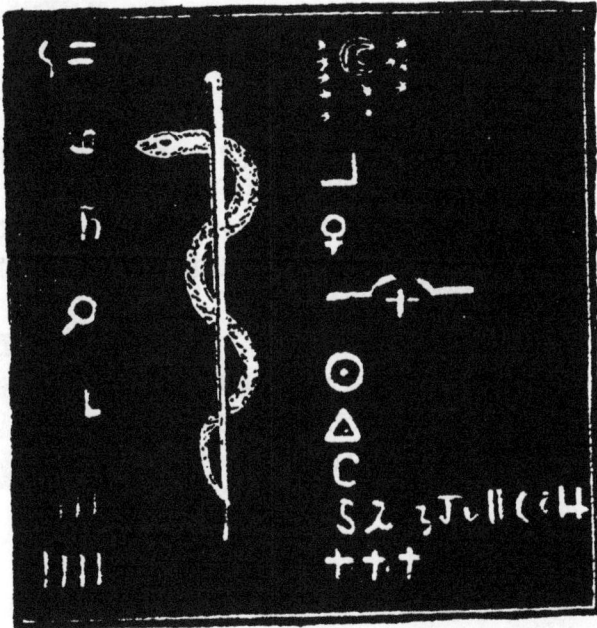

Ex Verbis Revelatis (II) Intellectui Sigillatis Verbis.

NUNC APOSTOLICA ✠ CONSECRATIONE

DE NOVO CONFIRMATO.

Script. de Ellbio.

ANNO MCCCLXXXIII.

TREATISE OF THE SIXTH BOOK OF MOSES.

Chapter I.—THE SPIRIT APPEARS TO MOSES IN A BURNING BUSH.

Chap. II.—MOSES CHANGES THE STAFF INTO A SERPENT.

Chap. III.—MOSES CHANGES WATER INTO BLOOD.

Chap. IV.—THREE NEW SIGNS WITH FROGS, LICE AND PESTILENCE.

Chap. V.—THREE SIGNS ON CATTLE, PESTILENCE, BLACK SMALL-POX AND HAIL.

Chap. VI.—THREE SIGNS OF GRASS-HOPPERS AND DARKNESS.

Chap. VII.—GENERAL CITATION OF MOSES ON ALL SPIRITS.

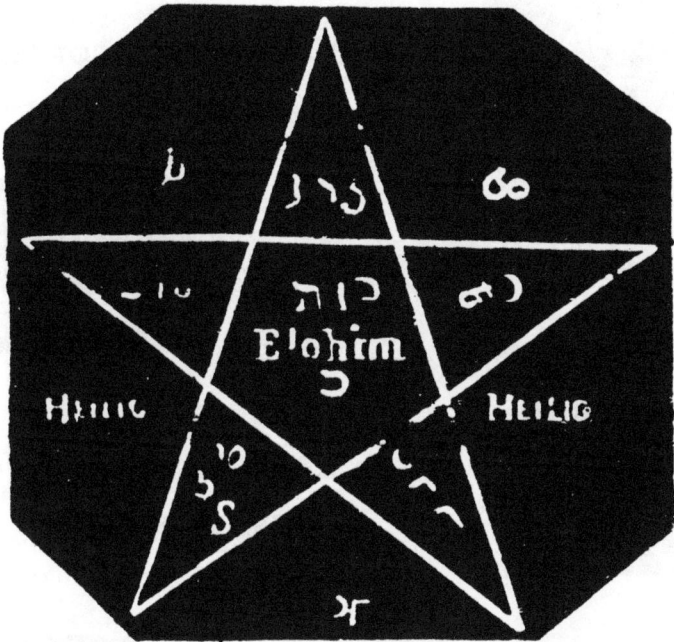

END OF THE SIXTH BOOK OF MOSES.

TREATISE SION.

THE SEVENTH BOOK OF MOSES.

Chapter I.—THE SPIRIT APPEARS IN A PILLAR OF FIRE BY NIGHT.

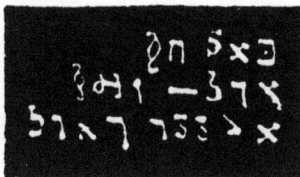

Chap. II. THE SPIRIT APPEARS IN A PILLAR OF CLOUD BY DAY

Ghap. III.—BALAAM'S SORCERY.

Chap. IV.—EGYPT.

Chap. V.—CONJURATION OF THE
LAW OF MOSES.

Chap. VI.—GENERAL CITATION OF
MOSES.

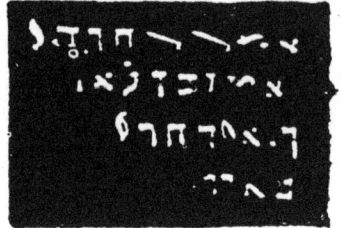

Chap. VII.—GENERAL CITATION OF
MOSES ON

Chap. VII.—CONJURATION OF ELEAZAR.

DISMISSAL.

Chap. VIII.—CITATION OF QUERNITHAY OR LEVIATHAN.

DISMISSAL.

Chap. IX.—MAGICAL LAWS OF MOSES.

Chap. X.—HELMET OF MOSES AND AARON.

Chap. XI.—BREASTPLATE OF MOSES.

Chap. XII.—BREASTPLATE OF AARON.

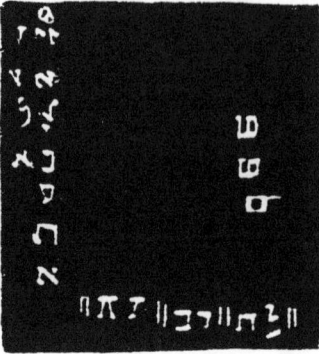

Chap. XIII.—THE CHALICE OF

HOLINESS.

FOR THE LEFT HAND.

FOR THE RIGHT HAND.

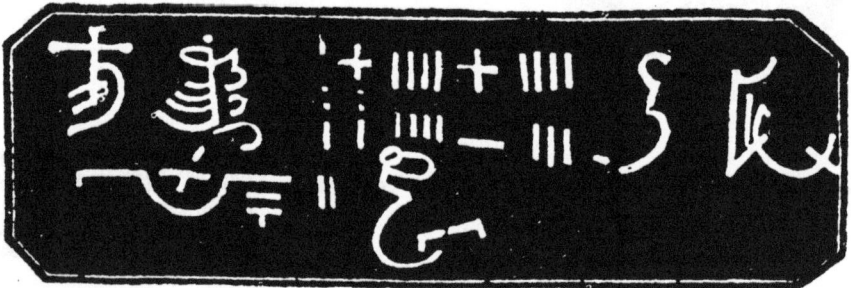

III.

EXTRACT

FROM THE

MAGICAL KABALA,

OF THE

SIXTH AND SEVENTH

BOOKS OF MOSES.

BY

S. T. N.

Translated for the first time from the Cuthan-Samaritan Language into English.

ANNO MDCCXXVI.

TRANSLATOR'S PREFACE.

SINCE the Oriental transcript of this work was imperfect in many parts, the translation of it had to be taken according to the great original book, on account of the purity of its text, and, therefore, it won for itself the advantage of understanding and completing the exercises with serenity and confidence. The translator, in the meantime believes, that no one, who feels honestly called to these things, can ever be made the subject of ill-fortune, or be deceived by the wiles and deceptions of the old serpent, the inevitable fate that will and must fall to his lot under any other exorcisms, and that he may cheerfully and safely move thence, because only the angels of God will perform the service required by Him.

The Vestibule of the Entrance.—The language and manuscript of this rare and eternal monument of light, and of a higher wisdom, are borrowed from the Cuthans, a tribe of the Samaritans, who were called Cuthim in the Chaldee dialect according to the Talmud, and they were so called in a spirit of derision. They were termed sorcerers, because they taught in Cutha, their original place of abode, and afterward, in Samaria, the Kabala or Higher Magic (Book of Kings). Caspar, Melchior, and Balthasar, the chosen arch-priests, are shining lights among the eastern Magicians. They were both kings and teachers—the first Priest-teachers of this glorious knowledge, and from these Samaritan Cuthans—from these omnipotent priests of the fountain of light, who were called Nergal, according to the traditions of Talmud, originated the Gypsies, who, through degeneracy, lost the consecration of their primordial power.

LAWS OF ENTRANCE.

1. Before you can enter the temple of consecrated light, you must purify your soul and body during thirteen days.

2. As a brother and disciple of the new covenant, or as a Christian, you must receive the holy sacrament for the glorification of three kings—Caspar, Melchior and Balthasar.

3. Three holy masses must be read as often as you make use of this Book in your priestly service with your intention fixed upon the three glorified kings.

4. You must provide yourself with a ram's horn, wherewith to call together the angels and spirits. This horn must be included in your intentions of the holy mass.

5. You must wear a breastplate of parchment, ten inches high and ten inches wide, inscribed upon it the names of the twelve apostles with the five-fold name of Schemhamforasch, in the same order that it is placed on the last leaf.

6. You must draw a circle around you upon white paper, or upon sky-blue silk. Its circumference shall be thirteen feet, and, at the distance of each foot, one of the following names must be written, viz: Moseh, Messias, Aaron, Jehova, Adoni, Jesus, Christus, Caspar, Melchior, Balthasar. Al. Al. Al.

7. Between each name you must place the holy symbol of Horet,—namely :—+—or—+—+.

8. The breastplate must be included in the intention of the holy mass.

9. Through consecration with holy triple king's-water and with three burning wax tapers, you must finally pronounce a benediction over this book, the horn, the breastplate, and the circle, after reading a well-selected mysterious ritual.

10. You may enter alone, or begin this great work with two companions, by day or by night, but always from the first to the thirteenth of the month, and during the thirteenth day, and through the whole night of the new moon, and also during full moon, when the three planets, Saturn, Mars and Jupiter, are visible in the heavens on the day of exorcism, either singly or together.

11. You must always stand with your face toward Zion, or toward the rising of the sun.

12. He who refuses a copy of this book, or who suppresses it or steals it, will be seized with eternal trembling, like Cain, and the angels of God will depart from him.

INTRODUCTION AND BEGINNING.

BREASTPLATE OF MOSES.

Schedusi, Weduse, Tiwisi.—I have sinned, I shall sin.

Prayer.—Eternal God of our all! Our God! hear our voice, spare and have mercy upon us. Accept our prayer in mercy and with pleasure. I have sinned. I have committed transgressions. I have sinned before Thee; I have done that which is displeasing unto Thee here in the earth. For the sake of Thy great name pardon me all the sins and iniquities and transgressions which I have committed against Thee from my youth. Perfect again all the holy names which I have blemished, great Champion, terrible, highest God, eternal Lord, God Sabaoth.

HELMET OF MOSES AND AARON.

Wochutu, Tukal, Beschufa, Gutal.—If I shall sin, I shall blow with the great horn.

Here the horn must be blown, three times in succession, toward the four corners of the earth, or toward the four quarters of the earth.

For the ram's horn, in the old covenant, is the symbol of omnipotence and of purification, or of beauty, truth and holiness.

BREASTPLATE OF AARON.

Dehutu, Euwsaltu, Bescholam.—You have sinned. I shall sin in peace.

Prayer.—The Lord, King of all Kings, holy and praised is He, the Father, God, Son of God, the Holy Spirit of God are three in one among these three. In the power of Thy might and Thy right, release those that are bound, receive the prayer of Thy people, strengthen us, purify us, oh, terrible Hero, us who worship Thy only name. Protect them as the apple of Thine eye, bless them, cleanse them, repay them always in mercy and justice. Mighty, holy Lord, reward Thy congregation with Thy great goodness. Thou, the only and exalted God, appear unto Thy people with Thy holy name; receive and remember our prayer; hearken unto our cries, Thou who knowest all secrets and who knowest our desire.

Here the horn must be blown as before.

MAGICAL LAWS OF MOSES.

Kuta-Al, Lewuwat.—We are great! Our hearts!

Prayer.—Oh, Lord, arise, that mine enemies may be destroyed and that they may fly; that those who hate Thee may be scattered like smoke —drive them away. As wax melteth before the fire, so pass away all evil-doers before God, for God has given Thee the kingdom. Pour out Thy wrath over them. Thy wrath seize them. Thou shalt stand upon leopards and adders, and Thou shalt subdue the lion and dragon. With God only can we do great things. He will bring them under our feet.

THE CHALICE OF HOLINESS.

Al, Al, Al. Arise, Thou eternal Angel!
This must be repeated three times in a loud voice, and also through the symbol of the horn, for he is an angel of the sanctuary.

Prayer.—Thou, that art, and wast, and wilt be in the old and new convenant! Eternal, Jehovah, Jesus Christ, Messia, All-beautiful, All-true, All-holy! All-loving and All-merciful in the old and in the new covenant. Thou hast said: Heaven and earth shall pass away, but my words shall not pass away. Thou hast said: I came not to destroy the old covenant, but to fulfil it. Thou hast said: He who sees me sees the Father. Thou hast said If ye have true faith, ye can perform the wonders which I have done, yea, ye will perform yet much greater wonders than I have done. Come also to me for the sake of my faith, come also unto me for the sake of Moses, Thy messenger of faith. Reveal also to me Thy mysterious name from Jehovah, as Thou once did to Thy fire prophet Moses, in solitude; come, and say unto me in love, through the heart of Moses and with the tongue of Aaron:

Scahebual! I shall come!

THE CONJURATION OF ELEAZAR.

Duwatu, Buwatie, Bemaim.—I come to you on the water!
Bring me up N. N.!

DISMISSAL OF ELEAZAR.

Orum, Bolectn, Ubajom.—Cursed by night and by day!

CITATION OF QUERNITHAY OR LEVIATHANS.

These, as well as the following exorcisms, contain only the peculiar names of the angels who will permit the conjured spirits to appear, or will compel them by force to appear. Here the three angels of omnipotence will be called up to drive forth the monsters of hell, namely Elubatel, Ebuhuel Atuesuel!
Each name must be repeated three times.

DISMISSAL.

I beseech and conjure thee, angel Elubatel, conduct N. N. from my presence.
Each angel's name must be called three times toward the four quarters of the earth, and three times must be blown with the horn.

CHAP. III.—BALAAM'S SORCERY.

Onu, Baschba, Nischoaz Hueretz.—In the name of God I conjure the earth.

CHAP. V.—CONJURATION OF THE LAWS OF MOSES.

Keisehu, Nischba, Lawemso.—How to be God, so swarest Thou to our parents.

Prayer.—Eternal of Eternals! Jehovah of Light, Adonai of Truth! Messiah of the All-merciful! Jesus Christ the beloved and All-redemption and love! Thou hast said: Who seeth me seeth also the Father. Father, eternal Father of the old and new covenant; triune Father, triune Son, triune Spirit, our Father, I beseech and conjure Thee by the eternal words of Thy eternal truth.

And now the seventeenth chapter of John, or the prayer of Jesus, must be prayed.

Closing Prayer of the Conjuration of the Law.—Eternal God Jehova, Thou hast said: Ask and it shall be given you. I pray that Thou mayest hear Thy servants Caspur, Melchior and Balthasar, the arch-priests of Thy fountain of light! I pray that thou mayest bid Thy angels to purify me from all sin; that they may breathe upon me in love, and that they may cover me with the shadow of their wings. Send them down! This is my prayer in peace!

CHAP. VI.—EGITGIM.

Conjuration of three angels, Gebril! Meachuel! Nesanel! By the lamp of the threefold eternal light, let N. N. appear before me.

Three calls with the voice and three with the horn.

CHAP. VII.—GENERAL CITATION OF MOSES ON ALL SPIRITS.

Tubatlu! Bualu! Tulatu! Labusi! Ublisi!—Let there appear and bring before me the spirit of N. N.

Each of these five omnipotent angels must be called three times toward the four corners of the world, with a clear and powerful voice, and when the name of each is pronounced three times, then three sounds must be made by the horn. The name of each angel therefore, must have three calls with the voice and three with the horn.

DISMISSAL OF MOSES.

Ubelutusi! Kadukuliti! Kebutzi!—Take away from my presence the spirit of N. N.

Twelve calls with the voice, and twelve with the horn, for each name.

FOR THE LEFT HAND.

These signs were used at the time of burnt-offering in the holy temple.

FOR THE RIGHT HAND.

These are also symbolical of the plagues of Pharaoh in Egypt.

Schema Israel Adonai Elhœjno, Ekat.—Hear, oh, Israel, the Lord our God is God alone.

THE SEVENTH BOOK OF MOSES.

CHAP. I.—THE REVELATION OF ZION.

THE SPIRIT APPEARS IN A PILLAR OF FIRE BY NIGHT.

Talubsi! Latubusi! Kalubusi! Alusi!

Arise and bring me the Pillar of Fire that I may see.

The name of each angel must again have three calls by the voice directed to the four quarters of the earth and an equal number by the horn.

CHAP. II.—THE SPIRIT APPEARS IN A PILLAR OF CLOUD BY DAY.

Bual! come! Aul! arise! Tubo! I come! Wegulo! arise!

In this place the blowing will be repeated.

CHAP. VII.—GENERAL CITATION OF MOSES ON ALL SPIRITS.

Adulal! Abulal! Lebusi!

Arise and bring before me the spirit N.

Calls with the voice and horn as already known.

Here follows the Pentagon, or, the Omnipotent Five-Corners.

This mysterious figure must be written before the exorcism, in the open air, and in the ground, with consecrated chalk or with the index finger of the right hand dipped in holy three-kings-water, the same as it is written up on the paper, but each line must be thirteen feet in length. The conjuror then kneels in the centre of the star, with un-covered head and with face turned toward Zion, and calls first in a loud voice, coming from the heart, the names of Caspar, Belchior and Balthasar, thirteen times, and after calling these thirteen times, he must also then call the high and sacred name of Elokim 375 times with equal fervor and faith. But only as has already been stated in the Laws of Entrance, No. 10, in the first three days or nights of the new moon, or full moon, or when Saturn, Mars and Jupiter appear in the heavens.

CHAP. IV.—THREE NEW SIGNS WITH FROGS, MICE, LICE AND SIMILAR VERMIN.

Adus! Baachur! Arbú! Ulu!
Frogs, mice, lice and similar vermin arise in our service.

CHAP. V.—THREE SIGNS AT CATTLE PESTILENCE, BLACK SMALLPOX AND HAIL.

Abull, Baa!
Pestilence, black smallpox, etc., arise in our service.

CHAP. VI.—THREE SIGNS WITH GRASSHOPPERS AND DARKNESS.

Ardusi! Dalusi!
Grasshoppers, Darkness, arise in our service.
These are the plagues which the Cuthians often employed in their exorcisms for punishment.

Revelation of the Sixth Book of Moses.

CHAP. I.—THE SPIRIT APPEARS UNTO MOSES IN A BURNING BUSH.

CONJURATION.

Kaluku! Ubesu! Lawisu!—Arise and teach me.

Calls with voice and horn as is already known.

CHAP. II.—MOSES CHANGES THE STAFF INTO A SERPENT.

Tuwisu! Kawisu! Lawisu!—Arise and change this staff into a serpent.

Calls with voice and horn as usual.

MOSES CHANGES WATER INTO BLOOD.

Akauatiu! Tuwalu! Labatu!—Arise and change this water into blood.

Calls with voice and horn as usual.

Here follows the Latin title of this book, from which these magical fragments are extracted.

BIBLIA

Arcana Magica Alexandri (Magi),

ACCORDING TO

(REVEALED) TRADITION OF THE SIXTH AND SEVENTH

BOOKS OF MOSES.

TOGETHER WITH THE

MAGICAL LAWS.

Ex Verbis H. (human) Intellectu Sigillatis Verbis.

Nunc Apostoli✠ ✠ (Anctoritate) Consecrata de Novo Confirmata ✠ ✠ ✠ (Licentia.)

Script de Eppbio.

ANNO MCCCXXXVIII.

Now Moses appears on the right of the silk, in a simple priestly garb, holding the tree of life, which has four leaves in the right hand, and the ram's horn in the left.

Upon his heart rests the cross; a wide, white band flows over his shoulder and breast, a broad, white girdle graces his loins. He stands upon a kind of hat, which is decorated with three flowers. On the right hand of the hat reposes a dove having a ring in her bill, on the left side and over the head of Moses a threefold tripod with magical hieroglyphics thereon rises upward.

1. Upon the leaves of the tree of life you read the words:

Besulo! Bedunim! Labatel!

That is, if you are not pure, or if you do not become pure as a virgin through the two angels Bunedraim and Lebutal, you cannot reach toward the tree of life.

2. A hat adorned with three flowers, upon which Moses stands, and from which a dove with ring in her bill appears to descend, that is:

If you preserve faith and hope with holy care, the spirit of omnipotence will emanate from you.

3. A threefold intertwined triangle, extending from the feet to the head, having inscribed upon it the names of the three angels, Meachuel, Labatel, Kautel, that is: And the three angels of the triune God, Meachuel, Lebatei, Ketuel, will surround and carry you upon their hands.

On the reverse side of the picture of Moses, or rather on the first leaf, according to Oriental reckoning, appears the elevated, winding and crowned serpent, holding a ring in her teeth. Around the serpent may be seen the moon, the stars, planets, water and many other magic hieroglyphical signs. On the left side of the tail may be seen seven nails, on the right side are magical hieroglyphics making the name of Schemhamporasch. To see Jesus Christ with the cross, that is to say: Jesus Christ, through his love, and by his seven wounds and through his death on the cross, for his love's sake, has overcome the kingdoms of this world, and thus took again from the old serpent, the devil the seal-ring of human omnipotence, or the happiness of man to all the eternal eternities, in order to fulfil the old covenant in the new covenant, for the eternal glorification of the eternal Father in the eternal Son, through the eternal Spirit. Amen.

VI.

Biblia Arcana Magica Alexander,

ACCORDING TO THE TRADITION OF THE

SIXTH AND SEVENTH BOOKS OF MOSES.

TOGETHER WITH THE MAGICAL LAWS.

Ex Verbis (H) Intellectui Sigillatis Verbis Nunc Apostolica ✠

Consecrat de Nove Confirmati ✠ ✠

SCRIPT DE ELSTRO.

MCCCLXXXIII.

BREASTPLATE OF MOSES.

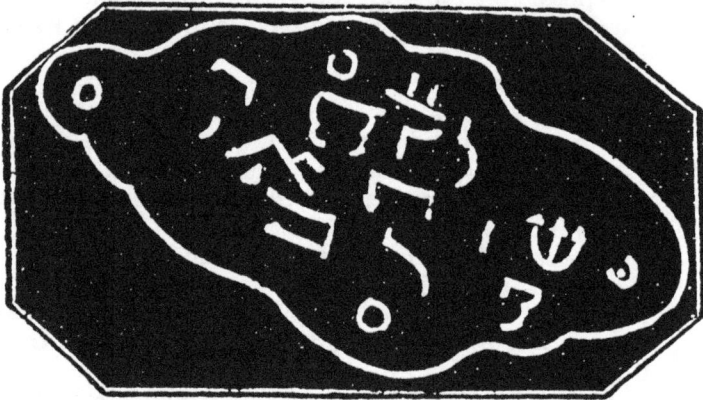

HELMET OF MOSES AND AARON.

BREASTPLATE OF AARON.

FOR THE LEFT HAND.

FOR THE RIGHT HAND.

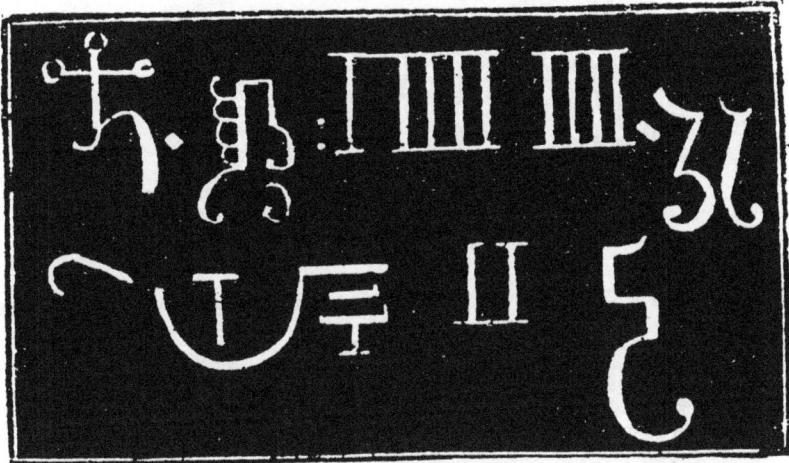

Hear, oh Israel, the Lord our God is God alone. Amen.

Tradition of the Sixth Book of Moses.

Chap. I.—THE SPIRIT APPEARS IN A BURNING BUSH, CITATION OF MOSES.

Chap. II.—MOSES CHANGES THE STAFF INTO A SERPENT.

Chap. III.—Moses Changes Water Into Blood.

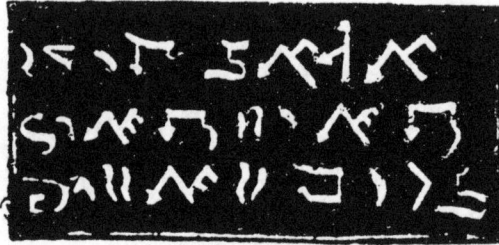

Chap. IV.—Three New Signs With Frogs, Lice, and Similar Vermin

Chap. V.—Three Signs at Cattle, Black Smallpox and Hail.

Chap. VI.—Three Signs With Grasshoppers and Locusts.

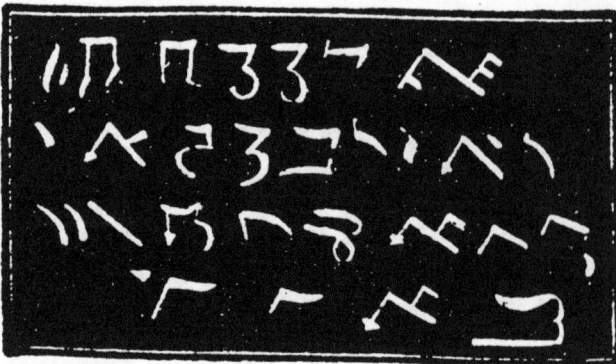

Chap. VII.—GENERAL CITATION OF MOSES ON ALL SPIRITS.

END OF THE SIXTH BOOK OF MOSES.

Tradition of the Seventh Book of Moses.

Chap. I.—THE SPIRIT APPEARS IN A PILLAR OF FIRE BY NIGHT.

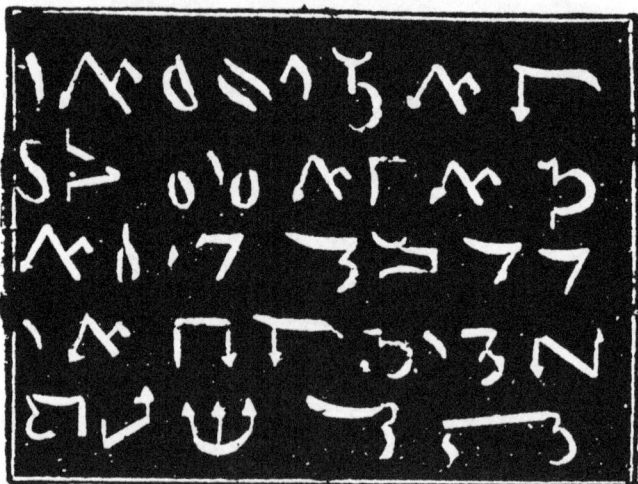

Chap. II.—THE SPIRIT APPEARS IN A PILLAR OF CLOUD BY DAY.

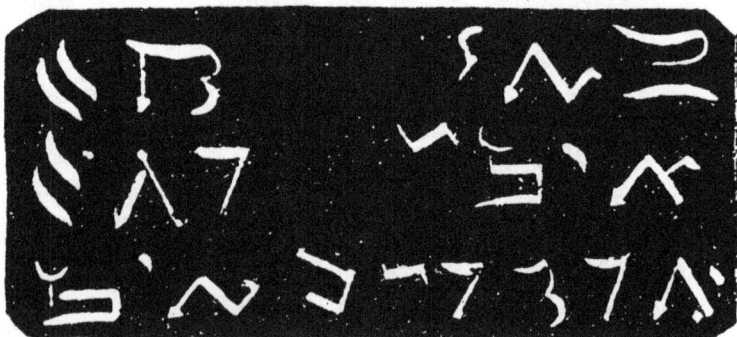

Chap. III.—BALAAM'S SORCERY.

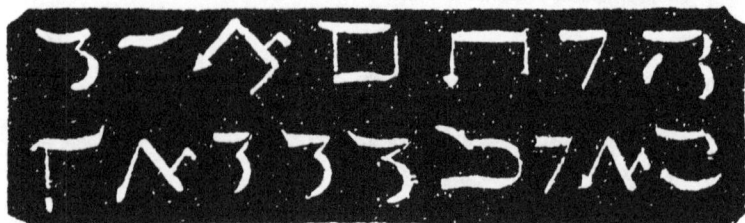

Chap. IV.—EGIFGIM.

Chap. V.—CONJURATION OF THE LAWS OF MOSES.

Chap. VI.—GENERAL CITATION OF MOSES ON ALL SPIRITS.

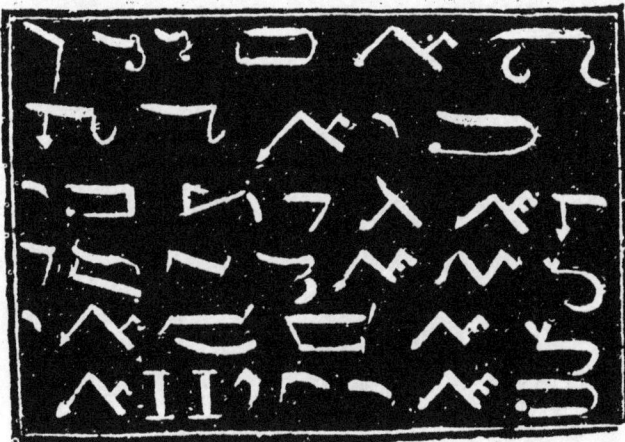

DISMISSAL

OF

MOSES.

MAGICAL

LAWS OF

MOSES.

CONJURATION OF ELEAZAR.

DISMISSAL OF ELEAZAR.

CITATION OF QUERMILLAM OR LEVIATHAN.

DISMISSAL OF QUERMILLAY OR LEVIATHAN.

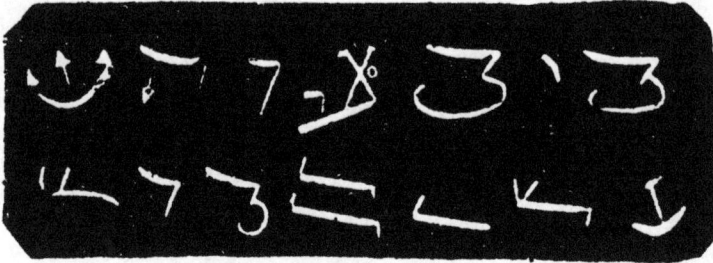

APPENDIX.

I.

Magical (Spirit-Commando) beside the Black Raven.
Romae ad Arcanum Pontificatus unter Popet Alexander VI., printed and anno (Christi) M. D. I.

PREFATIO.

Quiam per ILLVSTREM et Generosum D ARNOLDVM comnitem Bemthemi Tichelenburgi-steinfordii Dominum in Rhoed Wivelhoven magica Arcana originali celeberrimi D. Joannis FAUSTI in Germania ex Kundling oriundi Baroni HERMANNO in Mosa Ripa and Geldriae fines Batoburgico Episcopo fideliter admanuata et anno quadragesimo supra sesquimillesimum ad VATICANUM APOSTOLICUM NOS-TRUM ROMAN per eum transmissa sunt, volumus: ut hæc typis imprimantur, ad Arcanum Pontificatis mandentur et sicut pupilla oculi in archivio Nostro serventur et custodiantur atque extra Valvas Vaticanus non imprimantur neque inde transportentur, si vero quiscunque temere contra agere ansus fuerit, DIVINAM maledictionem latæ sententiæ ipso facto servatis. Nobis solis reservandis oa incursurum sciat, ita mandamus et constituimus Virtute Apostolica. Ecclesiae JESU CHRISTI sub pœna Excommunicationis et supra Anno secunda Vicariatus Nostri. ROMAE VERBI INCARNATI Anno M. D. I. ALEXANDER VI.

D. G. PONTIFEX,
F. Piccolomepus Cardinalis Caneefi.

APPROBATIO.

numuiet structio Vaticana Sapienti paucis maxima praeterea assecuratur a sua Sanctitate desuper facto Consecratio Canonica.

LECTOR.

Ne spernas librum, si non intelligis esto,
Si contra captum est, satis esti, quod vota secundet.
Frigidus in pratis cantaudo rumptiur anguis.   Ec. 8 virg.
Quidlibet audendi semper fuit acqua potestas
Hoc lege lector opus sacra hæc monumenta polorum
Hinc optata sarass hæc te tua vota docebant,
Fide cave, sapienter age, et virtute labora,
Sicque heabit opus pia CONSECRATIO facta.

✠ ✠ ✠

D. I. F.

INSTRUCTIONS.

If you want to cite and compel spirits to appear visibly before you and render you obedience, then observe the following instructions :

1.   Keep God's commands as much as you can possibly do.
2.   Build and trust solely upon the might and power of God ; believe firmly on his omnipotent help in your work, and the spirits will become your servants and will obey you.
3.   Continue your citations, and do not cease, even if the spirits do not appear at once.   Be steadfast in your work and faith, for the doubter will obtain nothing.
4.   Take especial notice of the time, viz :

Monday night, from eleven until three o'clock.
Tuesday night, from ten until two o'clock.
Wednesday night, from twelve until three o'clock.
Thursday night, from twelve until two o'clock.
Friday night, from ten until three o'clock.
Saturday night, from ten until twelve o'clock.

The Sabbath keep holy to the Lord Sabaoth, Adonai, Tetragrammaton.
5.   It must, at the same time, be new moon.   Perhaps you may say, "Why these hours and signs—are they not all the days of the Lord?" It is true ; but not all hours, and all signs, are favorable to rule over their spirits.
6.   Complete the following circle, described in this work, on parchment, written with the blood of young white doves.   The size of the circle may be at your own option.
7.   If you wish to undertake the operation, be sure to consecrate the circle previously.

✠ ✠ ✠

(See this Circle.   Fig. 24.)

Ego N. N., consecro et benedico istum Circulum per Nomina Dei Attissimi in ec Scripta, ut sit mihi et omnibus Scutum at Protectio

Dei Fortissimi Elohim Invincibilie contra omnes malignos Spiritus, earumque Potestates. In Nomine Dei Patris Dei Filii Dei Spiritus Sancti. Amen.

Upon your entrance into this Circle speak as follows: Tetragrammaton, Theos, Ischiros, Athanatos, Mes'as, Imas, Kyrie Eleison. Amen.

After you have entered the Circle begin your operation with the following prayer from the Ninety-first Psalm.

He that dwelleth in the secret place of the Most High shall abide under the shadow of the Almighty. I will say of the Lord, He is my refuge and my fortress, my God, in Him will I trust. Surely he shall deliver me from the snare of the fowler and from the noisome pestilence. He shall cover thee with his feathers, and under his wings shalt thou trust. His truth shall be thy shield and buckler. Thou shalt not be afraid for the terror by night, nor for the arrow that flieth by day. Because thou hast made the Lord, which is my refuge, even the Most High, thy habitation. There shall be no evil befall thee, neither shall any plague come near thy dwelling. Because he hath set his love upon me, therefore will I deliver him. I will set him on high because he hath known my name. He will call upon me and I will answer him; I will be with him in trouble, I will deliver him and honor. With long life will I satisfy him and show him my salvation, even so help me and all them that seek thy holy ✠ God the Father ✠ God the Son ✠ God the Holy Ghost. Amen.

Citation

OF THE

SEVEN GREAT PRINCES

FROM THE

Sixth and Seventh Books of Moses Biblia Magical.

CITATIO AZIELIS.

Agla Cadelo, Samba, Caclem, Awenhatoacoro, Aziel, Zorwot. Yzewoth, Xoro, Quotwe, Theosy, Meweth, Xosoy, Yachyros, Gaba, Hagay, Staworo, Wyhaty, Ruoso Xuatho, Rum, Ruwoth, Zyros, Quaylos, Wewer, Vegath, Wysor, Wuzoy, Noses,* Aziel.*

CITATIO ARIELIS.

Yschyros, Theor Zebaoth, Wyzeth, Yzathos, Xyzo, Xywetuo.owoy, Xantho, Wiros, Rurawey, Ymowe, Noswathosway, Wuvnethowesy, Zebaoth, Yvmo, Zvswethonowe, Yschyrioskay, Ulathos, Wyzoy, Yrsawo, Xyzeth, Durobijthaos Wuzowethus, Yzweoy, Zaday, Zywaye, Hagathorwos, Yachyros, Imas, Tetragrammaton, Ariel.

✠✠✠

CITATIO MARBUELIS.

Adonay, Jehova, Zebaoth, Theos, Yrhatheroewa, Weheoymathos, Zosim, Ygthoroy, Vegerym, Abaij, Weges, Gijghijm, Zowolj, Yhenowe, Wothym, Kijzwe, Uijwotu, Cenegres, Hehgewe, Zebaoij, Wezater, Zibuo, Sijbetho, Ythos, Zeatijm, Wevoe, Stijwoljmwethij, Pharveij, Zewor, Welges, Ruhen, Mrhatheroes, Stawows, Zijen, Zijwowij, Haroe, Worse, Yswet, Zebaeth, Agin, Marbuel.

CITATIO MEPHISTOPHILES.

Messias, Adonaij, Weforus, Xathor, Yxewe, Soraweijs, Yxaroa, Wegbarh, Zljhalor, Weghaij, Wesoron, Xoxijwe, Zijwohwawetho, Ragthoswatho, Zebaoth, Adonaij, Zijwetho, Aglaij, Wijrathe, Zadaij, Zijebo Xosthoy, Athlato, Zsewey, Zyxyzet, Ysche, Sarsewu, Zyzyrn, Deworonhathbo, Xyxewe, Syzwe, Theos, Yschaos, Worsonbesgosy, Gesgowe, Hegor, Quaratho, Zywe, Messias, Aharabi, Mephistophiles.

CIDATIO BARBUELIS.

Yschiros, Imns, Zebaoth, Otheos, Kuwethosorym, Zylohym, Zaday, Yschowe, Quyos, Zenhatorowav, Yzwesor, Xywoy, Yzyryr, Zalijmo, Zabaoth, Adonaii, Messios, Aglaabaij, Stoweos, Hijwetho, Ycoros, Zijwetho, Uwoim, Chamoweo, Zijzobeth, Sotho, Emnohalj, Zedije, Huwethos, Chorij, Yzquoos, Lijraije, Weghoijm; Xiixor, Waijos, Gofaljme, Toroswe, Yeijros, Emanuel, Imas, Barbuel.

CITATIO AZIABELIS.

Thoeos, Ygweto, Yzgowoij, Quiseo, Wijzope, Xorsoij, Nowetho, Yxose, Haguthou, Xoro, Theos, Magowo, Wijzosorwothe, Xaroshaij, Zebaoth, Emanuel, Messia, Yzijwotho, Zadaij, Xexhatosijmeij, Buwatho, Ysewet, Xijrathor, Zijbos, Malhatou, Yzos, Uzewor, Raguil, Wewot, Yzwewe, Quorhijm, Zadob, Zibethor, Weget, Zijzawe, Ulijzor, Tretragaammaton, Aziabel.

CITATIO ANIQNELIS.

Thoeos, Aba, Asba, Aba, Agathoswaij, Yzoroij, Ywetho, Quardos, Quasoai Uschjjros, Cijmoe, Qowathim, Gefoij, Zarobe, Weghatj, Ohe gathorowaij, Mesows, Xslose, Waghthorsowe, Wephatho, Yzebo, Sto ilwethonaij, Quorathon, Sijbo, Mephor, Wijhose, Zaloroa, Ruetho Zebaathonaijwos, Zijweth, Ycarij, Ruwethonowe, Ruiathosowaij Zebaoth Messias, Aniquel.

[Now follow the four leaves—Figs. 24, 25, 26, 27, 28.]

CIRCLE WRITTEN ON PARCHMENT

WITH THE

BLOOD OF WHITE YOUNG DOVES.

(Fig. 24.)

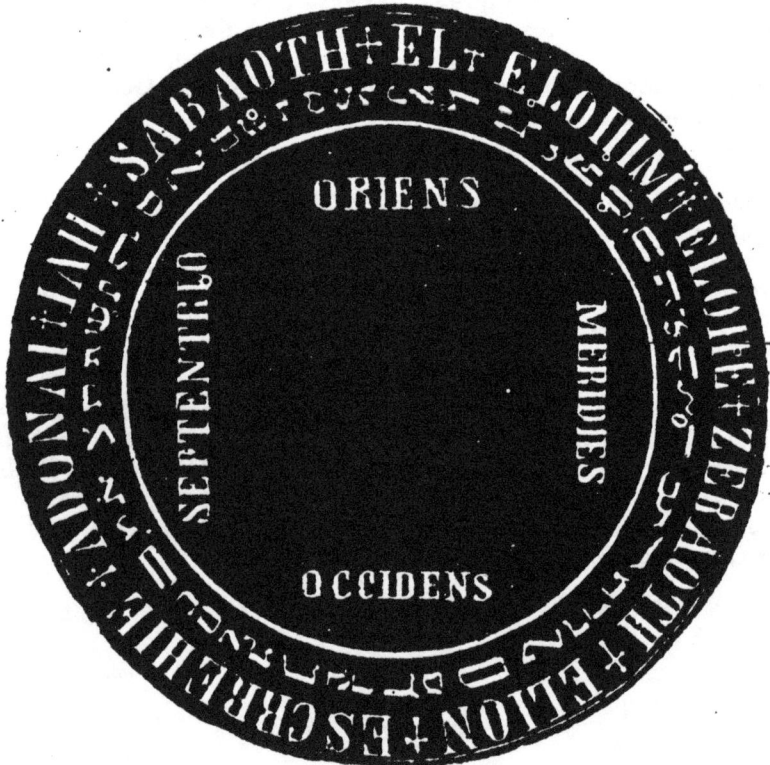

AZIELIS

Seal or Character for Coercion and Obedience.

(Fig. 25.)

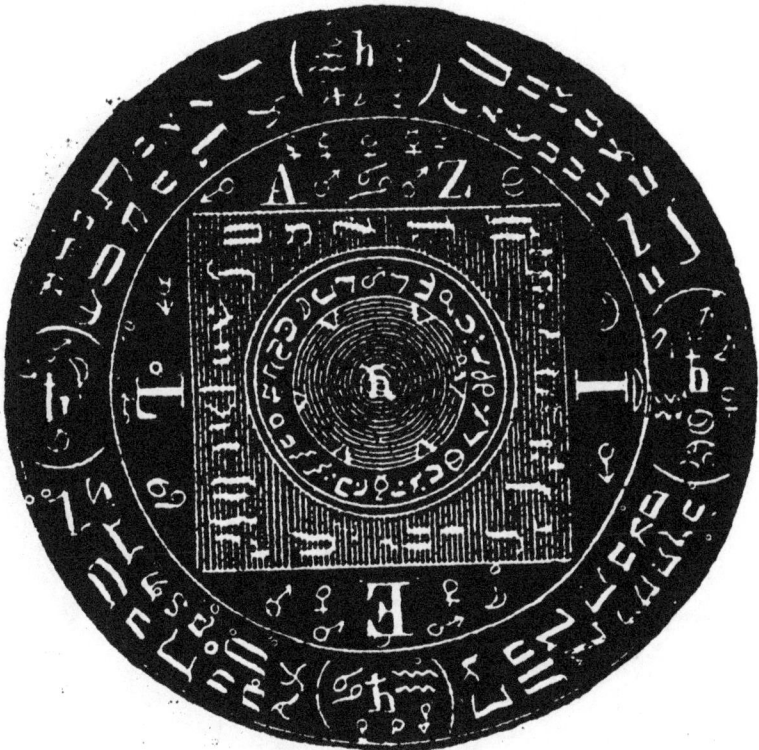

✠   ✠   ✠

ARIELIS

Seal or Character for Coercion and Obedience.

(Fig. 25.)

✠   ✠   ✠

MARBUELIS

Seal or Character for Coercion and Obedience.

(Fig. 26.)

✠   ✠   ✠

MEPHISTOPHILIS

Seal or Character for Coercion and Obedience.

(Fig. 26.)

BARBUELIS

Seal or Character for Coercion and Obedience.

(Fig. 27.)

✠   ✠   ✠

AZIABELIS

Seal or Character for Coercion and Obedience.

(Fig. 27.)

✠ ✠ ✠

ANTQUELIS

Seal or Character for Coercion and Obedience.

(Fig. 28.)

✠   ✠   ✠

NOTE.

THE USE OF THE SEALS.

When these great princes do not appear immediately on the foregoing Citations, or if they hesitate in their obedience, then take frankincense and myrrh, and cast them upon burning coals, and when the smoke arises, place the spirit-seal thereon, with the following mysterious words:

✠   ✠   ✠

Ex VI. and VII. Libro
MOSIS.
Bibliae Arcano
MAGICAE.

ALTISSIMA DIE VERBA.

SPIRITUUM CACTIVA MOSIS AARON ET SALOMOINS.

Zijmuorsobet, Noijm, Zavaxo, Quehaij, Abawo, Noquetonaij, Oasaij, Wuram, Thefotoson, Zijoronaifwetho, Mugelthor, Yzxe, Agiopuaij, Huzije, Surhatijm, Sowe, Oxursoij, Zijbo, Yzweth, Quaij, Salarthon, Qaij, Qeahaij, Qijrou, Sardowe, Xoro, Wugofhoswerhij, Kaweko, Ykquos, Zehatho, Aba. Amen.

APPARITIO, OR THE APPARITION,

Is almost instantaneous upon these mysterious words and procedure. As soon as they appear, however, address them and compel them to obedience with the following coactionis

BINDING OF MOSES.

Zebaoath, Abatho, Tetragrammaton, Adonaij, Abathoij, Xijhawe, Aglaij, Quohowe, Agla, Muijroshoweth, Phalowaij, Agla, Theos, Messias Zijwethororijm, Feghowo, Aba, Mowewo, Choe, Adonaij, Cewoe, Christohatos, Tetragrammaton.

A ✠ m ✠ c ✠ n.

INSTRUCTIONS.

Since the spirits will now appear quickly, bring your desires forward honestly, as if before your fellow-man, without fear, for nothing can harm you, much rather, all must serve you and yield obe dience and serve you according to your wishes. In this connection, be careful that you do not compromise in any degree with the spirit for all this power, and word of might, which Moses, Aaron and Solomon used according to the revelations of God, are sufficient to compel the spirits to reveal to you the treasures of the earth and sea, and to give them to you without harm and deception.

✻ Mihi ✻ Fausto ✻ Crede (✠) Experto ✻

REMARKS.

AZIEL is a very prompt treasure-spirit of the earth and of the sea. He appears in the form of a wild ox.

ARIEL is a very serviceable spirit, and appears in the form of a ferocious dog. He commands the lost treasures of the land and sea.

MARBUEL appears in the form of an old lion. He delivers the treasures of the water and the land, and assists in obtaining all secret knowledge and honors.

MEPHISTOPHILES is ready to serve, and appears in the form of a youth. He is willing to help in all skilled arts, and gives the spiritus Servos, otherwise called "familiares." He brings treasures from the earth and from the deep very quickly.

BARBUEL is a master of all arts and all secret knowledge, a great master of all treasure. He is very accommodating, and appears with alacrity in the form of a wild hog.

AZIABEL is a prince of the water and mountain-spirits and their treasures. He is amiable, and appears with a large crown of pearls.

ANITUEL appears in the form of a serpent of Paradise. He confers great wealth and honors according to wish.

APPENDIX ✻ MAGICUS

The Seals or General Characters of the Seven Great Princes of Spirits must be written upon virgin parchment, with the blood of butterflies, at the time of full moon; besides this, know that the Seven Great Princes of Spirits have among them some of the legions of crown-spirits which were expelled from Heaven, ita ex Revelatinoe Traditio. VI. et VII. libri Mosis. Amen. †††

> Mundus ater cum illis
>   Me pactum dicit habere,
> Sed me teque Deus
>   Te illo custodiat omnes.

D. I. F.
VALEDICTIO OR DISMISSAL OF THE SPIRITS.

Since the spirits have now served you according to your wish, dismiss and discharge them as follows:

Zebaoth, Theos, Yschyres, Messias, Imas, Weghaymnko, Quoheos, Roveym, Christoze, Abay, Xewefaraym, Agla.

And now depart in the name of God; praise, live and thank God to the

E. N. D.

Peter. James. John. Andrew. Philip. Thomas.

1. 𝔄 𝔅. 1.

J e h o v a

Messias Urim Thummim

A—⌢—

Bartholomew, Matthew, James, Alpheus, Simon the Canaanite, Judas, Thaddeus, Matthias.

This Table belongs to the Chapter of the Laws.

II.
TABELLAE RABELLINAE

SPIRITI-COMMANDO,

id est
MAGIAE ALBAE et NIGRAE CITATIO ✠ GENERALIS
Upon all Spirits, Good and Evil.
ROMAE
Vaticano ad Arcanum Pontificatus under Pope Alexander VI., printed in the year 1501.

CITATIO GENERALIS MOSIS, AARONIS ET SALOMONIS CANONIZATA AB ALEXANDRO VI.

Aba, Alpha, Omega, Hewozywetony, Xewerator, Menhatoy, Queo, Zuwezet, Ramcy, Ruwetze, Quano, Duzy, Xenthono-Rohmatru, Xono, Xonoxehehoos, Zebaoth, Aglay, Tetragammaton, Adonay, Theos, Yschyroroseth, Zumquvos, Nywe, Athanatos, Thoy, Quyhet, Homor, Wethoum, Ywae, Ysgeboth, Oray, Zywo, Ysgewot, Zururogos, Zuy, Zywethorosto, Rurom, Xuwye, Xunewe, Keoso, Wecato, Zyweso, Tetragrammaton.

Pronounce the name of the good or evil ††† spirit distinctly, when he will appear very suddenly; you may then address him.

COARCTIO OR THE BINDING OF SPIRITS.

Theohatatos, Quyseym, Gefgowe, Phagayr, Messias. Amen.

MONARCHIA OF THE GOOD SPIRITS FAMILIARES

to cite for all human ministration are the following:

Seraphim Urlel, Cherubim Raphael, Thronus Oriphiel Dominatio Zachariel, Potestas Gabriel, Virtus Barbiel, Principatus Requel, Archangelus Anael, Angelus Phaleg.

These are the Princes of the (IX.) Choir of Angels. They have among them many

1,000 times 1,000 without end
Millia Millium sine Fine Dicentium
Sanctus, Sanctus, Sanctus.

These angel princes appear very willingly to human beings to help and serve them in all things, as well as the following:

✠ ✠ ✠

BONI SPIRITUS, OR GOOD SPIRITS.

Chymchy, Asbeor, Yzazel, Xomoy, Asmoy, Diema, Bether, Arfose, Zenay, Corowe, Orowor, Xonor, Quiheth, Quato, Wewor, Gefowe, Gorhon, Woreth, Hagyr, Welor.

†††

ACHARONTICA SPIRITUS

Even though Evil, they are still Familiar or Ministering Spirits, and Ready to Serve.

Thebot, Wethor, Quorthonn, Ywote, Yrzon, Xysorym, Zuwoy, Puchon, Tulef, Legioh, Xexor, Woryon.

*** † ***

INSTRUCTION.

Concerning the Magia Albia, take notice, that all good spirits must be cited when the moon is full, the Princes of the (IX.) Choir of angels as well as other good angel-spirits.

Concerning the Magia Nigra, take notice, that the VII. Princess of Devils must be cited in new moon, other evil spirits are cited the most readily in the dark of the moon, or at the time of an eclipse of the sun or moon. The circle already described, as coercive of hell, is for all spirits.

VALEDICTIO, OR DISMISSAL,

of all good and bad spirits according to the tradition of the Tabella Rabellini, out of the Sixth and Seventh Books of Moses.

Theos, Zebaoth, Adonay, Ischiros, Zaday, Messias, Salomon, Yweth, Thoros, Yzheto, Thyym, Quowe, Xehatoym, Phoe, Tetragrammaton.

Now pronounce the name of the spirit and let him depart in peace. Deus Principium et Finis.

(Front side—Fig. 29.)

TREASURE ELEVATION

AND

SPIRITUAL REDEMPTION,

AUTHORIZED, DEDICATED AND CONSECRATED IN

High Domstift,

AT

BAMBERG.

J. E. S. U. S.

IN

N ADOYAH.
Chananyah.
Ahmen

OF GOD,

The Father ✠ God the Son ✠ ✠ God the Holy Spirit. ✠

YES CHAYA HETH   RACHMYEL AYSCHER.

The Innocent, holy blood of Jesus Christ, the Son of God, cleanses us from all sin and give you spirits of eternal rest and peace through Jesum Christum ✠ the Son of God.

AWEL . . . . YIHEYE.

Therefore, may the spirits of Jesus Christ redeem you from all pain and suffering, and give us the treasures that are here, through the shed blood of I. N. R. I. Eei Elyon Jesus Christi Eheyoha. Amen.

Optimo Successu Remissum.

THE

Schemhamforas

Which will certainly bring to light the Treasures of Earth, if buried
in the Treasure-Earth.

From the Arcan Bible of Moses.

FROM

P. HOFFMAN, Jesuit.

Composed ad Proxim.

L. MISCHINSKY, at RAOL, MDCCXLVI.

SCHEMHAMPHORAS,

No. 1.

Seu septuaginta duo Divina Nomina in lingua Hebraic, denotant semper Nomen deisive legantur a principo fine veladextrisant sonistris suntque ingentie virtutis.

SCHEMHAMPHORAS,
No. 2.

III.

SEMIPHORAS AND SCHEMHAMPORAS

KING SOLOMON.

WESAL, DUISPBURG AND FRANKFORD:

Printed and Published by ANDREW LUPPIUS, Licensed Bookseller in the above Cities.
1686.

AN HUMBLE PRAYER FOR THE ATTAINMENT OF WISDOM AND UNDERSTANDING.

" For the Lord giveth wisdom, out of his mouth cometh knowledge and understanding."—PROVERBS ii. 6.

" If any of you lack wisdom let him ask of God, that giveth to all men liberally, and upbraideth not."—EPISTLE OF JAMES i. 5.

OH, God my Father and Lord of all goodness, who didst create all things by Thy word, and who didst prepare man in thy wisdom to rule over all creatures that were made by Thee, that he should rule over the world with holiness and righteousness, and judge with an upright heart. Give unto me that wisdom that is constantly around Thy throne, and cast me not out from among Thy children. For I am Thy servant, and the son of Thy hand-maiden, a weak creature of a short existence, and too weak in understanding, in right, and in the law. Send it down from Thy high heaven and from the throne of Thy glory that it may abide with me and labor with me, that I may know and do the things that are pleasing unto Thee. For Thy wisdom knoweth and understandeth all things, and let it lead me in my works and protect me in its glory, and my labors will be acceptable unto Thee. When I was yet in my youth I sought wisdom without fear in my prayer. I prayed for it in the temple, and will seek it fo my end. My heart rejoiceth over it as when the young grapes ripen. Thou art my Father, my God, and my Shepherd, who helpest me. Thy hand created and prepared me; teach me that I may learn Thy commandments; open my eyes that I may behold the wonders of Thy law. Remember, Lord, Thy covenant, and teach me what to say and think. Instruct me and so shall I live. Lord, show me Thy ways, lead me in Thy truth, and teach me. I am Thy servant, teach me that I may understand Thy evidence. Console me again with Thy help and let the happy spirit sustain me. Thou lover of life, Thy immortal spirit is in all things. Teach me to work in a manner that is well pleasing unto Thee, for Thou art my God. Let Thy good spirit lead me in pleasant paths. With Thee is the living fountain and in Thy light we see the light. Let my goings be established, and let no unrighteousness rule over me. Teach me wholesome manners and enlighten me, for I believe Thy commandments. Lead me in Thy truth and teach me, for Thou art the God who helps me, and I wait daily before Thee. Let Thy countenance shine upon Thy servant and teach me to know Thy justice. Let me behold Thy glory, for Thou, Lord, art my light, and Thou wilt turn my darkness into day. Wilt Thou join Thyself with me in eternity, and trust me in righteousness and in judgment, in grace and mercy, yea, wilt Thou join me in faith that I may know Thee, the Lord. Lord, let my complaints come before Thee. Instruct me according to Thy word. Let my prayers come before Thee, rescue me according to Thy word. Show me Thy ways, oh, Lord, that I may walk in Thy truth. Keep my heart in singleness that I may fear Thy name. I will remember Thy name from childhood, therefore, all people will thank Thee forever and ever. Amen.

In the name of the highest, almighty Creator, I, King Solomon, hold to the interpretation of the name of (God) Semiphoras, in other words, the First and the Greatest, the oldest and hidden mystery of great power and virtue, to obtain all that which is asked of God, for God must be worshipped in spirit and in truth, which consists not in many and vain words, because each word and name of God is self-existent, and therefore the name and prayer must agree, and no strange name must be used unnecessarily if anything fearful or wonderful is intended to be accomplished, in order that the divine quality may pour into our soul and spirit His grace and gifts—that is the consciousness of God in His name through which he comes near and abides with those who know His name. Therefore, this name must be held in the highest honor and should be hidden from all frivolous and unworthy persons, since God says himself in Exodus: Out of all places will I come unto thee and bless thee, because thou rememberest my name. Therefore, have the Hebrew Maccabees seventy-two names for God, and named and wrote Schemhamphora, the name of seventy-two letters.

First, it must be known that the names of God cannot be taught and undersood except only in the Hebrew language, neither can we pronounce them in any other dialect, as they were revealed to us through the grace of God. For they are the sacrament and emanation of divine omnipotence, not of man, nor of angels, but they are instituted and consecrated through the (generent) of God, to instil divine harmony in a certain manner according to the characters of his immovable number and figure, and of which those that are appointed over the heavens are afraid. The angels and all creatures honor them and use them to praise their Creator, and to bless Him with the greatest reverence in His divine works, and whosoever will apply them properly with fear and trembling and with prayer, will be powerfully enlightened by the spirit of God—will be joined with a divine unity—will be mighty according to the will of God—that he can perform supernatural things—that he can command angels and devils—that he can bind and unbind the things of the elements, over which he may elevate himself through the power of God. Therefore, he, who has purified and improved his understanding and morals, and who, through faith, has purified his ears, so that he may without spurious alterations call upon the divine name of God, will become a house and a dwelling-place of God, and will be a partaker of divine influences, etc., etc.

On the other hand, the order of God should be known, that God makes use of other words among angels and also others among men, but the true name of God is known neither to men nor to angels, for He has reserved it and will not reveal it until His order and exhibition are fulfilled and perfected. After that the angels will have their own tongues and speech, about which we need not concern ourselves, because it is not necessary for us to examine them.

In the third place, all the names of God are taken by us from His works, as indicating a communication with God, or are extracted out of the divine scriptures through the art of Cabalisticam, Calculatoriam, Notariacam and Geometriam.

The beginning of the name and word Semiphoras, which God the Creator, Jehovah gave in Paradise, embraces three Hebrew letters, Jehovah the inscrutable Creator of the world, almighty Providence, and all-powerful strong Deity.

After this there are four parts of the earth which are the most subtle light of the spiritual world: 4. Hierarchus, Cherubim et Seraphim, Potestates et Virtutes, Archangelos et Angelos, Spiritus et Animus Hominum, which come before God. This part of the world has also four angels that stand upon the four corners of heaven; they are Michael, Raphael, Gabriel, Uriel; four angels stand for the elements, namely, Seraph, Cherub, Tharsis, Ariel; four highly enlightened men full of the light of God.

For the other light or part of the world is the heaven of all the stars; has four Triplicitates of the twelve signs, under which the sun revolves yearly, making the change of seasons, the Spring, Summer, Fall and Winter of birth and corruption, and changes the fourth element.

In the third part of the work are the elements and everything that is subordinate to them, in which is the small world, man. He again has four elements within him. Anima is in the head, per nemos; Spiritus is in the heart, and operates through the arteries; Corpus is the whole body with the veins; Genius, a spark of fire, is in the kidneys, and governs birth. He has four spiritual and strong working faculties, as facultates actiones, or spiritus, as his Animali, Vitalis, Naturalis, Genitions. The soul has inward senses, as sensum communene; in which faith takes hold as (fides) and other senses Intellectus in the brain.

2. Imaginatrix, the imagination is another soul-operation or phantasie, which draws a picture of power and accomplishes all things.

3. Rativtanatio repeats the Species on the mind on all causes and judgments, Scientia; if the soul will now turn to real reason, it will obtain a knowledge of all worldly wisdom.

4. Memoratrix, the memory, retains all things which pertains to the faculties and operations of the spirit, to bring an experimentum et Sensus; through agitation of the nerves the increase of the human race is effected

by God. The living spirit of the heart embraces within itself four virtues: Justitia, Temperantia, Prudentia, Fortitudo, and these lie in the arterial blood and connect the soul with the body. Appetitus Sensitivus; the natural spiritual action and power lies in the liver and arteries, and effect motion and attraction, support and subsistence; the proper spirit of strength and sap lies in the kidneys . . . to multiply through divine perfection.

The body has four elements, namely, spirit, fruit, flesh and bone—four complexions or temperaments, warm, wet, dry; attraction is produced by warmth, dryness, dampness; rel retentio is produced by coldness and dryness; Lien Cactio by warmth and wet, id est stomachus: four wet, gall, blood, mucus and melancholia.

In the fourth quarter of the world there is darkness, instituted for condemnation in wrath and for punishment. Four princes of devils are injurious in the four elements: Samael, Azazel, Azael, Mehazaer, four princes of devils over the four quarters of the earth, Oriens, Pagmon, Egyn, Amayon.

The first Semiphoras is that of Adam, because he spoke with the Creator in Paradise.

The second Semiphoras, because he spoke with angels and spirits.

The third, because he spoke with devils.

The fourth, because he spoke with the creatures of the four elements, the birds, the fishes, the animals, and the creeping things of the earth.

The fifth, because he spoke with inanimate objects, as herbs, seeds, trees, and all vegetation.

The sixth, because he spoke with the winds.

The seventh, because he spoke with the sun, moon and stars.

By the power of the seven Semiphoras he could create and destroy all he desired.

The first Semiphoras was acknowledged by Adam, since God created him and placed him in Paradise, where he was allowed to remain only seven hours. The name is Jove, which name must be pronounced only in the greatest need, and then only with the most devout feelings toward the Creator. In this case you will find grace and sure help.

The second Semiphoras, in which Adam spoke with angels, and which gave him the expression, yeseraye, that is, God without Beginning and without End, must be pronounced when speaking with angels, and then your questions will be answered and your wishes fulfilled.

The third Semiphoras, in which Adam spoke with the spirits of the departed, and inquired of them, who gave him satisfactory answers upon the word, Adonay Sabaoth, cadas adonay amara; these words must be uttered when you wish to collect winds, spirits or demons, Aly, Adoy, Sabaoth, amara.

The fourth Semiphoras, Layamen, Iava, firin, Iavagellayn, Lavaquiri, Lavagola, Lavatasorin, Layfialafin, Lyafaran; with this name he bound and unbound all animals and spirits.

The fifth Semiphoras, Lyacham, Lyalgema, Lyafarau, Lialfarah, Lebara, Lebarosin, Layararalus; if you wish to bind equals, as trees and seeds, you must pronounce the above words.

The sixth Semiphoras is great in might and virtue; Letamnin, Letaylogo, Letasynin, Lebaganaritin, Letarminin, Letagelogin, Lotafaloain. Use these when you desire the elements or winds to fulfil your wishes.

The seventh Semiphoras is great and mighty. They are the names of the Creator, which must be pronounced in the beginning of each undertaking: Eliaon yoena adonay cadas ebreel, eloy ela agiel, ayoni, Sachado, essuselas eloyrn, delion iau elynla, delia, yazi, Zazael, paliel man, umiel, onela dilatan saday alma paneim alym', canal deus Usami yaras calipix calfas sasna saffasaday aylata panteomel auriel arion phaneton secare paneriony, emanuel Joth Jalaph amphia, than demisrael mu all le Leazyns al; phonar aglacyei qyol paeriteron theferoym barimel, jael haryon ya apiolet, echet.

These holy names pronounce at each time in reverence toward God, when you desire to accomplish something through the elements or something connected therewith, and your wishes will be fulfilled, and what is to be destroyed will be destroyed, for God will be with you because you know his name.

☞ The following is another name of Semiphoras which God gave to Moses in seven parts.

The first is, when Moses concealed himself and spoke with God, when the fire burned in the forest without consuming it.

The second, as he spoke with the Creator on the mountain.

The third, when he divided the Red Sea, and passed through with the whole people of Israel, etc.

The fourth, when his staff was turned into a serpent which devoured the other serpents.

The fifth, are the names which were written on the forehead of Aaron.

The sixth, when he made a brazen serpent and burned the golden calf to divert pestilence from the Israelites.

The seventh, when manna fell in the wilderness and when water gushed from the rock.

In the first are the words which Moses spake as he went on the mountain, when he spoke to the flames of fire: Maya, Affaby, Zien, Jaramye, yne Latebni damaa yrsano, noy lyloo Lhay yly yre Eyivi Zya Lyelee, Loate, lideloy eyloy, mecha ramethy rybifassa fu aziry scihiu rite Zelohabe vete hebe ede neyo ramy rahabe (conoc anuhec). If you pray this word to God devoutly your undertaking will be fulfilled without a doubt.

In the second are the words which God spake to Moses as he went on the mountain: Abtan, Abynistan, Zoratan Juran nondieras, potarte faijs alapeina pognij podaij sacroficium. In these words the prophet spoke to the angels with whom the four quarters of the earth are sealed, through which the temple was founded Bosale. If you wish to pronounce these you should fast three days, be chaste and pure, and then you can perform many wonders.

In the third are words which Moses spake in order to divide the Red Sea: Oua claiie saijec holomomaatl; bekahn aijclo inare asnia haene hieha ijfale malieha arnija aremeholbna queleij, Lineno feijano, ijoije malac habona nethee hijcere. If you have lost favor of your master, or if you wish to gain the good-will of some one, speak these words with fervor and humility, etc.

In the fourth are words which Moses spake when he changed his staff into a serpent: Micrato, raepijsathonich petanith pistan ijttn ijer hijgarin ijgnition temayron aijcon drnsnas castas Lacias astas ijecon cijna caihera natu facas. Pronounce these names when you wish to have your desires fulfilled:

In the fifth are the written names of the forehead of Aaron as he spake with the Creator: Sadaij haijlves Lucas elacijus jaconi hasihaia ijein ino, sep, actitas barne lud doncnij eija iehhu reu, vaha, vialia, eije. Vie haija hoij asaija salna hahai, cuci ijaija. Elenehel, na vena; setna. The names are powerful in satisfying each request.

In the sixth are names which were written upon the staff of Moses, when he made the brazen serpent and broke the golden calf: Tane mare syam, abijl ala, nuno, hija actenal tijogas ijano, eloim ija nehn ijane haij ijanehn, ahijaco mea. With this name destroy all sorcery and evil. You must not pronounce it with levity in your works.

In the seventh are words which Moses employed in leading the Israelites out of Egypt, with which he brought manna from heaven and caused the water to flow from the rock: Sadaij amara elón pheneton eloij eneij ebeoel messias ijahe vehu hejiane, ijanancl elijon. Pronounce these words when you desire to do something wonderful, or when you are in great need, and call earnestly on God, etc.

PRAYER.

Oh, thou living God: thou great, strong, mighty, holy and pure Creator full of mercy—a blessed Lord of all things; praised be thy name. I implore Thee, fulfil my desire. Thou canst work. Permit us to accomplish this work. Grant us thy grace and give us thy divine blessing, that we may happily fulfil this work. Thou, holy, merciful and gracious God, have mercy upon us. Thy name, Jeseraire be adored forever and ever. Amen, etc.

In the name of the Almighty Creator, I, Solomon, hold to the declaration of the divine names: Agla. Thou art a mighty God to all eternity. He who bears upon his person this name, written upon a gold plate, will never die a sudden death. Ararita—a beginning of all unity. Ahen— thou solid rock, united with the Son. Amen, etc. Thou, Lord, a true king, perfect it, etc.

The names consist of the beginning of the chapters Adonay, which the Hebrews made·use of instead of the unutterable name, Asser Eserie.

The seven mighty names may be obtained at a favorable hour and place: Comiteijon, sedc aij, throtomas, sasmagata bij ijl ijcos.

The four names of the Creator: Jva, Jona, eloij, Jeua. He who calls often upon God in faith and with fear, and carries with him the golden letters, will never want for an honorable subsistence and good clothing. The name which Adam uttered at the entrance to hell is mephenaij pha ton. He who bears this name with him is unconquerable.

The name which God communicated to Moses on Mount Sanai, Hacedion, will put away all causes for sorrow.

The name which Joshua prayed when the sun stood still, baahando, heltaroir, dealzhat, brings vengeance upon enemies.

The ten names of Sepiroth, I, Solomon, spoke in my prayer to God, and he gave me wisdom: Ethor, Hoehmal, binach, baesed, Geburah, thipheret, nezath, hod Jehod malchut.

Now follow the ten names of God: Eseie, Jod teragrammaton, Tetragrammaton Saboth, elohim Sabaoth, Sadaij Adonaij nulech, all with ten letters. Tetragrammaton Vedath have eight letters. Ehoie, the self-existence of God, Arerite Aser, ehele, the names of God of seven letters.

Eseh, used by Moses as the fire of God, Elion has five letters and they are all Hebrew characters.

Emeth, the true God, is God's seal. The explanation of the ten names of God and the ten Sephiroth, is given in Cornel Agrippa de occulta Philosophia, Lib, 3, Cap. 10.

Hacaba, the holy and adored God.

Hu, himself the power of the Deity.

Hod, Jod, a divine being.

Jah, a just God, comparing himself with man.

Inon.

Jesuba, the Messiah will come in the golden age.

Jaua, he who created the light.

Isaia, with the name El, resembles the changed era (each made up of 31).

Mettatron for Sadai, each name composed of 314.

Icuru Maapaz, both names are derived from a transposition of the name Jehova.

Messiah is derived from a transposition of the letters in Jisma Macom.

Na, the name of God, should be used in tribulation and oppression.

Oromasim, Mitrim, Araminem, signify God and the Spirit. These are three princes of the world.

Pele, he who worketh wonders, etc.

These names must be selected out of each letter constituting the work, for the accomplishment of which the help of God should be implored. Similar to a certain text, in Exodus xiv., consisting of three verses which are always written with seventy-two letters, beginning with the three words: Vaijsa, Vaiduo, Vaiot, which, when placed in a line, one and three, from left to right, the middle one transposed from the right to the left, as in a reverse order, constitutes one name, the seventy-two letters of which are named Schemhamphoras.

If now the divine names, El or Jad, are added, there will be seventy-two names of God, each of them syllables, for it is written: My angel goeth before me, behold him, for my name is in him. These are seventy-two deacons of the five departments of heaven, there are so many nations and tongues, so many bodily functions, working with the seventy-two disciples of Christ. And this is one method which Cabalists use in making up these names.

Another method to make the Schemhamforas is when the three verses are written in regular order from right to left subalternatim, without selecting this method from the tables of Zimph, or as it is selected from the table Commutationem.

Vehuiah, Jeliel, Sitael, Elemiah, Mahasia, Lehahel, Achuiah, Cahetel, Haziel, Aladiah, Laviah, Caliel, Leuniah, Pahaliah, Nelchael, Leiaiel,

Melahel, Hahuiah, Mittaiah, Haaiah, Jerathel, Scehia, Rauel, Omael, Lecabei Vasarias, Jehujah Labahiah Chauakiah Mahadel Aniel Haamiah. Richael, ieiazcl hahael Michael, Vehuel, Daniel, Hahasias Imamiahs, Nanael, Nitael Behahia, Poiel Nemamiah; Selalel, Harael, Mizrael, Sahhel Annanuel Mehael damabiah menkiel Eliapel, Habuiah. Rochel Tabamiah Haianel. Maniah.

In the first period of nature God was addressed by the name of Sadai Tvigrammaton. In the second period of the law he bore the unutterable name of Tetragrammaton, which is spoken Adonaij. In the period of grace he was called upon as Pentragrammaton effabile Jesu, which is also written Jusu, with four letters, and JHS with three letters.

The Father gave all power to the Son, the angels received heaven, but in the name of God and Jesus, which is the first power in God. Afterward it spreads into the twelve and seven angels through which it was communicated to the twelve signs and seven planets, and consequently into all the servants and instruments of God, even to the humblest. Therefore, said Jesus: Everything which ye ask of the Father in my name, that will he give unto you, if ye pray unto him with a pure heart and a fervent spirit, for there is no other name given to man whereby he can be saved but the name of Jesus. Amen.

OF THE BENEFIT AND USE OF THE SEMIPHORAS.

That man who lays hold in strong faith and trust in the first Creator, must first implore the divine help and blessing, not only with the lips, but also with holy gestures and humble heart, praying fervently and continually, that he may enlighten the mind, and take away from the soul all darkness of the body. For, precisely as when our souls are moved by some ordinary cause, so the soul moves all the members of the body to contribute something toward the accomplishment of a contemplated work. Therefore, the great Creator, when he is worshipped in spirit and in truth, and when no unnecessary things are asked of Him, when the prayer is devoutly preferred, will cause the lower order of creatures to yield obedience to the wishes of man, according to their state, order and calling, for man was made in the image and likeness of God, and endowed with reason and working under the favor of God, he will obtain his desire through faith and wisdom: first, from the stars and from the heavens by the rational reflections of His spirit; second, by the animal kingdom, through his senses; third, by the elements, through his fourfold body.

Therefore, man binds all creatures through comparison, by calling upon the higher power, through the name and power which governs one thing, and thereafter through the lower things themselves, etc.

And now, he who desires to become master of the working of the soul, must become familiar with the order of all things, just as they are obtained by God in their proper state, from the highest to the lowest, through natural connections, that he may descend as if from a ladder. On this account the Heathens committed the error of worshipping the planets and fixed stars, not because they heard but because they were moved by the powers which governed them and were, at the same time, impelled thereto by the influence of their founder and creator. And in this manner, likewise, Christian nations have committed the error of paying homage to departed saints and giving honor to the creature which belongs only to the Creator, and God is a jealous God and will not permit the worship of idols. The prayer of faith, therefore, in proper language, and for proper objects, is intimately related to the name of God, from which we descend by words, from one to the other, following each other out of a natural relationship, in order to accomplish something.

The son, therefore, prevails upon the father that he may support him although the father may not do so willingly; still since he is his offspring he must calculate to maintain him. How much greater care our heavenly Father must feel for us, if we serve him in a proper manner?

He who desires the influence of the sun, must not only direct his eyes toward it, but he must elevate his soul-power to the soul-power of the sun, which is God himself, having previously made himself equal to God, by fasting, purification and good works, but he must also pray in the name of the Mediator, with fervent love to God, and his fellow-man that he may come to the sun-spirit, so that he may be filled with its light and lustre, which he may draw to himself from heaven, and that he may become gifted with heavenly gifts and obtain all the desires of his heart; and as soon as he grasps the higher light and arrives at a state of perfection, being gifted with supernatural intelligence, he will also obtain supernatural might and power. For this reason, without godliness, man will deny his faith in Christ, and will become unacceptable to God, therewith often falling a prey to the evil spirits against whom there is no better protection than the fear of the Lord and fervent love to God and man.

Most people who are skilled in divine works, and who possess the right to command spirits, must be worthy by nature or become worthy by education and discipline for their calling—must keep all their works secret, but may not conceal it from a true and pious person. Dignity of birth comes from station, but it is due to Saturnum, Sol, Mercurium or Martem that he is made prosperous—that he is learned in Physics, Metaphysics and Theology.

If a man has a knowledge of God, as the first great cause, he must also acknowledge other causes or coöperative spirits, and determine what official station of dignity and honor to accord to them; and without which knowledge their presence and help cannot be enjoyed. Such honor and dignity must not be shown for the sake of the spirits but for the sake of their Lord, whose servants they are. In this manner the angels of God will encamp around those who fear and love the Lord, and, as Augustinus says: "Everything possesses a predestined angel-power." For this reason the Hebrew theologians, Mecubaes and Cabalists, named ten principle divine names as members of God, and ten Numerationes or Zephirot, as raiment and instruments of the Creator, through which he is infused into all his creatures, according to the order of the ten, Angelic and ten princely spirit-choirs, from which all things derive their power and quality.

The name EHEIE, aser Eheie, its number Cether elion, our Lord, is the simplest Deity, which no eye has seen, is ascribed to God the Father, gives influence through the order Setaphin haiath, heiadosch, gate of holiness or of life, that transmits life to everything through Elieic. From this he flows in through premum mohele so that all things must exist—that the heavens must revolve every twenty-four hours. This wonderful being is called Intelligentia Mettatron, that is, a prince of faces. His office is to lead others into the presence of the Sovereign, and through him God spake to Moses.

2. JEHOVAH, Jod, ve! Jah, his number Chochma—wisdom: The Deity full of spirit. The firstborn son through whom the Father redeemed man from his curse, is infused through the order of Cherubim, Hebrew Ophanim, of the form or Council. From these he flows into the star-bedecked heavens, and produces there many figures. Chavs of creatures, God, Jod, Tetragrammaton, through the peculiar Intelligentiam razielem, who was a representative of Adam, etc.

3. TETRAGRAMMATON ELOHIM, his number is called Binah. That is, caution or sense, and signifies pardon and rest, cheerfulness, repentance and conversion—the great trumpet, the redemption of the world and life in time to come, is adopted to the Holy Spirit and flows in his might through the order of Thronorum, which is called Arabim in Hebrew—that is, the great, strong and mighty angels, from thence through the Saturui Sphaeram it gives to liquid matter the form Stopsie, which was an Intelligentia Zaphekiel, was Noah's representative, and another Intelligentia Jophiel, Shem's representative, and these are the three highest and greatest Numerationes, as a throne of the divine Persons, through whose commands everything takes place, and which is completed by the other seven, which, in this account are called Numerationes fabrice, etc.

4. El, his number Haesed, that is, grace or goodness, and is called mercy, pity, great power, sceptre and right hand, and flows in through order Dominationum, Hebrew Hasmalin—confers peaceable justice through Spaeram Jovis and bestows in a general manner special Intelligentia; Zadkiel, Abraham's representative.

5. ELOHIM cuhor, a strong God, who punishes the guilt of the wicked. His number is Geburah, that is, might, gravity, strength, security, judgment. He inflicts punishment through the sword and through wars. To this is added the judgment-seat of God, the girdle of the Lord, a sword and left arm; also Pached, that is, fear before God; flows in through the order of Potestatum Hebrai Seraphin, so named, and from thence through the Sphaeram Martis, which has great wars and tribulation—moves the elements accordingly. His peculiar Intelligentia Gamael, Samson's representative.

6. ELOHA, the God of Alchemy; his number is Tipheret, grace, beauty, adornment, happiness and pleasure—signifies the word of life and flows in through the order Virtutum, which in Hebrew is Malachien: This angel, through Sphaeram Solis, gives perspicuity and life, and reveals metals. His particular Intelligentia, Raphael, was the representative of Isaac and of the youthful Tobias, and Pehel was the representative of Jacob.

7. TETRAGRAMMATON SABAOTH, or Adonaij Sabaoth, the

God of Hosts. His number is Nezaeh, that is, triumph and victory; to him is accorded the right pillar, and signifies eternity, the justice of God, and avenger; he flows in through the order of Principatum or through the Hebrew Elohem, that is, God in Sphaeram Veneris, love and justice. He produces all Vegetable growth and his peculiar Intelligentia Hamel, and the angel Cernaiul is David's representative.

8. ELOHIM SABAOTH, God of Hosts, not of war or wrath, but of pity, for he has both names and goes before his hosts. His number is called Hod, that is, honorable confession, ornament and renown. To him is accorded the left pillar, and he flows in through the order of Archangelorum, before the gods in Sphaeram Mercuri, adornment, safety and unanimity, and brings forth animals; His peculiar Intelligentia Michael, the representative of Solomon.

9. SADAI, the Almighty, who does all things abundantly, and Elhay, that is, the living God. His number is called Jesod, that is, a foundation, and is denominated good sense, redemption and rest. He flows in through the order of Angelorum, in Hebrew Cherubin in Sphaerem Lunae, to increase and decrease all things, supports and contributes the genius of man: his Intelligentiae Gabriel, a representative of Joseph, Joshua, and Daniel.

10. ADONAY MELECH, that is, a Lord and King. His number is called Malchat, that is, a kingdom and dominion, and is termed the Church and house of God, and the door flows in through the order of Animasticum of the believing soul—in Hebrew the life of princes, and they are inferior to the hierarchy. They afford information to the children of men, of the wonderful things of knowledge, guard them against prophesies. For their Anima Messiah Meshia, or according to others the Intelligentia Metratron, which is called the first creature—the soul of the world, is the representative of Moses, the fountain of all life.

Therefore, all the names of God and the ten Sephirot, are embraced in the Archetypum.

In mundo intelligibili are included the nine choirs of the angels, or according to Dionysius, the ten blessed orders:

1. Seraphim; 2. Cherubim; 3. Throni; 4. Deminationis; 5. Potestates; 6. Virtutes; 7. Principatus; 8. Archangeli; 9. Angeli; and 10, Animae Beatae.

The Hebrews, therefore, call them: Haioth, Hacades, Ophanim; Aralim; Hasmalim; Seraphim; Malachim Elohim, ben Elohim; Cherubim; Issim.

The ten representative angels are: Mattron, Jophiel, Zaphkiel, Camael, Raphael, Haniel, Michael, Gabriel, Anima Messiae.

The Nine Choirs of Angels divide Theology into Three Hierarchies.

In the first hierarchy are the Seraphim, Cherubim and Throni. These more than celestial spirits are called gods, or the sons of the gods, because they continually behold the order of divine providence. Being foremost in the goodness of God, they praise Him unceasingly and pray for us.

The second in the being of God, according to form, and the third, in the wisdom of God, stand continually before God.

In the middle hierarchy are the Dominationes, Potestates, Virtutes, as spirits of intelligence, to rule the whole world. The first command what the others perform. The second steer that which interfere with the laws of God. The third oversee the heavens and occasionally perform great wonders. These six orders of spirits are never sent upon the earth.

In the lower hierarchy are the Principatus, Archangeli et angeli, which are ministering spirits to oversee earthly affairs.

The first, in general, provide for princes and magistrates, and care for kingdoms and countries, each in his own especial sphere, as Moses declares in his song, Deut. xxxii. 8: "When the Most High divided to the nations their inheritance, when he separated the sons of Adam, he set the bounds of the people according to the number of the children of Israel." And Daniel says, chap. x. 13: "But the prince of the kingdom of Persia withstood me twenty-one days. And Jesus Sirach bears witness, that each nation has its angel as a director. Therefore did the Romans at all times invite the angel of their country. 2. The second are engaged in divine affairs, institute and regulate the worship of God among all men, and present the prayers, offerings and piety of men to God. 3. The third order all things of minor importance, and each one is appointed as a protector to every man.

For this reason the fourth hierarchy are added to the former as the souls of heavenly bodies; Animae Corporum Colestium, the souls of Hervos, vel Heroas and of the Martyrum. They first control the light, and the influence of the strong, so that their power may proceed from God to the lower regions. The second are the chosen souls of the redeemed. The third are the souls of the innocent martyrs and followers of God, who offered up their lives, amid pain and suffering, out of love to God.

Since God the Father gave to the Son, our Mediator, Saviour and Redeemer, all power in heaven and on earth, and the angels of the great name of God and Jesus, which is the first might in God, it flows, accordingly, into the twelve angels and twelve signs, through which it spreads into the seven planets, and, as a natural consequence, into all other servants and instruments of God, until it penetrates into the lower regions, so that even an insignificant herb may develop a peculiar power, even if it is decayed, and so the angel of man appears before God at all times bearing his prayers into his presence.

Without the name of Jesus the old Hebrew cabalists can accomplish nothing in the present day, with old arts as they were used by the Fathers Therefore, it is, that all creatures fear and honor him. All men who believe in him are enlightened through his brightness, our souls are united with him, and the divine power emanating from him is communicated to us.

OF THE MOVEMENT OF THE HEAVENLY POWERS.

The first course in Mundo Ceolesti watches day and night. Primum Mobile Rechet Hagallalim. It continues from morning until night.

From these the Heathens divided the angels into thirty-three orders.
The first great light, communicates light, life and station out of the first
course, and opposes others in the Saphaera Zodiaci, causes summer and
winter, the spring of all the things of the elements: Hebrew Masloth,
goes from evening to morning according to the twelve signs of the
heavens.

But even if all things have their existence from God, the great First
Cause, we should not despise other causes, according to changes in time,
in the year, in the month, day and hour, neither should we regard these
causes exclusively, and forget God, for in this manner heathen idolatry
was instituted.   For this reason God does not regard time, because it
robs him of his honor.   For the heathens experienced that the heavenly
spirits were not united with their bodies, as our souls are united with our
bodies, but they could rejoice in the presence of God, and prepare their
bodies without much labor to work with the lower creatures of God.
They regarded the celestial spirits as gods, and conferred divine honors
upon them.   Very often the Jews turned away from God and worshipped
the host of heaven, and therefore the wrath of God was kindled against
them.   But on account of the order of all things, God has set them before
us as his instruments, and which we, on account of their honorable office,
are to regard as the noblest creation of God, and that we should honor
them, next to God, according to their station, not as gods but as creatures.
which he has appointed as twelves princes over the twelve gates of
heaven, that they may admit what they received from the divine name,
transposed twelve times.

Ezekiel writes: "The laws of the twelve tribes of Israel were thus
written, and God Tetragrammaton ruled over them.   Thus it is written
in Revelations, that the stones in our heavenly city are planted in the
ground, or that the Church of Christ is represented by the twelve names
of the Apostles, including twelve angels and of them the name of Jesus,
who received all the power of the Father, so that the heavens will receive
what the angels give to them according to the will of God.   If then an
Intelligentia is ascribed to each heaven, each star and department of
heaven must have a distinct and separate power and influence and, therefore, must also have a distinct Intelligentiam.   Therefore, there are
twelve princes of angels, who represent the twelve signs of the Zodiac,
and thirty-six, who represent so many Decuriis, and seventy-two angels,
who represent so many Quinariis of heaven, of the seventy-two nations
and languages of man.   Likewise seven angels of the hosts for the seven
heavens of the seven planets, to rule the world, etc.   Also, four angels
who represent the Triplicitatibus of the twelve signs of the Zodiac and
the four elements.

All of these have their names and signs which the philosophers used in
their works, signs, images, clothes, mirrors, rings, cards, wax-figures, as
if they had a sun-work before them, and they called them the names of
the sun and his angels, and likewise of others, etc.

In the third place, they designated the lowest angels as servants.
These they distributed over the world, and named them after the seven
planets, and these have their special course after the four elements and
after the four parts of the air and earth—of the daytime several Diurnos

several Nocturnos, several Merailianos, not that they are subordinate to the influence of the stars as the body which they represent, but that they are more nearly related to the star-body-kind-time than others, otherwise they might be everywhere, as each human being has three angels, for God has ordained that each human being shall have his good angel as a protector, who also strengthens the spirit and urges and exhorts us to what is good and commendable, that we may fly from what is sati malignitatem. And so every man has also an evil spirit, who controls the desires of the flesh and awakens the lusts of the heart; between these two angels there is a constant struggle for supremacy, and to whichever man gives the preference, he will receive the victory; and if the evil angel triumphs, then man becomes his servant; should the good angel prove the stronger, then he will cleanse the soul and save man from destruction. The angel and his impulses come from the stars. In the third place are the Genii of man who govern birth, and are joined to each perfection in man. These are recognized from the star which is the Lord of the births. The Chaldeans seek this Genium in the sun and moon. Astronomers would have the good Genium out of the eleventh house, which, on this account, they call bonum Genium. The evil one out of the sixth house. But each one will learn to know him through natural inclination, to which every one was inclined from his youth. On this account he is called the birth-angel, who is sent into the world by God. Of this the Psalmist says: " Thou hast made the spirit of man as a flame of fire." For experience teaches us, that the flame of fire and the spirit of birth may be separated without injury to man, that we can learn hidden things from him if he is good and true. But he is powerless over the members of birth. If, however, a virgin or a companion becomes marriageable, he may be liberated from the glass, and our time of life will be extended.

Moreover, God has endowed man with a divine character, through the number Phahad—the left-hand sword of God, through which man becomes a curse to all creatures. And then again he has another character in the number of God, Hesed—the right and sceptre of God, through which he finds favor in the sight of God and all his creatures. An evil conscience is the judge of men, but a good conscience is his happiness. Therefore, through the other divine numbers, and through the angels and stars a man becomes impressed with signs and characters of conscience, which causes him to be happy at one time and unhappy at another.

On this account, if a man has committed murder, theft, or any other act which his conscience condemns, he can be brought to a confession of his guilt through persistent calling upon the name of God, for his conscience will then give him no rest until he returns what he has stolen, or until he has suffered the punishment due to his crime. Therefore, in the name of the Father, Son and Holy Spirit, take three small pieces of wood from the door-sill over which the thief passed in leaving the place where he committed the theft, place them within a wagon-wheel, and then through the hub of the wheel say the following words: " I pray thee, thou Holy Trinity, that thou mayest cause A, who stole from me B, a, C, to have no rest or peace until he again restores me that which he has stolen." Turn the wheel round three times and replace it again on the wagon. Nevertheless, all pious Christians, who have any regard for their future happiness, should carefully avoid all superstitious matters and should beware of using the holy name of God unworthily, holding it in the greatest reverence lest they bring upon themselves eternal punishment. If a man knows himself and realizes that he is created in the image and likeness of God, he will acknowledge God the Creator before all things, and afterward the world and all its creatures. From the high spirits, angels and the heavens, he has his portion, and from the elements, animals, vegetation and stones, he has within himself everything that he desires to obtain.

If a man knows how to appropriate the particular place, time, order, bulk, proportion and mental organization of any one, he can attract and draw them, just as a magnet attracts iron: but he must first be prepared, just as the magnet must be fashioned by the file and charged with electricity. To this end the soul must first be purified, and dedicated to God through faith; a pure heart and constant joy in the spirit are requisites. He must possess love to God and his fellow-man, and then he may arrive at a perfect state and become like unto the Son of God. He will become united with God, and will once more be like him. It is not given to angels nor to any creature to unite with God, but only to man, and he may become his son; and when this takes place, so that he overcomes himself, he overcomes and can draw to him all other creatures and command their obedience.

But our spirit, word and act, have no power in magic and knowledge, if they are not everywhere strengthened by the word of God, which we should hear often. We must pray to God without ceasing, live a sober, temperate and unstained life; we must live in a continual state of repentance, give alms and help the poor, for Christ has not said in vain: "Make unto you friends with the unrighteous Mammon, so that he will receive you into eternal habitations," that is, apply your wealth and abundance to the support of the poor, that they may receive their daily bread from you and be satisfied. Christ says: "What ye have done unto the least of mine, that have ye also done unto me." These are the friends that will lead us to a divine abode in heaven, where we shall receive a thousandfold and life eternal. On the other hand there are others who will be rejected. For Christ also says: "I was hungry and thirsty and ye gave me no meat and drink, depart from me ye workers of iniquity, into outer darkness."

Therefore, by fasting, praying, giving alms, preparing the souls of the believing for the temple, we may become co-heirs of heavenly gifts, which the Most High will confer upon us in this life if we know how to use them properly.

Since all things have their life and being from God, so the proper name of everything was taken from the being of that thing, and all things derive an influence from the Creator if they have been appropriately named, for as God brings forth all things through the influence of heaven and the operation of the planets, even so the names of all things have been given in accordance with some quality of the thing named by him who counts the stars. And thus God led all creatures to Adam in order to have them named, and their names indicated some peculiar quality or part possessed by each. Therefore, each name that has a meaning, shows by comparison with the heavenly influence an inherent qualification of the object, although it is frequently changed. When, however, both meanings of the name harmonize, then the will-power and natural power become identical. Moreover, the celestial office to which man is ordained by God, endows him with power to confer life, and tells him what to encourage, what to elevate, what to suppress in his cause Sphaera, and to perform wonderful works with full devotion toward God, etc.

What Man Receives from the Order of Angels.

Man becomes strengthened with wonderful power through the order of angels, so that he declares the divine will.

From the Seraphim, that we cling with fervent love.

From the Cherubim, enlightenment of the mind, power and wisdom over the exalted figures and images, through which we can gaze upon divine things, etc.

From the Thronis, a knowledge of how we are made and constituted, that we may direct our thoughts upon eternal things.

From Dominationbius, assistance to bring into subjection our daily enemies, whom we carry with us constantly, and enabling us to attain salvation.

From Potestatibus, protection against human enemies of life.

From Virtutibus, God infuses strength into us, enabling us to contend against the enemies of truth and reward, that we may finish the course of our natural life.

From Principatibus, that all things become subject to man, that he may grasp all power, and draw unto himself all secret and supernatural knowledge.

From Archangelis, that he may rule over all things that God has made subject to him, over the animals of the field, over the fishes of the sea, and over the birds of the air.

From the Angelis he receives the power to be the messenger of the Divine will.

What Man may Obtain from the Twelve Signs.

As each creature receives its spirit, number and measure from God, so also each creature has its time.

In the Ram, the vegetables of earth obtain new vigor, the trees sap, and females become better adapted to propagate the human species. In this sign the fecundity of all creatures is limited and regulated. It has Sunday for its peculiar time and end.

In the Bull, all transactions and enterprises are prospered and fostered, so that they may go forward according to the will of God, but to this end constant prayers are necessary, and particularly on Sunday.

In the Twins, the angels have power over bodily changes and travel from one place to another over the heavens and through the course of the stars—have power over the motion of the waters in rivers and in the sea, cause love between brethren, friends and neighbors, and give warning against dangers, persons and objects.

In the Scorpion, the angels rule over legacies and riches, over treasure and treasure-seekers—are calculated by nature to confer power, the art of speaking, and to enlighten the mind in holy things, in like manner as did the apostles in their unceasing prayers to God at Pentecost.

In the Lion, the angels have power to move every living thing, to multiply their species, to watch, and in certain manners to judge. And through the gift of God they confer Physicam, Medicinam and Alchymiam.

In the Virgin, the spirits have power to subvert kingdoms, to regulate all conditions, to discriminate between master and servant, to command evil spirits, to confer perpetual health, and give to man Musicum, Logicam and Ethicam.

In the Balance, the angels derive from God great power, inasmuch as the sun and moon stand under this sign. Their power controls the friendship and enmity of all creatures.

They have power over danger, warfare, over quarrels and slander—lead armies in all quarters of the earth, cause rain, and give to man Arithmeticam, Astronomiam, Geometriam.

In the Scorpion, the angels have power over suffering and terror, over which man makes against God, over common privileges. They compel the conscience to obedience, and also force devils to keep their agreements with men, and *vice versa*. They govern the life and death of all creatures, have power over departed souls, and give to man Theologiam, Metaphysicam and Geomantiam.

In the Archer, they have power over the four elements, lead the people from one far country to another, regulate the changes of the elements and the propagation of animals.

In the Goat, the angels give high worldly honors, worthiness and virtue, such as Adam enjoyed in Paradise in his innocence. They also enlighten the understanding and confer human reason.

In the Aquitarius, angels keep man in good health, and teach him what is injurious to him, make him contented, and teach him through the command of God the mysteries of heaven and of nature.

In the Fish, the angels compel the evil spirits to become subject to man, protect the pious, so that the great enemy cannot harm him.

The Twelve Signs are Divided into Four Triplicitates.

The twelve angels, which represent the twelve signs, are called in the Apoc. Malchidael, Asmodel, Ambriel, Muriel, Verchiei, Hamaliel, Zuriel, Barbiel, Aduachiel, Hanaeb, Gambiel, Barehiel. Over this the angels also received names from the stars over which they rule as the twelve signs: Teletial, Zariel, Tomimil, Sartimel, Ariel, Bataliel, Masuiel, Aerahiel, Ehesatiel, Gediel, Doliel, Dagymel, which means the same as if expressed in Latin: Ariel, Tawnel, Geminiel, Cancriel, Leonial, Virginiel, Libriel, Scorpiel, Sagitariel, Capriel, Aquariel, Pisciel.

This method of obtaining all kinds of things with peculiar power, in the twelve signs, is described in many kinds of books. The seal of Hermetis teaches how the powers of the heavenly influence may be obtained under each sign in a crystal or gem; that they are constellated, and then, at each period of the twelve signs the appropriate character of each is divided into four parts, each of which is represented by an angel. Therefore, each of the twelve stories in the badge of office of Aaron (Solomonis) was constellated, and the Amorites possessed a constellated stone for each idol, and to this end they consecrated the book.

Further, King Solomon teaches a hidden Almadel or a Geometrical figure bearing upon the twelve signs of heaven, which he calls heights, and gives to each height seven or eight names of princes. There are also many other methods for seeking after the powers of heaven in the twelve signs, which, for good reasons, must not be made known, because they are not mentioned in the Holy Scriptures and were kept secret.

The Planets have Seven Heights and Seven Angels.

The heights are named as follows:

1. Samaym. 2. Raaquin. 3. Taaquin. 4. Machonon. 5. Mathey. 6. Sebul. 7. Arabat.

Of the operations of these, and their angels, office, order, number and measure, an account may be found in a work by Rasiel, which constitutes the Sixth Book Physicum Salomonis and Elementia Magica Petri de Aïano, page 574. From this book the book of the angel Tractatu takes its source. (2 Cornel. Agrippa, Lib. 3, page 24; Philosophiae Occul, 377, 575.)

There are seven exalted Throne Angels, which execute the commands of Potestates, viz:

1. Ophaniei. 2. Tychagara. 3. Barael. 4. Quelamia. 5. Anazimur. 6. Paschar. 7. Boel.

These are named with the name of God, through which they were created, belong to the first heaven.

SCHAMAYM GABRIEL.

The second heaven, Raaquiae, has twelve lords, or twelve heights of angels, who are placed over all. Zachariel, Raphael.

The third heaven, Saaquin, has three princes, Jabniel, Rabacyel, Dalquiel; they rule over fire, and each has his subordinate angel. The principal prince of angels in this height in called ✠ Anahel, Avahel.

The fourth heaven, Machon, by his angels leads the sun by day, and through other angels by night. The chief angel is called Michael.

The fifth heaven, Matthey, aly Machon, has the prince Samael who is served by two millions of angels. These are divided among the four quarters of the world; in each quarter three, who control the twelve months, and over these are twelve chief angels.

The sixth heaven, Zebul, has for its prince, Zachiel, with two millions of angels. The angel Zebul is placed over these during the day, and another angel, Sabath, during the night. They rule over kings, create fear, and give protection from enemies.

Arabath, the seventh heaven, has for its prince the angel Cassiel.

The names of the angels of the seven planets are as follows:

Zaphiel (Saturn), Zadkiel (Jupiter), Camael (Mars), Raphael (Sun), Haniel (Venus), Michael (Mercury), Gabriel (Moon).

There are seven princes who stand continually before God, to whom are given the spirit-names of the planets. They are called Sabathiel, Zedekiel, Madimiel, Semeliel, or Semishia, Nogahel, Coahabiath or Cochabiel, Jareahel or Jevanael, for the planets are called for themselves:

Sabachay, through which God sends hunger and tribulation upon the earth.

Sodeck, through him come honor and favor, right and holiness of man.

Modym, through him wrath, hate, lies, and war.

Hamnia, from him comes light, and the power of distinguishing between time and life.

Noga, from him food and drink, love and consolation.

Cochab, from him proceeds all trade and commerce.

Lavahan, causes all things to increase and decrease.

I, Solomon, acknowledge that in the hours Sabachay Madym it is burdensome to labor, but in the hours Zadeck and Noga labor is light. During other hours labor is middling, sometimes good and occasionally bad.

Some writers, as for example, Cornelius Agrippa, Occult, Philos, Lib. 3, chap. xvi., call the seven regents of the world by other names, which are distributed among the powers of other stars as Orphiel, Zechariel, Samael, Michael, Anael, Raphael, Gabriel, and each of these rules the world three hundred and fifty-four years and four months. A few give the Angel-year at three hundred and sixty-five years—as many years as there are days in our year. Others, one hundred and forty-five years, Apac, twenty-one Spiritu, Septem in Conspectu Dei Throni sunt quos reperi etima presidere Planetis.

The names of the seven angels over the seven heavens must be uttered first, and afterward the names of those over the seven planets, over the seven days of the week, over the seven metals, over the seven colors, these must be uttered in the morning of each day of the week.

Invocation of Angels.

Oh, ye aforesaid angels, ye that execute the commands of the Creator; be willing to be present with me in the work which I have undertaken at this time, and help me to finish it, and be ye my attentive hearers and assistants, that the honor of God and my own welfare may be promoted.

Over this there are twenty-eight angels who rule over the twenty-eight houses of the moon, viz: Asariel, Cabiel, Dirachiel, Sheliel, Amnodiel, Amixiel, Ardesiel, Neriel, Abdizriel, Jazeriel, Cogediel, Ataliel, Azerniel, Adriel, Amutiel, Iciriel, Bethuael, Geliel, Requiel, Abrunael, Aziel, Tagried, Abheiel, Amnixiel. And each moon has her own guardian and ruler, and these are described in Lib. 2, Razielis.

A man must also know how to divide the months, days and hours into four parts, for God has ordained that all things can best be perfected on suitable days and at proper hours.

The angels placed over the four parts of heaven are: Scamijm, Gabriel, Cabrael, Adrael, Madiel, Boamiel.

Alscius, Loquel, Zaniel, Hubaiel, Baccanael, Janael, Carpatiel.

Elael, Unael, Wallum, Vasans, Hiaijel, Usera, Staijel.

Ducaniel, Baabiel, Barquiel, Hannu, Anael Nahijmel.

In the second heaven, Raquie, the following angels serve.

Nathan, Catroije, Betaabat.

Yeseraije, Yuacon:

Thiel, Jareael, Yanael, Venetal, Vebol, Abuionij, Vetameil.

Milliel, Nelepa, Baliel, Calliel, Holij, Batij, Jeli.

There are also, over the four quarters of the globe, four high angels.

Over the morning winds, Michael rules.

Over the evening winds, Raphael rules.

Over the midnight winds, Gabriel rules.

Over the noonday winds, Nariel or Uriel rules.

THE ANGELS OF THE ELEMENTS ARE:

Of the air, Cherub.

Of the earth, Ariel.

Of the water, Tharsis.

Of the fire, Seruph or Nathaniel.

These are all great princes, and each has many legions of angels under him; they have great power in governing their planets, times, signs of the year, month, day, and hour, and in their part of the world and wind.

In the third heaven, Saaquin, the Angels are:

Sarquiel, Qnadissu, Caraniel, Tariescorat, Amael, Husael.

Turiel, Coniel, Babiel, Kadie, Maltiel, Hufaltiel.

Faniel, Peneal, Penac, Raphael, Carniel, Deramiel.

Porna, Saditel, Kyniel, Samuel, Vascaniel, Famiel.

In the fourth heaven, Machon, the Angel of the Divisions serves:

Carpiel, Beatiel, Baciel, Raguel, Altel, Fabriel, Vicnatraba.

Anahel, Papliel, Uslael, Burcat, Suceratos, Cababili.

In the fifth heaven, Machijn, the following Angels serve in four divisions:

Friagne, Cnael, Damoel, Calzas, Arragon.

Lacana, Astrgna, Lobquin, Sonitas, Jael, Jasiael, Naei.

Rahumiel, Jahijniel, Baijel, Seraphiel, Mathiel, Serael.

Sacriell, Majaniel, Gadiel, Hosael, Vianiel, Erastiel.

In the sixth heaven, Zebul; and seventh, Arabat, over the fifth heaven.

Should no Spiritus Aeris or divisions be found, then pronounce in the direction of the four quarters of the world, the following words:

Oh, great exalted and adored God, from all eternity.

Oh, wise God, day and night I pray unto Thee, oh, most merciful God, that I may complete my work to-day, and that I may understand it perfectly, through our Lord Jesus Christ, Thou that livest and reignest, true God from eternity to eternity.

Oh, strong God, mighty and without end.

Oh, powerful and merciful God.

On Saturday call upon God in the words which he gave in Paradise in which is the name of God.

Oh, holy and merciful God of Israel, the highest terror and fear of Paradise, the Creator of heaven and earth (as before).

✠✠✠ Quere hoc signum.

END OF THE FIRST DIVISION.

SECOND DIVISION.

I.

Sepher Schimmusch Tehillim;

OR,

Use of the Psalms,

FOR THE PHYSICAL WELFARE OF MAN.

A fragment out of the PRACTICAL KABALA, together with an Extract from a few other Kabalistical Writings. With five Illustrations upon Four Tables.

Translated by GODFREY SELIG, Lect. Publ. Acad. Lips.: 1788.

This eminent publisher and translator insists stringently that only persons of a moral character can expect success in the use of the foregoing method.

FROM THE PREFACE OF THE TRANSLATOR.

IT cannot be denied that true, wise and enlightened Kabalists lived at one time, and that some still live. But such do not wander from place to place, offering their art for sale, in order that they may accumulate wealth, but they are satisfied to remain quietly in the pillared palace of Solomon, where they are constantly employed in gathering divine wisdom, so that (as they express it), they may finally become worthy to receive the hidden gifts from above. I myself know such a man, who obtained exalted wisdom from the Kabala, and who, notwithstanding his extreme poverty, never undertakes a kabalistic process for money. When I once asked him why he refused to write a desired amulet for a noble lord, who offered him a large sum for his services, he answered me with an adage from the well-known Pirke Awoth (Extract or Fragment from the Fathers):

" Deitschtammasch Betaggo Chalof," that is to say, " whosoever accepts the crown for his reward, will perish suddenly. Not for all the money in the world would I do such a thing. But if I can assist my needy neighbor therewith, then I will do what I can, trusting in the omnipotence of the Most Holy, without looking for a reward. For my necessary support I do not feel any concern, for the Almighty has methods to support me if I trust in Him. Why, he even cares for the sparrow."

It is particularly remarkable that the greatest and most genuine Kabalists of the Jewish nation were nearly all followers and disciples of the blessed Saviour of the world, and they are so still, as I can prove satisfac torily, by numerous passages from their writings and prayers. Let this suffice for this one kind of men. But that Kabalists live and still live, who engaged in experiments, and who performed wonderful works, and who will yet do wonderful things, is also an undeniable fact, unless we are prepared to condemn all that was ever said upon this subject by renowned men of wisdom.

The celebrated and well-known Prussian Hussar, Lord of Archenwood declares, in a description of London, that there lives a man in that city, whose name is Doctor Falcon, who is known to be a great Kabalist, and who is visited and consulted by the most honorable and intelligent people of London. He states further, that this same Dr. Falcon, lived not very long since in Brussels under the name of Jude Chayim Schmul Fulk, who according to the evidence of the French Duke of Nancy, in his published memoirs of kabalistical processes, performed the most astonishing feats.

I confidently hope and trust, and I can assert without hesitation, that my little book cannot have a tendency to foster superstition. Take it for granted that one of my readers should choose to employ one of the methods described in these pages in order to accomplish a desired object, his eagerness to satisfy curiosity will soon disappear when he takes into consideration the hard terms and strict morality which are required to avail himself of them in order to derive any benefit or be successful in their use.

Before concluding my preface, it is necessary to give the reader some instruction concerning the arrangement of this volume. We find in it, for instance, single words, names, sentences, and indeed entire experiments, printed in the Hebrew and Chaldean languages. This fact should not prevent any one from purchasing the book. Because all the words printed in Hebrew and Chaldaic, which are intended to be impressed upon the mind, are also printed in English in plain terms, and they have been carefully translated. So far as the Hebrew passages are concerned, the meaning of each passage and experiment follows immediately in English, or it is placed beneath the Hebrew expression. I have made this arrangement in compliance with a request from a number of prominent persons, to make sure that the translation is genuine and correct. The chapter and verse of Holy Scripture, where all passages quoted may be found, are also correctly recorded.

EXTRACT FROM THE PREFACE OF THE KABALISTIC PUBLISHER.

It is universally known and acknowledged, that we are named after the most holy name of the Ruler of the World, and that we receive the holy decalogue or the written law from him. It is further well known that in addition to the laws which he gave to Moses engraven upon stone, he also gave to him certain verbal laws, by which, through his protracted stay upon the mountain Sinai, where all doctrines, explanations of mysteries, holy names of God and the angels, and particularly how to apply this knowledge to the best interest of man, were entrusted to him. All these doctrines, which God pronounced good, but which were not generally made known, and which in the course of time were called The Kabala, or

Traditions, Moses communicated, during his life, to Joshua, his successor. Joshua handed them over to the elders, the elders gave them to the judges, and from the judges they descended to the prophets.   The prophets entrusted them to the men of the great synagogue, and these gave them unto the wise men, and so the Kabala was handed down from one to the other—from mouth to mouth—to the present day.   Therefore do we know that in the Thora are many names of the Most High and his angels, besides deep mysteries, which may be applied to the welfare of man, but which, on account of the perverseness of humanity and to guard against their abuse, have been hidden from the great mass of human beings.

Everything that I have here stated is as clear as the sun, and needs no further proof, and it is equally clear and incontrovertible that the All-merciful gave the Thora in the beginning to promote the best interests of the soul and the body of man at the same time.   Therefore has God endowed her with exalted talents, powers and virtues that, with a rational use of her, man may protect himself from danger when no other help is at hand and save himself simply by uttering the words of the living God. On this account, the expression. " For it is thy life," occurs frequently in the Thora.   And Solomon says in his Proverbs vi. 22: " When thou goest it shall lead thee, and when thou sleepest it shall keep thee."   That the Psalms and the Thora are equal in holiness and worthiness, will not be called in question.   Our wise men delare, " He who will daily live closer to God, who deserves to unite his soul with Him, and who is willing to live in the closest communion with him, should often pray the Psalms with fervor and devotion.   Happy the man who does this daily and hourly, for his reward will be great."   The Psalms are formed and divided into five books, just like the Thora.   We can, therefore, implicitly trust in the doctrines of the enlightened Kabalists, when they assert that the Almighty accorded equal talents and powers to the Psalms as he did to the Thora, and that in them many names of the Most High Majesty of God and his angels, besides, many mysteries, are hidden.

Yes, dear reader, you must not doubt.   Through a pious life and by a rational use of the Psalms you may obtain the grace of God, the favor of princes and magistrates and the love of your fellow-men.   You will be enabled to protect yourself from danger, to escape suffering, and to promote your own welfare.

That this is all true, the contents of the prayer, with which we end each Psalm, and which we are in duty bound to pray, will amply demonstrate.   But the correctness of it is also established by the teachings of the Talmud and of the old wise men, who assure us, that many of our famous forefathers availed themselves of apparently supernatural means from time to time, to protect their best interests.   The truth of this I can establish by the most trustworthy witnesses; yea, I could even mention some great men, who, by a proper use of the Psalms, performed great works.   Such examples are rare.   Let it suffice.   I present you with a few passages out of standard books, through which you will become fully convinced that the Almighty has given his revealed word true and unexampled talents and power, and that, in an extreme case of necessity, we are permitted to make use of this gift of God, for our own and our neighbor's welfare.   As for example, to cast out evil spirits, to relieve deep melancholy and to cure grievous diseases; to set free prisoners who have been unjustly imprisoned; to arrest and resist enemies, opponents, murderers and highway robbers; to quench the fiercest fires; to resist floods of water, to defend innocence and to reveal it, and to foster good fortune, well-being and peace in a general manner.

Read the treatise on this subject, of the excellent Rabbi Schimschon bar Abraham, in his book entitled "Responsiones Raschaba." Examine the words of the enlightened Rabbi Jochanan ben Sackas in his Treatise of the Talmud and Sanhedrin, Chap. ii., where he treats of magical conjurations, and where he asserts and proves that it is allowed, in dangerous and incurable diseases, to make use of words and passages in the Holy Scripture for their cure. You will find more or less similar references in the treatise of Sabbath in the Talmud, as well as in the Responsonibus, by Zemach, son of Simonis, in which the Ninety-second Psalm, with certain prescriptions added, are highly recommended as a certain means to avoid suffering and danger, even in cases of war, fire and similar instances, enabling us to escape unharmed, free, secure and without hindrance.

Under such happy circumstances, it is surely right and proper, that such wholesome knowledge, which up to this day was known but to a few men, and they only the learned, was yet free to all, but found only in the libraries and cabinets of the great, although not generally known, should at least, in some degree, be brought to light.

Since however, I cannot gain my object in any other way than by giving these pages to the world in a printed form, and since they will unavoidably fall into unclean hands, I feel myself constrained, in order to prevent an unworthy use of them, to extend this preface, which might otherwise, very properly have ended here, in laying down a few rules and limits. Do not, however, be discouraged for I am really endeavoring to promote your best interests and shield you from harm.

1. If you are willing to avail yourself of the means indicated, I warn you not to attempt it in a case of extreme necessity, and when there is no other help at hand.

2. If this be so, in experimenting, place your trust in the goodness and power of the Most High and ever blessed God, upon whom you may perhaps have hitherto called under an unknown holy name.

3. The ordained Psalm, for this or the other undertaking, besides the appropriate prayer, you must pray with a broken and contrite heart to God, and in addition to this keep in mind the added holy name with its letters, which are given the wise Kabalists. At the same time you must have your undertaking continually before your eyes.

4. I must say to you, if you wish to console yourself with this help, that you must live in such a manner that no crime or wilful sin can trouble your conscience, for it is well known, that the prayer of the ungodly is not acceptable to God. And herewith I commit you to the protection of the Most High.

THE USE AND EFFICACY

OF

The Psalms,

AND

THE MANY PURPOSES TO WHICH THEY MAY BE APPLIED.

Psalm 1.—When a woman is pregnant and fears a premature delivery, or a dangerous confinement, she should write or cause to be written, on a piece of parchment prepared from the pure skin of a deer, the three first verses of the above Psalm, together with the hidden holy name and appropriate prayer contained therein, and place it in a small bag made expressly for that purpose, and suspend it by a string about the neck, so that the bag will rest against her naked body.

The holy name is called Eel Chad, which signifies, great, strong, only God, and is taken from the four following words: Aschre, verse 1; Lo, verse 4; Jatzliach, verse 3; Vederech, verse 6.

The prayer is as follows:

May it please thee, O Eel Chad, to grant unto this woman, N., daughter of R., that she may not at this time, or at any other time, have a premature confinement; much more grant unto her a truly fortunate delivery, and keep her and the fruit of her body in good health. Amen! Selah!

Admonition of the Translator.

Before I proceed further with the translation of the Psalms, it is necessary to insert in this place an admonition, which the author, who wrote only for his own nation, deemed unnecessary, and which, nevertheless, should be addressed to every one.

"Each human being," says the celebrated Kabalist, Rabbi Isaac Loriga, "except only the ignorant idolator, can by a pious and virtuous life enter into the consecrated temple of the true Kabala, and can avail himself of its benefits without being able to speak or understand the Hebrew language. He can pray, read and write everything in his mother tongue; only the holy name of God and the angels that may occur in the experiment, must, under all circumstances, be written and retained in the mind in the Hebrew tongue (for they must in no case be uttered), because, on the contrary, a wrong direction might otherwise easily be given to the experiment, and consequently it would lose all its holiness, worth in) efficiency.

With this pronunciation we must all be well satisfied, and, therefore, I must write all similar words and names, from the letters of which the holy names are taken, in Hebrew. In order, however, that the reader may read all similar occurring names and words in his mind and retain them, I have written all the Hebrew words with English letters together with their meaning.

Psalm 2.—Should you be exposed to danger in a storm at sea, and your life threatened, then recite this Psalm without delay and with becoming reverence, and think respectfully of the holiest name contained therein, namely, Schaddei (which means, mighty God), then immediately utter the prayer belonging thereto, after which write everything together on a fragment of a pot, and in full confidence in the Omnipotent, who fixes the boundary of the sea and restrains its power, throw it into the foaming waves, and you will see marvelous wonders, for the waves will instantly cease their roaring and the storm will be lulled.

The words, the letters of which constitute this holy name, are taken from Rageschu, verse 1; Nossedu, verse 2; and Jozes, verse 9.

The prayer is as follows: "Let it be, Oh, Schaddei! (Almighty God!) Thy holy will, that the raging of the storm and the roaring of the waves may cease, and that the proud billows may be stilled. Lead us, oh, all-merciful Father, to the place of our destination in safety and in good health, for only with Thee is power and might. Thou alone canst help, and Thou wilt surely help to the honor and glory of Thy name. Amen! Selah!

This Psalm is also an effectual remedy against raging headache. The direction is as follows: Write the first eight verses of this Psalm together with the holy name and appropriate prayer, upon pure parchment, and hang it upon the neck of the patient; then pray over him the Psalm with the prayer arranged for it. Do this in humble devotion, and the sufferer will be relieved.

Psalm 3.—Whosoever is subject to severe headache and backache, let him pray this Psalm, with the leading holy names and appropriate prayer contained therein, over a small quantity of olive oil, anoint the head or back while in the act of prayer. This will afford immediate relief. The holy name is, Adon (Lord), and is found in the words, Weatta, verse 3; Baadi, verse 3; Hekizoti, verse 5; and Hascheini, verse 7. The prayer is as follows: Adon (Lord) of the world may it please thee to be my physician and helper. Heal me and relieve me from my severe headache and backache, because I can find help only with Thee, and only with Thee is counsel and action to be found. Amen! — — Selah — — Selah!

Psalm 4.—If you have been unlucky hitherto, in spite of every effort, then you should pray this Psalm three times before the rising of the sun, with humility and devotion, while at the same time you should impress upon your mind its ruling holy name, and each time the appropriate prayer, trusting in the help of the mighty Lord, without whose will not the least creature can perish. Proceed in peace to execute your contemplated undertaking, and all things will result to your entire satisfaction.

The holy name is called: Jiheje, (He is and will be,) and is composed of the four final letters of the words. Teppillati, verse 2; Selah, verse 5; Jehovah, verse 6; and Toschiweni, verse 9. The prayer is as follows: May it please Thee, oh, Jiheje, to prosper my ways, steps and doings. Grant that my desire may be amply fulfilled, and let my wishes be satisfied even this day, for the sake of Thy great, mighty and praiseworthy name. Amen! — Selah!—

If you wish to accomplish an undertaking by or through another, proceed in all things as already stated above, with this exception: you must
change the prayer as follows: Let me find grace, favor and mercy in the
eyes of N., son of R., so that he may grant my petition, etc.

Again, if you have a cause to bring before high magistrates or princes,
you must pray this Psalm and the closing prayer arranged for it, seven
times in succession before the rising of the sun.

By the Translator.

I must be permitted in this place to insert another caution. When it
is said N., son or daughter of N., it must be understood that we must
first mention the name of the person by whom we wish to be served, and
afterward the name of his mother, as, for example, Isaac, son of Sarah,
or Dinah daughter of Leah.

Psalm 5.—If you have business to transact with your magistrates or
with your princes, and desire to obtain their special favor, then pray this
Psalm early at the rising of the sun and in the evening at sunset. Do
this three times over pure olive oil, while at the same time you think unceasingly, upon the holy name of Chananjah (merciful God), anoint your
face, hands and feet with the oil and say: Be merciful unto me, for the
sake of thy great, adorable and holy name, Chananjah, turn the heart of
my prince to me, and grant that he may regard me with gracious eyes,
and let me find favor and courtesy with him. Amen! — — Selah! — —

The holy name is found in the words: Chapez, verse 5; Nechini,
verse 9; Nechona, verse 10; Hadichemo, verse 12; and Kazinna, verse
14.

Still another peculiarity of this Psalm is, when you find notwithstanding the utmost industry and care, your business does not prosper, and you
have reason to fear that an evil Masal, that is, an evil star, spirit or destiny is opposing you, then pray this Psalm daily, even to the last verse
with great devoutness, and you will soon find yourself in more favorable
circumstances.

Psalm 6.—With this Psalm all diseases of the eye may be healed.
Read the Psalm for three days successively, and pray the prescribed
prayer seven times slowly, in a low tone, and with devotion, and with
this keep continually in your mind the holy name of Jaschajah (which
means help is with the Lord); believe without a doubt that the Lord can
and will help you. The prayer is as follows: Jehovah my Father, may it
please Thee, for the sake of the great, mighty, holy and adorable name,
Jeschajah Baal Hatschna, that is, Help is with the Lord, (for he is the
Lord of help, he can help,) which name is contained in this Psalm, heal
me from my diseases, infirmities, and from the pain of my eyes, for thine
is the power and the help, and thou alone art mighty enough to help; of
this I am certain, and therefore I trust in thee. Amen! — Selah! —

Further it is said: If a traveler encounters danger by land or sea, he
shall, when there is no other help to hope for, pray this Psalm seven
times, and each time with full confidence in the mighty and sure help of
the Almighty, and add thereto: Jeschajan, Lord of help! may it be thy

holy will and pleasure to assist me in this extremity and to avert this danger from me.   Hear me for the sake of thy great and most holy name, for thine is the power and the help.   Amen! — Selah! —

The five letters of this holy name contain, according to the prayer, the words: Jehovah al, verse 2; Schuba, verse 6; Oschescha, verse 8; Bewoshn and Vejibbahaln, verse 11.

Psalm 7.—When evil persons conspire to render you unfortunate, if your enemies watch for an opportunity to overthrow you, if they pursue you in order to harm you, then take upon the spot where you stand a handful of earth or dust, pray this Psalm and keep in your mind the holy name of Eel Elijon, great, strong, highest God! then throw the dust in the direction of your enemies, uttering a prayer prescribed for this case, and you will find that your enemies will cease their persecutions and leave you undisturbed.   The letters of the holy name are found in the words: Aisher, verse 1; Ode, verse 18, (according to the order of Al, bam, and the letters must be transposed), Hoshenei, verse 2; Eli, verse 7; Jadin, verse 9; Jashuf, verse 13; Elijon, verse 18.

The prayer is as follows: Oh, Eel Elijon! great, strong and highest God! may it please thee to change the hearts of my enemies and opposers, that they may do me good instead of evil, as thou didst in the days of Abraham when he called upon Thee by this holy name. (Gen. xiv. 22.)   Amen! — Selah! —

If you have incurred the ill-will of an enemy, whose cunning power and vengeance you have reason to fear, you should fill a pot with fresh water from the well, and pronounce over it the twelve last verses of this Psalm, namely, the words: "Arise, Jehovah! in thy wrath!"   Pronounce these four times, and at the same time think of the holy name of Eel Elijon, and of your enemy, and pray each time.   "Humble and overthrow, Oh! Eel Elion, mine enemy, N., son of R., that he may not have the power to provoke or to injure me."   Amen!   After this prayer, pour the water upon a spot at your enemy's residence, or at a place where he must pass over it, and by doing this you will overcome him.

If you have a case to decide before the court, and you have reasons to fear an unfavorable or partial verdict, then pray this Psalm slowly before you appear in the presence of the judge, thinking at the same time of Eel Elijon and of the righteousness of your cause, and as you approach the judge pray as follows: Oh, Eel Elijon! turn thou the heart of the judge to favor my best interests, and grant that I may be fully justified when I depart. Give unto my words power and strength and let me find favor.   Amen! —Selah! —

Psalm 8.—If you wish to secure the love and good will of all men in your business transactions, you should pray this Psalm three days in succession after sundown, and think continually of the holy mame of Rechmial, which signifies great and strong God of love, of grace and mercy.   Pronounce at each time the appropriate prayer over a small quantity of olive oil, and anoint the face as well as the hands and feet. The letters composing the holy name are found in the words: Addir. verse 2; Jareach, verse 4; Adam, verse 5; Melohim, verse 6; Tanis chilebu, verse 7. . The prayer reads as follows: May it please thee, Oh, Rechmial Eel to grant that I may obtain love, grace and favor in the eyes of men according to thy holy will. Amen!—Selah!—

Psalm 9.—The principal attribute of this Psalm according to the precept is, that it is an unfailing remedy in the restoration of male children, who are feeble in health, when no medicines and help are at hand. This Psalm should also be prayed against the power and malignity of enemies. In the first instance write this Psalm, with its holy name, upon pure parchment, with a new pen, and hang it around the patient's neck. Afterward repeat the prayer with reverence, and think at the same time of the holy name of Eheje Aischu Eheje, that is, I am he that will be, and utter the following prayer: All-merciful Father! for the sake of thy mighty, adorable and holy name, Eheje Aischer Eheje, may it please thee to take away from N., son of R., the illness [here name the disease] from which he suffers, and relieve him from his pains. Make him whole in soul, body and mind, and release him during his life from all plagues, injury and danger, and be thou his helper. Amen.

In the second case repeat this Psalm and pray devoutly: May it be agreeable to thy will for the sake of thy most holy name Eheje Aisher Eheje, to release me from the power of my enemies and opposers, and to protect me from their persecutions, as thou once didst protect the Psalmists from the enemies who pursued him. Amen.—Selah!

The letters of this holy name are in the words: Ode, 2; Haojeff, verse 7 and verse 16, and in alphabetical order in the At Basch.

Psalm 10.—If any one is plagued with an unclean, restless and evil spirit, let him fill a new earthen pot with water from the spring, and, in the name of the patient, pour into it pure olive oil, and pronounce over it this Psalm nine times, keeping in mind constantly the adorable name of Eel Mez, which means Strong God of the oppressed, and at each ending of the Psalm: May it be thy most holy will, Oh, Eel Mez, to heal the body and soul of N., son of R., and free him from all his plagues and oppressions: wilt thou strengthen him in soul and body and deliver him from evil. Amen!—Selah!

The holy name may be found in the words: Alah, verse 6; Lamma, Anawin, verse 16, and Haasez, verse 17.

Psalm 11.—Whoever prays this Psalm daily with feelings of devotion, and with it keeps constantly in mind the holy name of Pele, that is, Wonderful, and who besides utters a suitable prayer to God, he will be safe from all persecution, and will not have any great evil to fear.

The holy name is in the words: Ofel, verse 2; Paal, verse 3, and Adam. The closing prayer may be as follows: Adorable, mighty and holy God Pele! with thee is advice, action and power, and only thou canst work wonders. Turn away from me all that is evil, and protect me from the persecution of evil men, for the sake of the great name Pele. Amen.—Sela.

Psalm 12.—This Psalm possesses similar power, action and worth

as the foregoing. The holy name is Aineel, which means Strong God!
my Father! and is found in the words of the sixth verse of Ewjonim,
Akum Lo. The prayer is as follows: Almighty Father, my God Aineel!
grant that all conspiracies against me may be set at naught; turn away
from me all danger and injury, and thine is the kingdom and the power.
Amen.— Selah!

Psalm 13.—Whoever prays this Psalm daily with devotion, together
with the proper prayer belonging thereto, and thinks at the same time of
the powerful name of Essiel, that is, My help is the mighty God, will be
safe for the next twenty-four hours from an unnatural death and from all
bodily sufferings and punishments. The prayer is as follows: Protect me
according to thy good will and pleasure from violent, sudden and unnatural death, and from all other evil accidents and severe bodily afflic-
tions, for thou art my help and my God, and thine is the power and the
glory. Amen.—Selah.

According to tradition this Psalm is also a good cure for dangerous and
painful diseases of the eyes. The patient must procure a plant that is
good for the eyes, and with this must pray this Psalm with a suitable
prayer, trusting firmly in the certain help of the mighty Essiel, and then
bind the plant upon his eyes. The letters composing this holy name are
contained in the words: Ezoth, verse 3; Mismor, verse 1; Jarum, verse
3; Aneni, verse 4; Ojewi, verse 5, and Jagel, verse 6.

Psalm 14.—Whoso prays this Psalm in childlike faith and trust in
the most holy name, Eel enunet, that is, the true God, or God of Truth,
and prays the prayer belonging to it daily, will find favor with all men,
and will be free from slander and mistrust. The prayer is as follows:
"May it please thee, Oh! Eel summet, to grant me grace, love and favor
with all men whose help I need. Grant that all may believe my words,
and that no slander may be effective against me to take away the confidence of men. Thou canst do this, for thou turnest the hearts of men according to thy holy will, and liars and slanderers are an abomination to
thee. Hear me for the sake of thy name. Amen.—Selah!
The letters composing this holy name are found in the words: Elohim,
verse 1; Maskiel, verse 2; Echad, verse 3; Ammi, verse 4, and Azat,
verse 6.

Psalm 15.—Against the presence of an evil spirit, insanity and melancholy, pray this Psalm with the prayer belonging to it, and the holy
name Iali, which means: My Lord! or, The Lord, too, is mine, over a
new pot filled with well-water that was drawn for this express purpose,
and with this water bathe the body of the patient. The prayer which
must be repeated during the process of washing, is as follows: May it be
thy will, O God, to restore N., son of R., who has been robbed of his
senses, and is grievously plagued by the devil, and enlighten his mind for
the sake of thy holy name Iali. Amen.—Selah.
The three letters of this holy name are found in the words: Jagur,
verse 1; Ragal, verse 3, and Jimmot, verse 5.

He who otherwise prays this Psalm with reverence will be generally received with great favor.

Psalm 16.—This Psalm is important and can be profitably employed in different undertakings. As for example, 1st, If any one has been robbed, and wishes to know the name of the robber, he must proceed as follows : Take mud or slime and sand out of a stream, mix them together; then write the names of all suspected persons upon small slips of paper and apply the mixture on the reverse side of the slips; afterward lay them in a large and clean basin, filled for this purpose with fresh water from the stream—lay them in the water one by one, and at the same time pray this Psalm over them ten times with the prayer adapted to it keeping in mind at the same time the name of Caar, that is, Living, which name is found in the words of the sixth verse, as follows: Chabalim, and Alei, and if the name of the real thief is written upon the slips, that upon which his name is written will rise to the surface. The prayer is as follows: Let it be thy will, Eel Caar, the Living God to make known the name of the thief, who stole from me (here name that which was stolen). Grant that the name of the thief, if it is among the names, may arise before thy eyes, and thus be made known to mine and all others who are present, that thy name may be glorified: grant it for the sake of thy holy name. Amen.— Selah !

2. Whoever prays this Psalm daily with reverence, and childlike trust upon the eternal love and goodness of God, directed to circumstances, will have all his sorrows changed into joy.

Finally, it is said, that the daily praying of this Psalm will change enemies into friends, and will disperse all pain and sorrow.

Psalm 17.—A traveler, who prays this Psalm early in the morning, with ardor, together with the proper prayer, in the name of Jah, will be secure from all evil for twenty-four hours. The prayer is as follows: May it be thy holy will, Oh, Jah, Jenora, to make my journey prosperous, to lead me in pleasant paths, to protect me from all evil, and to bring me safely back to my loved ones, for thy mighty and adorable name's sake. Amen.

The two letters of the holy name Jah are taken from the words, Shod-dini, verse 9, and Mirmah, verse 1.

Psalm 18.—If robbers are about to attack you, pray this Psalm quickly but frevently, with the prayer belonging to it, with confidence in the holiest name of Eel Jah, that is, mighty, all-merciful and compassion-ate God, the robbers will leave you suddenly, without inflicting the slightest injury upon you. The letters necessary to make the holy name of God are contained in the words, Aisher, verse 1; Shoal, verse 1; Tamin, verse 33, and Haol, verse 47.

The prayer is the following : " Mighty, all-merciful and compassionate God, Eel Jah ! may it be pleasing to thy most holy will, to defend me against approaching robbers, and protect me against all enemies, opposers and evil circumstances, for thine is the power and thou canst help. Hear me for the sake of thy most holy name, Eel Jah. Amen.—Selah !

Is there a sick person with you, with whom the usual bodily remedies have failed, fill a small flask with olive oil and water, pronounce over it, with reverence, the eighteenth Psalm, anoint all the limbs of the patient, and pray a suitable prayer in the name of Eel Jah, and he will soon recover.

Psalm 19.—During a protracted and dangerous confinement take earth from a crossroads, write upon it the five first verses of this Psalm, and lay it upon the abdomen of the parturient; allow it to remain until the birth is accomplished, but no longer, and in the meantime pray this entire Psalm seven times in succession, with the proper holy name of God and the appropriate prayer. The holy name of this Psalm consists of two letters from the most holy name Jehovah He, which, according to the tradition of the Kabalists, are of great power, and which embrace the so-called ten Sepiroth or reckonings and other deep mysteries.

The prayer is as follows: Lord of heaven and earth! May it please thee graciously to be with this parturient, N., daughter of R., who is fluctuating between life and death; ameliorate her sufferings, and help her and the fruit of her body that she may soon be delivered. Keep her and her child in perfect health and grant her life, for the sake of the holy name, He. Amen.—Selah!

Do you desire your son to possess an open and broad heart, so that he may become an apt student and understand the lessons placed before him readily, then speak this Psalm over a cup filled with wine and honey, pronounce also the holy name and an appropriate prayer over it, and let the lad drink of it, and your desires will be realized.

Finally, it is claimed that this Psalm is effectual in driving away evil spirits. It is necessary, however, to pray this Psalm, with the holy name and an appropriate prayer, seven times over the person possessed of the evil spirit. The letters of the name He are contained in the words Hashamaijim, verse 2, and Begoaeli, verse 6.

Psalm 20.—Mix in a vessel, rose-oil, water and salt, pray over it seven times in the most holy name Jeho, this Psalm and a suitable prayer, in a low voice and with reverence, then anoint with this oil your face and hands, and sprinkle it on your clothing, and you will remain free from all danger and suffering for that day.

Are you summoned to appear before the judge in person, in a judicial trial, you should avail yourself of the above means shortly beforehand, and by so doing you will surely be justified and depart without restraint. The prayer in the last case is as follows: Lord and judge of all the World! Thou holdest the hearts of all men in thy power and movest them according to thy holy will; grant that I may find grace and favor in the sight of my judges and those placed above me in power, and dispose their hearts to my best interests. Grant that I may be favored with a reasonable and favorable verdict, that I may be justified by it, and that I may freely go from hence. Hear me, merciful, beloved Father, and fulfil my desire, for the sake of thy great and adorable name, Jeho. Amen.—Selah.

The letters of the holy name Jeho are contained in the words: Jaanah, verse 2; Sela, verse 4, and Korem, verse 10.

Psalm 21.—During an existing storm at sea, when there is danger at hand, mix rose-oil, water, salt and resin, pronounce over it slowly this Psalm, and the holy name Jehaen, and then pour the consecrated salve into the foaming sea while uttering the following prayer: Lord of the world! Thou rulest the pride of the foaming and roaring sea, and calmest the terrible noise of the waves. May it please thee, for the sake of thy most holy name, Jehach, to calm the storm, and to deliver us mercifully from this danger. Amen. Selah!

The letters of this holy name are contained in the words: Jehovah, verse 2; Duma, verse 14, and Ki, verse 13.

If you have a petition to present to the king, or to some other person in high power, pronounce this Psalm over a mixture of olive oil and resin, and at the same time think of the holy name of Jehach, anoint your face, and pray in faith and in confidence a prayer suitable to your circumstances, and then you may comfort yourself with the assurance that you will be favorably received and receive grace.

Psalm 22.—If a traveler prays this Psalm seven times daily, with the appropriate divine name, Aha, and a prayer arranged according to surrounding circumstances, in full trust in the mighty protection of our exalted and most merciful God, no misfortune will happen to him. Should he travel by water neither pirates nor storms can harm him, and if he travels by land he will be safe from harm, by beasts and men.

The letters of this holy name are found in the words: Eli, verse 2; Assah, verse 33.

Psalm 23.—Should you desire to receive reliable instructions in regard to something through a vision or in a dream, then purify yourself by fasting and bathing, pronounce the Psalm with the holy name Jah seven times, and pray at the end of each repetition: Lord of the World! notwithstanding thy unutterable mighty power, exaltation and glory, thou wilt still lend a listening ear to the prayer of thy humblest creature, and wilt fulfil his desires. Hear my prayer also, loving Father, and let it be pleasing to thy most holy will to reveal unto me in a dream, whether (here the affair of which a correct knowledge is deserved must be plainly stated) as thou didst often reveal through dreams the fate of our forefathers. Grant me my petition for the sake of thy adorable name, Jah. Amen. Selah!

The letters of the holy name Jah, contain the words: Jehovah, verse 1; Napschi, verse 3, and according to the alphabetical order Aasch Bechar, according to which the letters He and Nun become transposed.

Psalms 24 and 25.—Although the contents of these two Psalms differ materially, in respect to their mystical uses, they are equal and alike in power and action. Whoever repeats these Psalms daily in the morning with feelings of devotion, will escape from the greatest danger, and the devastating flood will not harm him.

The holy name is called Eli, and is found in the words of the twenty-fifth Psalm: Elecha, verse 1; Lemaan, verse 11, and Mi, verse 12.

Psalm 26.—When imminent dangers threaten, whether by land or by water, or if some one should be called upon to undergo severe imprisonment, he should pray this Psalm with the indicated holy name of Elohe, and with an appropriate prayer, and then he may confidently look forward to an early release from prison.

You will find the letters of this holy name in the words: Aischer, verse 10; Lischmoa, verse 7; Lo, verse 4 (after the order of At Basch), and Chattaim, verse 9.

Psalm 27.—If you wish to be well and kindly received in a strange city, and desire to be hospitably entertained, repeat this Psalm upon your journey again and again, with reverence, and in full confidence that God will dispose the hearts of men to receive and entertain you kindly.

Remark by the Translator.

Since the author has neither a holy name nor prayer for the above Psalm, it may be presumed that the frequent repetition of the Psalm is sufficient for all purposes intended.

Psalm 28.—Do you wish your enemy to become reconciled to you, pronounce this Psalm, with the appropriate holy name He, and a suitable prayer, trusting in the power and readiness of the Great Ruler of hearts, and so your wish will be fully realized.

The two letters of this holy name are contained in the words: Ledavid, verse 1, and Haolam, according to the order of At Basch.

Psalm 29.—This Psalm is highly recommended for casting out an evil spirit. The manner of proceeding is as follows: Take even splinters of the osier and seven leaves of a date palm that never bore fruit, place them in a pot filled with water upon which the sun never shone, and repeat over it in the evening, this Psalm with the most holy name of Aba, ten times with great reverence; and then in full trust in the power of God, set the pot upon the earth in the open air, and let it remain there until the following evening. Afterward pour the whole of it, at the door of the possessed, and the Ruach Roah, that is, the evil spirit, will surely depart.

The two letters of this holy name are contained in the words Jehovah, verse 11, and according to the alphabetical order called Ajack Bechar and Habre, verse 2.

Remarks by the Translator.

With this Psalm also there is no prescribed prayer given.

Psalm 30.—Whoever prays this Psalm daily, shall be safe from all evil occurrences. The holy name is Eel, and may be found in the words Aromimdha, verse 2, and Lemaan, verse 12.

By the Translator.

This Psalm and the following are also without a prescribed prayer.

Psalm 31.—Would you escape slanders, and are you desirous that evil tongues may do you no harm or cause you vexation, repeat this Psalm in a low voice, with commendable devotion, over a small quantity of pure olive oil, and anoint your face and hands with it in the name of Jah.

The letters constituting this holy name are found in the words: Palteni, verse 2, and Hammesachlim, verse 22.

Remark.

The translator regards it necessary to remark once for all, that prayers especially adapted to these as well as many of the following Psalms are wanting, and that the author undoubtedly thought that the prayers already given would enable each one to extemporize a suitable prayer. This presumption is the more probable, since we find further on in the work, that the author exhorts all to engage in prayer to God, without prescribing any particular form. Another circumstance, however, relates to the holy names, and if these are wanting it was so ordered by the ancient Kabalists, and on this account it should be particularly noted at all times.

Psalm 32.—Whoever prays this Psalm daily receives grace. Love and mercy. With this Psalm will be found neither holy name nor prayer.

Psalm 33.—Have you been unfortunate in respect to the constant death of your children at birth, pronounce this Psalm with the holiest name Jehovah, over pure olive oil and anoint your wife therewith, and the children born to you thereafter will live.

At the time of a general famine, the inhabitants of the afflicted district should pray this Psalm with united hearts and powers, and they will surely be heard.

The letters of this holy name you will find in Lajehovah, verse 2; Hodu, verse 3; Azath, verse 9, and Hejozer, verse 14.

Psalm 34.—Have you resolved to visit a prince or another person high in authority, pronounce this Psalm and the holy name Pele, that is, Wonderful, briefly before appearing in their presence and you will be received pleasantly and find favor.

The letters of this holy name are found in the words: Paude, verse 23; Lifne, verse 1, and Kara, verse 7.

Even so this Psalm is highly recommended to each traveler, for if he prays it diligently he will surely finish his journey in safety.

Psalm 35.—Have you a lawsuit pending in which you are opposed by unrighteous, revengeful and quarrelsome people, then, pray this Psalm with its holy name Jah, early in the morning for three successive days, and you will surely win your case.

The letters composing this holy name are contained in the words: Lochmi, verse 1, and in Wezinna, verse 2.

Psalm 36—Against all evil and slanderous libels pray this Psalm, and they will cause you no injury.

The holy name of this Psalm is found in the words: Arven, verse 6; Mischpatecha, verse 7, and Tehom, verse 7.

Psalm 37.—If any one has drunken so much wine as to lose his reason, and in consequence, fears are entertained for his safety, then quickly pour water into a pitcher, pronounce this Psalm over it, and bathe his head and face with the consecrated water, and give him also to drink of it.

Psalms 38 and 89.—If you have been so much slandered that the king and the officers of the law have been turned against you, and are taking measures to punish you, arise early, at the break of day and go out into the fields. Pray these Psalms and their holy name seven times with great devotion, and fast the entire day.

The holy name of the first Psalm is Aha, and of the second He, taken from the words Hascha, verse 14, and Amarti, verse 2.

Psalm 40.—The principal characteristic of this Psalm is, that we can, by its use, free ourselves from evil spirits, if we pray it daily.

The holy name is Jah, and is found in the words: Schauaiti, verse 2, and Chuscha, verse 14.

Psalms 41 to 43.—If your enemies have despoiled you of credit and caused you to be mistrusted, and thereby reduce your earnings, or perhaps, deprive you of your office and installed another in your place, you should pray these three times a day for three successive days, together with a prayer that is appropriate to your circumstances, and by doing this you will perceive incredible things. Your enemies will be put to shame and you will be unscathed.

The 42d Psalm possesses this peculiar characteristic. If you wish to be sure in regard to a certain cause, and desire to obtain information through a dream, you must fast one day, and shortly before retiring to rest you must pray this Psalm and the holy name, Zawa, (which means the Lord of Hosts,) belonging to the Psalm, seven times, making known your desires, each time, in an appropriate prayer, in which your wishes should be plainly named.

Psalm 44.—If you wish to be safe from your enemies the frequent praying of this Psalm will, it is said, answer your expectations.

Psalms 45 and 46.—These two Psalms are said to possess the virtue of making peace between man and wife, and, especially, to tame cross wives. The saying is, namely: Whoever has a scolding wife, let him pronounce the 45th Psalm over pure olive oil, and anoint his body with it, when his wife, in the future, will be more lovable and friendly. But if a man has innocently incurred the enmity of his wife, and desires a proper return of conjugal love and peace, let him pray the 46th Psalm over olive oil, and anoint his wife thoroughly with it, and, it is said, married love will again return.

The holy name is Adojah, (this name is composed of the first syllables of the two most holy names of God. Adonai and Jehovah).

The letters are in the words: Elohim, verse 2; Meod, verse 2; Jehovah, verse 8, and Sela, verse 12.

Psalm 47.—Do you wish to be beloved, respected and well received by all your fellow-men, pray this Psalm seven times daily.

Psalm 48.—If you have many enemies without cause, who hate you out of pure envy, pray this Psalm often, and with it think of the holy name Sach, which means Pure, Clear and Transparent, and your enemies will be seized with fear, terror and anxiety, and in future they will no more attempt to injure you.

The letters of the holy name are to be found in the words: Achasatam, verse 7, and Ki, verse 14.

Psalms 49 and 50.—Is one of your family burdened with a severe and perhaps incurable fever, then take a new pen and ink prepared for this purpose, and write the 49th Psalm and the first six verses of the 50th Psalm, together with the appropriate holy name Schaddi, which signifies Almighty, and which belongs to these Psalms, upon pure parchment prepared for this particular case, and hang it around the patient's neck with a silken string.

The letters composing the divine name, Schaddei, can be found in the words of the 49th Psalm Schimma, verse 1; Adaw, verse 3, and Wikas, verse 8.

Remarks by the Translator.

(Should some one choose to write and wear a talisman such as is described above, we would kindly advise him to procure parchment, ink and pen from a Jewish writer of the ten commandments.)

It is asserted that whosoever wears the 50th Psalm, written as above described, upon his person, will be safe from all danger, and escape from all the machinations of robbers.

The holy name is Chai, which signifies, Living, and the letters are taken from the words: Sewach, verse 5, and Anochi, verse 7.

Psalm 51.—Is any one troubled with an anxious and restless conscience on account of the commission of a heavy sin, then let him pronounce this Psalm with the word Dam connected with it in the mind, three times a day, namely, early at noon and in the evening over poppy-oil, and at the same time utter a prayer suitable to the occasion in which the evil deed must be mentioned in deep humility and sorrow, which must be obtained from the just yet merciful Judge of all men through a contrite heart, then let him anoint himself with the consecrated oil over the body, and he will find in a few days that he has found grace and that the heavy burden has been removed.

The letters of the word Dam, through the transposition of the B and M in the words Parim, verse 20, and Bebo, verse 2, are taken according to the order of the alphabet, Al Bam, in which the B is taken for M.

Psalm 52.—He who is so unfortunate as to be disturbed through frequent slanders is advised to utter this Psalm daily in the morning, and no special prayer or holy name is needed to obtain the benefit of the Psalm.

Psalms 53 to 55.—These three Psalms are ordained to be uttered by him who is persecuted without cause by open and secret enemies. If he desires only to quiet his enemies, or fill them with fear, he must daily repeat the prescribed 53d Psalm with the holy name Ai. The letters of this name are the first letters of the two blessed names of God, Adonai, Jehovah, and are found in the words Amar, verse 2, and Jiszmach, verse 6.

If, however, he wishes not only to be secure from their malice, but if he also desires to revenge himself upon them, then he must repeat the 54th Psalm with the prescribed holy name, Jah. The letters of this are found in the last words of this Psalm, Eeni, and in the word Immenu, verse 2, and indeed according to the Kabalistic rule Gematria, inasmuch as the letter, He, when it is written out signifies six in number, and in this manner may very easily be taken for the letter Vav, which, in counting, also numbers six.

Should he desire to render his enemies evil for evil, he shall repeat the 55th Psalm with the name Vah, which contains both of the final letters of the name Jehovah. The letters of this name are found in the words: Weattah, verse 12, and Haasinad, verse 2.

Psalm 56.—This Psalm is recommended to him, who is desirous of freeing himself from the bonds of passion and of sense, and who is anxious to be delivered from the so-called Jezer Horra, which means, the evil lusts or the desire to commit sin.

Psalm 57.—Whosoever wishes to be fortunate in all his undertakings should pray this Psalm daily after the morning prayer in the church, and with it the holy name Chai, signifying Living, which name he should keep constantly in his mind.

The two letters of this name are contained in the words: Chonneni, verse 2, and in Elohim, verse 6.

Psalm 58.—If you should be attacked by a vicious dog, pray this Psalm quickly, and the dog will not harm you.

Psalm 59.—Would you be entirely free from the Jezor Horra, that is, from the inclination which all men possess to do evil, and the sinful appetites and passions which often overcome them, then pray this Psalm from the second verse to the end, for three days in succession, at early noon and in the evening, and the holy name belonging thereto, namely Paltioel, which signifies Strong God, My Rescuer and Saviour; also pray the prescribed prayer, and you will become aware of the most wonderful changes within yourself.

The prayer is as follows: Lord, my Father and the Father of mine, mighty God! May it please thee for the sake of thy great, holy and adorable name, Paltioel, to release me from the Jezer Harra (from my evil desires and passions and from all evil thoughts and acts), as thou didst the author of this Psalm when he prayed to thee. Amen.— Selah!—

The letters of the holy name of Paltioel may be found in the words: Pischii, verse 3; Elohim, verse 5; Chattati, verse 3; Jehovrh, verse 8; Aschir, verse 15, and Maschel, verse 14.

Psalm 60.—If you are a soldier in an army, and are about marching into the field, repeat this Psalm, keeping in mind the holy name of Jah, and at the conclusion of each repetition of the Psalm, utter a suitable prayer in full reliance upon the endless omnipotence of Him, who can give the victory where he will, and you will be enabled to return to your home uninjured.

The two letters of the holy name Jah, are contained in the word Zarenu, verse 14, as the last word of this Psalm, and in Lelammed, verse 1.

Psalm 61.—When you are about taking possession of a new dwelling, repeat this Psalm just before moving in, with a suitable prayer, trusting in the name of Schaddei, and you will experience blessing and good fortune.

The letters composing this name are taken from the words Schimmu, verse 2; Ken, verse 9; and Jom, the last word of this Psalm. It should, however, be remarked that both the last letters are selected according to the alphabetical order of Ajack Bechar.

Psalm 62.—Speak this Psalm with proper reverence on Sunday immediately after the evening prayer, and on Monday after vespers, and at the same time think of the holy name Ittami, which means " concealed, hidden, or invisible " (which most probably refers to the invisible God, who covers the transgressions of penitent sinners), and utter the following prayer: Great, mighty and merciful God! may it be thy holy will to pardon me all my sins, transgressions and offences; wilt thou cover them, and blot them out as thou didst the sins and transgressions of him who uttered this Psalm in thy presence, wilt thou do this for the sake of the adorable name of Ittami. Amen.—Selah!

The letters of this name may be found in the words: Achi, verse 2; Jeschuate, verse 2; Emot, verse 3; Lelohim, verse 6, and Leisch, verse 13.

Psalm 63.—If you have reason to believe that your business-partners are about to take unfair advantage of you, and that you will suffer loss through them, and if you desire, on this account, to withdraw from the firm, repeat this Psalm, and with it think of the holy name Jach, and you will not only be able to withdraw without loss, but you will obtain further good fortune and blessings.

The letters of this holy name are contained in the words Jasjmach, verse 11, and Jechuda, verse 1.

Psalm 64.—In reference to this Psalm it is only necessary to say, that seafarers who daily pray it with devotion will complete their voyage without accident, and reach their place of destination in good health. As for the rest, neither holy name nor especial prayer have been considered necessary.

Psalm 65.—Whosoever utters this Psalm with its appropriate name Jah, persistently, will be fortunate in all his undertakings, and everything he attempts will result to his best advantage. It is particularly recommended to one who has a petition to prefer, for it is asserted that he will certainly obtain his desires.

The two letters of this holy name are taken from the words Joschira, verse 14, and Dumijah, verse 2.

Psalm 66.—If any man is possessed of a Ruack Roah (evil spirit), write this Psalm on parchment and hang it upon him ; then stretch your hands over him and say : Save me, O God, for the waters are come into my soul.   Psalm lxix. 2.

Psalms 67 and 68.—Both these Psalms contain the divine name of Jah.   The letters composing it are found in the first Psalm and are selected from the words ; Jechonnenu, verse 2, and from the last word of the fifth verse, Sela.   In the second, on the other hand, from Jakum, verse 2, and from Aora, verse 36.   The first should be prayed in a protracted case of fever, or in severe imprisonment.   The second, on the contrary, should be prayed over a vessel filled with water upon which the sun never shone, in a low voice, and in the name of the patient, and then work his body with the water, and the evil spirit will depart from him.

Psalms 69 and 70.—The first of these Psalms should be uttered daily over water, by the libertine and sensualist, who is so confirmed in his evil habits, as to become a slave to them, and who, however much he may desire to escape these habits, is unable to do so.   After having prayed this Psalm over the water he should drink of it.

The second should be prayed by him who desires to conquer his enemies.

Neither of these two Psalms have prescribed holy name or prayer.

Psalm 71.—With this Psalm there is likewise neither holy name nor prayer, but it is said to have the power to liberate any one from prison, who will for a time pray it reverentially seven times a day.

Psalm 72.—Write this Psalm with the name Aha, in the usual manner, upon pure parchment, and suspend it around your neck, and you will become a universal favorite, and find favor and grace from all men; you may then live unconcerned, for you can never come to poverty.

The letters of the holy name are taken from the words : Elohim, verse 1, and Jeasshruhu, verse 17.

Psalms 73 to 78.—Since these eleven Psalms have neither holy names nor particular closing prayers, I shall, in order to economize space, record the peculiar virtues ascribed to each one for the good of mankind.

The 73d Psalm should be repeated reverently seven times daily by those who are compelled to sojourn in a heathen, idolatrous or infidel country, and by doing so, no one need feel afraid that he will be induced to deny his faith.

The frequent and earnest prayer of the 74th Psalm is said to defeat the persecution embittered by enemies, and will frustrate the oppressions of the self-mighty, wealth-seeking, hard-hearted people, and will at the same time bring them to a terrible end.

The devout prayer of the 74th Psalm will effect the forgiveness of sins.

The 76th Psalm is said to be the quickest and most effective defence against danger from fire and water

Whosoever prays the 77th Psalm daily will not be overtaken by want or danger.

Whosoever prays the 78th Psalm earnestly and often, will be beloved and respected by kings and princes and will receive favor from them.

The frequent prayer of the 79th Psalm, it is said, is fatal to enemies and opponents.

The constant and industrious prayer of 80th and 81st Psalms is said to be a happy means of saving men from falling into unbelief and saves them also from other errors.

The prayer of the 82d Psalm will assist an envoy to transact his business to the satisfaction of his employers, and his business affairs will succeed and prosper.

You should write the 83d Psalm properly, upon pure parchment, and suspend it around your neck, and by so doing you will abide safely in war, avoiding defeat and captivity. If you should, however, be overcome, your captors will not harm you, for even in captivity no harm can befall you.

Psalm 84.—When a man, through a severe and protracted illness, has acquired a repulsive, disgusting and bad odor, he should pronounce this Psalm with the prescribed holy name of Af, which means Father, over a pot of water upon which the sun never shone, and then pour the water all over himself, and then the bad smell will leave him.

The letters of the holy name Af, are found in the words: Zebarth, verse 2, and in Bach, verse 6.

Psalm 85.—Do you wish that your former friend, but who now lives at enmity with you, should again be reconciled to you, if you can discover no disposition on his part to make it up with you, then go out into an open field, turn your face toward the South, and pronounce this Psalm, with its prescribed holy name Vah, seven times in succession, and he will approach and receive you in great friendship.

Psalms 86 to 88.—These three Psalms again are left without a holy name, and there is nothing further said about them, than that a person should accustom himself to pray them often, because by so doing much good can be done and much evil avoided. The frequent praying, of the 85th Psalm especially, is said to promote the welfare of the community and the congregation.

Psalm 89.—Should one of your own family or near friends waste away so rapidly, in consequence of a severe illness, so that they are already nearly helpless and useless, speak this Psalm over olive oil and pour the oil over the wool that has been shorn from a wether or a ram, and with it anoint the body and limbs of the patient, and he will speedily recover.

If your friend is under arrest, and you desire his liberation, go into an open field, raise your eyes toward heaven and repeat this Psalm, with a prayer suited to the circumstances, which should be uttered in full confidence in God.

Psalm 90.—Should you accidentally encounter a lion in the forest, or should you be deceived, cheated or plagued by an evil spirit or ghost, then grasp in your mind the name of God (Schaddei) and repeat this

Psalm, and they will withdraw themselves. But you will be still more secure when such a danger should arise, if you pray the following 91st Psalm in connection with the 90th, at one and the same time.

Psalm 91.—The holy name of this Psalm is El, which means Strong God. After speaking this Psalm, and the preceding one, over a person tormented by an evil spirit, or one afflicted by an incurable disease, in the name of Eel Schaddei, then pray humbly : Let it be thy holy pleasure, oh my God ! to take from N., son of R., the evil spirit by which he is tormented, for the sake of thy great, mighty and holy name El Schaddei. Wilt thou presently send him health and let him be perfectly restored. Hear his prayer as thou once did that of thy servant Moses when he prayed this Psalm. Let his prayer penetrate to thee as once the holy incense arose to thee on high. Amen. Selah !

The two letters of the name Eel are contained in the words Jeschuti, verse 16, and Orech, verse 16.

Again write this Psalm in connection with the last verse of the previous Psalm upon clean parchment, and conceal it behind the door of your house, and you will be secure from all evil accidents.

Kabalists ascribe to this Psalm when taken in connection with the above verse, the most wonderful virtue, when it is used in accordance with the nature of existing circumstances, and when it is combined with other scriptural passages, holy names of angels, characters and prayers, it is said, for example :

Prayer through which all distress, danger and suffering may be turned aside. If any one should be in danger of his life, or become distressed, be it what it may, such as being attacked by an incurable disease, pestilence, fire or water, overwhelmed by enemies or murderers, in battles, sieges, robberies, close imprisonment, etc., let him confess his sins first of all, and then speak the Vihi Noamprayer (the name by which the 91st Psalm with the aforesaid verse is usually known), ninety-nine times, according to the number of the two holiest names of God, Jehovah Adonei. Each time when he comes to the fourteenth verse, " Because he hath set his love upon me," etc., he shall keep in mind the holy name, and then pray devoutly each time : " Thou art the most holy, king over all that is revealed and hidden, exalted above all that is high, sanctify and glorify thy adorable name in this thy world, so that all the nations of the earth may know that thine is the glory and the power, and that thou hast secured me from all distress, but especially out of the painful emergency (here the object of the prayer must be distinctly stated), which has overtaken me N., son of R. And I herewith promise and vow that I will now and ever after this, as long as I shall live upon the earth, and until I return to the dust from which I was taken." (Here the vow must be verbally stated,—stating what we will do, perform or give in the service of our Creator. The vow may consist in fasting, giving alms, or in the daily reading of several chapters of the Holy Scriptures, Psalms, of the Sohar or of the Talmud, releasing of captives, nursing the sick and burying the dead.) " Praised be Jehovah, my Rock and my Salvation. Thou wilt be my representative and intercessor, and wilt help me, for thou helpest thy poor, feeble and humble creature, and in time of need releasest from fear and danger, and dealest mercifully with thy people; merciful and forgiving, thou hearest the prayer of every one. Praised art thou, Jehovah, thou who hearest prayer." (The last words should be repeated seven times at each ending of the prayer.)

And now, whoever will punctually observe the foregoing instructions three days in succession, in full trust in the mighty help of God, he may rest assured of the assistance which he desires.

Kabalists, and especially the celebrated Rabbi Isaac Loria have assured us that in a time of pestilence or general emergency, the Vihi Noam-prayer should be prayed seven times daily, connecting with it in the mind the figure of the golden candlestick, when it is composed of the forty-one holy and important words and names of this Psalm, with which we should especially consider the holy names in their order. The following are the names:

Vean,	Alm,	Bich,	Iba,	Wich,	Ika,	Aan,	Beni,
Mii,	Tmol,	Veal,	Ktaz,	Ilu,	Mehoh,	Imi,	Becha,
Im,	Retak,	Betu,	Lir,	Uma,	Ima,	Miz,	Mehi,
Aki,	Lakad,	Mili,	Ibak,	Rul,	Leta,	Afcham,	Pesch,
Aab,	Schin,	Aki,	Acchu,	Kuck,	Vetat,	Raasch,	Jaub,

Ana.

(See Fig. A.)

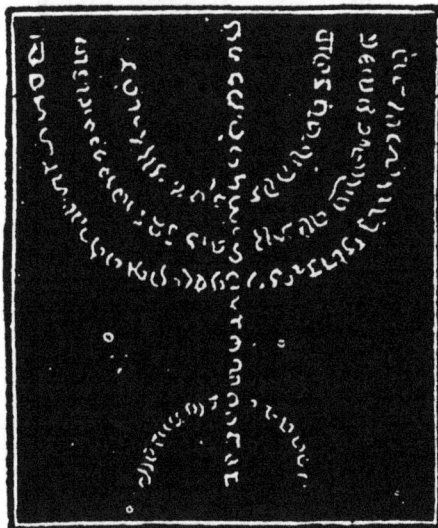

Fig. A.

After this should be spoken verses 21–28, chapter xii. of Exodus, and with them keeping in mind the names contained in the 23d and 28th verses, in the following order:

Awal, Jahel, Ito, Huj Husch, Aha, Imo, Vil.

As also Vohu, Uha, Bam, Bili, Zel, Holo, Vesop, and finally the holy name: Nischaszlas.

And now, he who observes all these things to the very letter, and who can keep in his memory all the letters, points or vowels, he shall be safe from all danger, and shall be as strong as steel, so that no firearms can harm him. The certainty of this is shown by the Kabalists, because the letter Seijid is not to be found in the entire Psalm, and since the word Seijin or Kie Seijin embraces within its meaning all deadly weapons, this conclusion is entirely correct.

Remarks by the Translator.

The extraordinary powers ascribed to the 91st Psalm may all be right and proper enough, but it is to be regretted that the reader cannot avail himself of its benefits, especially in the last experiment, because all the recorded holy names consist of the first letter of all the words of the 91st Psalm, and likewise of the 23d and 28th verses of Exodus, chapter xii., a passage which has already been quoted. It is, therefore, impossible to pronounce this name properly, neither can it be translated into English or into any other language. And how shall we then memorize the first letters of each word of the Psalm together with the points or vowels belonging to them? If any one, notwithstanding the difficulties attending the use of this Psalm, should desire to avail himself of its virtues, then he must undertake the burdensome task of learning the Hebrew language, or he must write it, and wear it upon his heart as an amulet.

Psalm 92.—He who desires to attain to high honors, let him take with this object in view, a new pot filled with water. Place in it myrtle and vine leaves, and pronounce over it, with perfect trust, the following Psalms, namely, the 92, 94, 23, 20, 24, and 100, three times in succession, and at each time let him wash himself out of the pot and afterward anoint his face and whole body with the water; then turn his face toward the north, pray to God for the fulfilment of his desires, and he will see wonderful things. He will be astonished with his ever-increasing good fortune. He will also, in a wonderful manner, advance from one post of honor to another.

Psalm 93.—There is nothing special recorded of this Psalm, other than that it is highly recommended to any one who has a suit with a stern and unjust opponent. The proper use of this Psalm, it is said will surely win him his cause.

Psalm 94.—If you have a hard, unyielding and bitter enemy, who oppresses you sorely and causes you great anxiety, repair to an open field on Monday, take some incense into your mouth, turn with your face toward the East and West, and repeat first the 94th Psalm and then the 92d, seven times, keeping in mind at the same time the holy name Eel Kanno Taf, which signifies great, strong, zealous and good God, and pray each time at the ending of these Psalms: "May it please Thee, O great, strong, zealous and good God, to humble my enemy N., son of R., as thou once did the enemies of our great teacher Moses, who rests in peace, and who completed this Psalm to thy glorification. Let my prayer arise to thee as did the sweet smell of incense from the altar of incense, and let me behold thy wonderful power. Amen!—Selah!—

Psalm 95.—The appropriate holy name of God and peculiar to this Psalm is Eel, which is, great, strong God, and the letters are found in the words: Eel, verse 3, and Lezur, verse 1.

The pious believer should pray this Psalm for his erring and unbelieving brethren.

Psalms 96 and 97.—The holy name of these two Psalms is Jah, and the letters of the first are found in the words, Jeschuato, verse 2, and Hawn, verse 7, and those of the other in the words, Jismechu, verse 1, and Atta, verse 9. Whosoever will pray these two Psalms three times daily, will cause his family great joy and contentment.

Psalm 98.—The holy name of this Psalm is also Jah, and should be pronounced in order to establish peace and unity between families. The letters of the holy name are taken out of the words: Israel, verse 3, and Haschiah, verse 1.

Psalm 99.—With this Psalm there is no holy name recorded, and all who wish to become really pious are advised to pray it often with proper devotion.

Psalm 100.—The holy name Jah, so often mentioned already, is also appropriate to this Psalm, and whoever prays it several days successively seven times, will overcome all his enemies. The two letters of this holy name are recorded in verse 3, and in Aetodah, verse 4.

Psalm 101.—Whoever bears this Psalm in addition to the 68th upon his person, written upon parchment, is secure from the persecution of evil spirits and vindictive persons.

Psalms 102 and 103.—Both these Psalms are said to be very good for barren women by the use of which they may receive grace and favor from God. The holy name of the one is called Jah, and is taken from Anneni, verse 3, and the name of the other one is Aha, and is taken from the word Adonai, verse 12, and from Sela, verse 20.

Psalm 104.—The frequent and earnest prayer of this Psalm is said to be attended with such great power, that through it the Masick may be destroyed.

Remarks of the Translator.

The word Masick signifies, according to its root, only something hurtful, something that will cause harm, it may be by spirits, beings or animals. Generally, however, the Jews understood the term to mean the Devil, and with its connections in this place the word must mean original sin and the propensity to commit sin.

Psalms 105 to 107.—To these three Psalms the holy name of Jah is ascribed, and according to the original writing, it is said, that the 105th Psalm will cure three days' fever; the praying of the 106th Psalm will cure the four days' fever, and finally the praying of the 107th will cure the daily fever.

The letters of the holy names are taken from Lejaikof, verse 7, and Hodu, verse 1, and further from Sochreni, verse 4, and from Tehillato, verse 2 of the 106th Psalm, and finally from Jischlach, verse 19, and Verinna, verse 21.

Psalm 108.—Write this Psalm with its proper holy name, Vi, (two letters from the most holy name of Jehovah, in which Kabalists seek through its many divisions, great secrets,) upon clean parchment, and hide it in a secure spot behind the door of your house, and then your going and coming will be blessed, and you will be successful in all your business transactions.

The two letters of the holy name Jehovah, by a transposition of Vav and Jod, are contained in the words: Zarenn, verse 14, and in Nachon, verse 2.

Psalm 109.—Have you a mighty enemy, who plagues and oppresses you, fill a new jug with new, sparkling wine, add some mustard to it, and then repeat this Psalm three days successively, while at the same time you keep in mind the holy name of Eel (great and strong God), and afterward pour the mixture before the door of your enemy's dwelling. Be careful, however that you do not sprinkle a single drop upon yourself when in the act of pouring it out.

The letters of the name Eel are found in the words, Elohim, verse 3, and in Ki Jamood, verse 5.

Psalms 110 and 111.—The first of these Psalms is marked with the holy name Jah, and by its frequent use in the form or a prayer, and a man may compel all enemies and opposers to bow to him and beg for quarters and peace.

Through praying the 111th Psalm a man may acquire many friends without the necessity of keeping constantly in mind any special holy name.

Psalms 112 and 113.—By praying the first of these Psalms a man will increase in might and power from time to time, and by praying the second devoutly it is possible to check growing heresy and infidelity. Neither of these Psalms has a peculiar holy name.

Psalm 114.—The holy name of this Psalm consists of two letters, taken together from the names Adonai (Lord), and Jehovah, namely, Aha, which may be found in this Psalm in the words Jiszraoel, verse 1, and Jehuda, verse 2. If you desire success in your trade or business, write this Psalm with its appropriate holy name upon clean parchment, and carry it about your person constantly in a small bag prepared especially for this purpose.

Psalm 115.—If you are determined to dispute with infidels, heretics and scoffers at religion, pray this Psalm devoutly beforehand.

Psalm 116.—Whoever prays this Psalm daily with devotion, trusting fully in God, will be safe from violent death, neither will he be overtaken by a sudden death.

Psalm 117.—Did you make a vow to obtain a certain commandmen/

or perform a good work, and fail in the performance of them through forgetfulness or carelessness, as soon as you recollect your remissness pray this Psalm with a broken and contrite heart.

Psalm 118.—If you pray this Psalm often and devoutly, you will be able to silence all free-thinkers, scoffers of religion and heretics, who labor to lead you astray.

Psalm 119.—This it is well known is the largest of all the Psalms, and consists in the Hebrew of eight alphabets, but in such a manner, that each letter appears in undisturbed regularity, and through this there arose twenty-two special divisions, which are included in each eight verses, because a particular power is ascribed to each division, which I cannot present to the reader in clearer manner than by placing each letter before him which forms the particular division.

Aleph.—The eight verses of this letter, which all begin with Aleph, should be pronounced over a man whose limbs shake and quiver, and if this be done in a low and even tone of voice, he will be relieved. If any one has made a vow, which has become burdensome to fulfil, it will be easy for him to keep his promise.

Beth.—It is said that through the second division from the ninth to the sixteenth verse, a man may obtain a good memory, an open heart, desirous to learn, and an extended intelligence. Whosoever desires to attain this must begin as follows: Remove from a hard-boiled egg the shell deftly and cleanly, so that the inside shall remain uninjured, and write upon it the above eight verses as well as the fourth verse of Deuteronomy, xxxiii., and eight verses of Joshua i., and also the holy name of the angels, Chosniel, Schrewniel and Mupiel. The translation of these three angel-names it is not necessary to know, because they must not be pronounced, but since it will be of interest to the reader to know the meaning of them, it will not be superfluous to give them here. Chosniel, signifies Cover, or overshadow me, mighty God! (namely, with the spirit of wisdom and knowledge). Schrewniel, turn me, again, mighty God! that is, change me, convert me into a better man or woman, as David once said, "Create in me, oh God," etc. Mupiel means: Out of the mouth of the mighty God (namely, let me attend upon the decrees of thy laws, as if I heard and received them from the mouth of God himself). Finally, the following must also be written upon the egg: Open and enlarge my heart and understanding, that I may hear and comprehend everything that I read, and that I may never forget it. All this must be done on a Thursday evening, after fasting the entire day, and then the egg must be inserted whole into the mouth, and when it is eaten, the four first verses of this division must be repeated three times in succession.

Gimel.—The division of the third letter, verses 17 to 24, should be prayed seven times in succession, in a low, solemn tone and with full confidence in the omnipotence of God, over the seriously injured eye of a friend, so that the pain may cease and the eye restored.

Daleth.—By the earnest praying of this division, verses 25 to 32, a painful injury of the left eye can be cured in the first place, in the same manner as is described above, and in the second place, if a man is engaged in a lawsuit, or is vexed by a change of occupation, or residence, or if he desires to make an advantageous selection, or make a resolution, he should repeat these eight times in succession. On the other hand, however, if a man must avail himself of the advice and assistance of many persons in order to accomplish an undertaking successfully, he should repeat this division ten times.

He.—The division of the letter He, verses 33 to 40, is said to make people refrain from committing sins. A sinful being, who has become so much accustomed to commit sin and vice, that he cannot refrain from them, notwithstanding his best resolutions, should write these eight verses upon parchment prepared from a clean deer skin, (or cause them thus to be written,) place it in a bag prepared for this purpose and hang it around his neck, so that he will carry it continually upon his breast.

Vau.—Speak these eight verses, 41 to 48, properly over water, and give it to your servant or dependent to drink, and then your rule and power over him will become easy and agreeable, and he will serve you willingly

Zain.—To the seventh division, verses 49 to 56, two different effects are ascribed. It is said, for example : If one of your friends or acquaintances is afflicted with melancholy, or becomes splenetic, or has severe stitching in the side, write this division, with the holy name Raphael, which signifies, heal, mighty God, properly upon a small piece of clean parchment, and bind it upon the patient where the spleen is situated. If you have been led into an undertaking that promises evil results, through the misrepresentations of evil counsellors, repeat this division eighteen times, and you will find means to withdraw from the undertaking without injury to yourself.

Cheth.—Speak the division of this letter, verses 57 to 64, seven times over wine, and give a sick person, who has severe pains in the upper part of the body, to drink of it, and he will soon find relief.

Teth.—The division of the letter Teth, verses 65 to 72, is an easy, quick and tried remedy to cure the severest case of kidney or liver complaints, or to take away pain in the hips. Pronounce these eight verses properly, specially and reverently over the sick person and he will convalesce.

Jod.—Would you find grace and favor with God and man, pray at the close of each morning prayer the division of this letter, verses 70 to 80, trusting fully in the mercy and grace of God, and your prayer will be heard.

Caph.—If one of yours has a dangerous sore, or a burning swelling on the right side of the nose, pray the eight verses of this division, verses 81 to 88, ten times, in a low and conjuring voice, over the sore, and you will perceive to your astonishment and joy, that the otherwise incurable sore will be healed.

Lamed.—If you are summoned to appear personally before the Judge in a lawsuit, pray on the preceding day, just after the evening prayer, the division of the letter Lamed, verses 89 to 96, and you will obtain a favorable hearing, and will be permitted to leave the court justified.

Mem.—For pain in the limbs, and especially for paralysis in the right arm or hand, a man should pray this division, verses 97 to 104, seven times for three successive days, in a low conjuring voice, over the affected arm, and the pain will cease and the arm will be healed.

Nun.—Have you a mind to travel, pray this division, verses 105 to 112, which begins with the words: "For thy word is a lamp to my feet," a few days previous to starting upon your journey, each time after the morning and evening prayer, and you will accomplish your journey safely and will prosper in your avocation.

Samech.—If you have a favor to ask of a superior, pray, before presenting your petition, or before you attempt to ask the favor verbally, the eight verses of the letter Samech, verses 113 to 120, and you will not go away unheard.

Ain.—In the same way and manner as the prayer of the division of the letter Mem, heals pain in the right arm, so also the praying of the eight verses of the letter Ain, verses 121 to 128, will cure pain in the left arm and hand.

Pe.—The prayer of this division, verses 129 to 136, will prove of the same effect in the case of a boil or swelling on the left side of the nose, and the proceedings in both cases must be the same to effect a cure.

Tsaddi.—Since it frequently happens that persons in an official station are induced, through misrepresentations and other circumstances, to give a wrong and unjust decision, even against their better knowledge and desire, they are kindly advised to pray the eight verses of this letter, verses 137 to 144, three times devoutly before giving their decision, at the same time asking the help of the Judge of all Judges, to enlighten their minds.

Koph.—The mysterious operation of this division, verses 145–152, relates to the cure of a dangerous and painful injury at the left leg. These eight verses should be pronounced in a low and conjuring voice over a quantity of rose-oil and the injury anointed with the oil.

Resh.—Are you burdened with a painful, constantly running boil in the right ear, pronounce the eight verses of the division of the letter Resh, verses 152–160, in a low and conjuring voice, over onion-water or juice, and let one drop run into the ear, when you will experience immediate relief.

Schin.—Against severe and burning headache speak the division of this letter, verses 161 to 168, in a low conjuring voice, three times over pure olive oil, and anoint the place where the pain is the most severe.

Tau.—The last division of this Psalm, verses 169–176, should be used in the same manner as the division of the letter Resh, that is, it should be spoken over onion-water, and by its use a boil in the left ear may be cured.

Finally, it is stated at the end of this Psalm, that whosoever is afflicted with a tearing pain in both arms, in the sides, and in the legs at one and the same time, should repeat this whole Psalm in the following order: 1. The eight verses of the letter Aleph; of Tau and Beth. 2. Those of the letter Schin. 3. The division of the letter Gimmel. 4. The eight verses of the letter Resh. 5. The division of the letter Daleth. 6. That of the letter Kuf. 7. The eight verses of the letter He. 3. Those of the letter Zain. 9. The division of the letter Vau. 10. The eight verses of the letter Pe. 11. The division of the letter Zain. 12. The division of the letter Ain. 13. The eight verses of the letter Cheth. 14. Those of the letter Tamech. 15. Those of the letter Teth. 16. Of Nun. 17. The eight verses of the letter Jud, and finally, 18, the division of the letter Mem, Caph, and Lamed. This remedy has been tried, and has proved infallible. Should any one become afflicted with tearing pains in the loins, make for him, at the conclusion of this Psalm, knots, combinations, or magical knots in water, with or under the names of: Adam, Seth, Enoch, Canaan, Mahalleel, Jared, Methusaleh, Lamech, Noah, Shem.

[The translator is compelled to admit honestly, that he does not comprehend this latter clause, and much less is he able to give any directions in regard to the method employed in making magical-knots, he does not presume that any one will be interested in this matter.]

Psalm 120.—If you must appear before the judge, repeat the Psalm beforehand, and you will receive grace and favor.

If a traveler should find himself in a forest infested with many poisonous snakes, scorpions and other poisonous reptiles as may easily happen, and thus be exposed to danger, let him pray this Psalm as soon as he comes in sight of the forest seven times, and he will be able to proceed on his journey without any harm.

Psalm 121.—Are you compelled to travel alone by night, pray this Psalm reverently seven times, and you will be safe from all accidents and evil occurrences.

Psalm 122.—If you are about to address a man high in station, repeat this Psalm thirteen times beforehand, and you will be received graciously and find favor. Also, pray this Psalm each time that you are present in church, and you will obtain a blessing.

Psalm 123.—If your servant or journeyman has run away from you, write this Psalm, together with his name, on a leaden or tin plate, when he will return to you.

Psalm 124.—If you are about to cross a swollen stream, or undertake a journey by water, pray this Psalm before entering the ship, and then you may commence your journey without fear.

Psalm 125.—If you are compelled to travel in a country, where you have avowed enemies whom you have reason to fear on account of threatened injury to yourself, then take, before entering the country, both your hands full of salt, pronounce this Psalm seven times over it, and then scatter it into the air toward the four quarters of the globe, and by so doing, not one of your enemies will be able to bring any harm against you.

Psalm 126.—Are you so unfortunate, that your children are taken away from you in their infancy, and that you are not able to raise any of them, then, when your wife again becomes pregnant, write this Psalm upon four amulets made out of clean parchment, and add to the last line of each amulet the names of the following angels: Sinui, Sinsuni, and Semanglaf, and afterward hide the amulets in the four walls of your house, when your child will live.

Psalm 127.—Write this Psalm upon pure parchment. place this amulet in a clean bag, and hang it about the neck of a newborn son immediately after birth, and no evil will ever befall him afterward.

Psalm 128.—Write this Psalm upon clean parchment, and hang it upon a pregnant woman, when she and the fruit of her body will always be secure from unlucky accidents, and she will have a fortunate confinement.

Psalm 129.—Whoever accustoms himself to repeat the Psalm daily after the morning prayer, will finally prepare himself to live piously and virtuously, and will be able to carry out many remunerative and good works.

Psalm 130.—If you are living in a besieged city, to and from which no one can go without danger, and if you have urgent business, so that you feel constrained to venture on a journey, then, just as you are about to leave the city, pray this Psalm in a low and abjuring voice toward the four quarters of the earth, and then you will be able to pass all the sentries without being seen or harmed. A heavy sleep will overcome them, so that they will not be conscious of your presence.

Psalm 131.—He who is so strongly possessed of the evil spirit of pride that he regards all other people with scorn, but who, upon sober reflection, desires to occupy a middle path, if his intolerable pride would only permit him, is advised to pray this Psalm reverently three times daily, after the morning and evening prayer. His pride will receive a certain check.

Psalm 132.—if you have sworn to perform anything punctually, and notwithstanding your oath you neglect to perform your obligation, and in this manner have perjured himself, you should, in order to avoid a future crime of a similar kind, pray this Psalm daily with profound reverence.

Psalm 133.—Whoever prays this Psalm daily, will not only retain the love and friendship of his friends, but he will also gain many more friends.

Psalm 134.—This very short Psalm, consisting of only three verses, should be repeated by every learned man, and especially by every student before entering college.

Psalm 135.—Whoever is desirous of repenting sincerely from sin, and of consecrating his life to the service of God, should pray this Psalm daily after the morning and evening prayers, and then his heart and spirit will be daily renewed, and he will become more closely united with God from day to day.

Psalm 136.—Whosoever desires, on account of wilful sins and transgressions, to make a penitent confession of his misdeeds, should pray this Psalm beforehand, and then make his confession with an humble and broken heart and with great reverence.

Psalm 137.—The praying of this Psalm, it is said, will root out of the heart the most inveterate hate, envy and malice.

Psalm 138.—Praying this Psalm, it is stated, will produce love and friendship.

Psalm 189.—This Psalm should be prayed to increase and preserve love among married people.

Psalm 140.—Praying this Psalm, is said to be a powerful means to remove growing hatred between man and wife.

Psalm 141.—Whoever is often oppressed with heartfelt fears should pray this Psalm frequently.

Psalms 142 and 143.—Praying of the first of these two Psalms will cure pain in the thighs, and praying the other will remove tearing pains in the arms.

Psalm 144.—When any one breaks an arm this Psalm should be prayed, and the perfect cure of the arm cannot be delayed or interrupted by untoward circumstances.

Psalm 145.—He who fears ghosts and evil spirits, should pray this Psalm in connection with the 144th, with reverence, for the praying of these Psalms will drive away all ghosts and apparitions instantly.

Psalm 146.—Whoever has been dangerously wounded by a sword or other deadly weapon, he shall, during the time he is receiving surgical assistance, pray this Psalm reverently daily, and especially when the wound is being dressed and the bandages renewed, and he will shortly find reason to rejoice in a perfect restoration from his injuries.

Psalm 147.—For the cure of dangerous and deadly wounds, bites, stings of a salamander, lizard, snake, scorpion or other poisonous reptile, the earnest prayer of this Psalm is said to possess the same power of healing as the former Psalm, already described.

Psalms 148 and 149.—These two Psalms are said to possess the desirable virtue of checking fire, when they are prayed in childlike trust on the unfailing help of the Almighty.

Psalm 150.—This happy Psalm of Praise should be uttered by every God fearing, thankful being, after having escaped a great danger, or received a peculiar grace in answer to a prayer to the Lord of Hosts, and it should be repeated with a thankful heart to His praise and glory.

END OF THE PSALMS.

SUPPLEMENT.

Finally, the author adds the following as a supplement:

I.

Whoever prays the five appended verses daily and hourly to God, will receive grace from God and man, and will obtain prosperity and blessing in all his undertakings.

The verses must be spoken in the following order:

Psalm cxxi. verse 2; Psalm lv. verse 23; Psalm xxxvii. verse 37; Psalm xxxvii. verse 3; Psalm cxviii. verse 13

II.

A truly mysterious wonder-working formula is contributed by the celebrated Kabalist Raf Amram, which is said to possess the especial virtue to protect and defend him, who, after the morning prayer, prays it with proper reverence during a whole day of twenty-four hours, whether at home or on a journey, from all evil power or accident, from robbery, murder, and injury by guns, or other weapons. No man will be able to attack him or to injure him, and no gun can harm him. This wonderful saying is as follows:

See and know, that I am He! I am He, and besides me there is no other God. I am He, who can kill and make alive; I wound, and I am he that can heal, and no one can escape my hand or my power. For I stretch out my hand toward heaven (that is, I swear by heaven), and say: I am He that liveth forever.

Animon, Animon, Alimon, Kirvtip, Taftian! The Lord can and will watch and keep, Amen. After a man has uttered this three times in succession, and with it has kept in mind the three names of angels added thereto, he should say the following: Happy art thou people of God! Who is like unto thee; a people whose help is Jehovah. He is the breastplate of thy help, and the strong sword of thy pride. Thy enemies will deny themselves before thee (that is, will hide themselves or retreat from thee), but thou wilt stand in their high places. Lord of the earth let it be agreeable to thy holy will to command thy angels to protect me and defend me in all my ways. Amen!

Remarks by the Translator.

The above Hebrew words are Kabalistic names of angels, and are very hard to understand, and yet harder to translate. Thus for example, the letters of the word Alimon, mean Eel Leolam, Jehovah, Melech Waaed, Netzach, that is, Jehovah is an eternal God! he is a victorious king to all eternity. This prince or king according to the belief of Kabalists, is entrusted with the superintendency of all weapons and guns in the whole world, for the letters of the word Alimon, according to the signification of numbers aggregate 137, and the two small words Klo Sajin, under which all kinds of guns and weapons are understood, likewise contained, according to the signification of number, 137 letters, viz:

Aleph	 1	Beth	 20
Lamed	 30	Lamed	 30
Jod	 10	Jod	 0
Mim	 40	Zani	 7
Vav	 6	Jod	 10
Nra	 50	Jod	 10
	———	Nun	 50
	137		———
			137

According to this, there are under the power of this field-general all cannons, howitzers, mortars, guns, rifles, pistols, all lances, spears, sabres, swords, and dirks in the whole world, and whenever he thinks proper, none of these will be able to do the least harm. Whoever, therefore, knows how to obtain the favor of the mighty Alemon, it will be very easy for him to make himself invulnerable against gun-shot wounds and against sharp instruments of all kinds. The words Reivtip and Tafthi are also full of mysterious meaning and are the names of two angels who are servants of Alimon.

The letters of the holy name Animon, are contained in the words Ani, Nelech, Raaed, Ne-Zachim, that is, I am King from Eternity to Eternity! Generally this angel claims a much higher rank than the angel Alimon, for he is first named, and is called upon twice in succession, through which he takes, according to the signification of numbers 314, letters, or as many as the holy name of the Schadai, the name of the Almighty.

III.

I here present you (writes the celebrated Rabbi and great Kabalist Moses, son of Nochman, who is also known as Ramban), a great and useful remedy, Leraue, Weacuo, Nirch, which means, that a man, (especially upon a journey) may see everything and yet remain invisible himself. It is said, that through this mysterious means a man may be able to see and know all watching or hidden enemies, persecutors, thieves, robbers and murderers, without being seen by them, and he may remain invisible to them. This means has been tried and tested, says the author, " and I have tried it myself on occasions and at places where my life and limbs were in danger, and at each trial, with the help of God, I escaped without injury. It is truly a blessed remedy! you must know, however, that the power of this means will last only from the morning until after vespers. (evening prayer.)

THE REMEDY IS:

After you have offered your devoted traveling prayer to God, early before commencing your journey, leave your lodging or dwelling, and when you arrive on the highway upon which you intend to travel, stand still and cover your eyes with the fingers of your right hand in the following manner : Lay the index finger on the right eye, the middle finger on the nose, and the third finger on the left eye, and then say three times: Through the word of Almighty God. But then also the following passages from the holy scriptures, Genesis, chap. i. verse 1 : "In the beginning God created heaven and earth." Deuteronomy, chap. xxxiv. and last verse: "And in all that mighty hand, and in all the great terror which Moses showed in the sight of all Israel." Genesis, chap. xxxii. 1, 2. "And Jacob went on his way, and the angels of God met him. And when Jacob saw them, he said, This is God's host, and he called the name of that place Mahanaim," that is, two hosts or camps, namely, God's and his own. Deuteronomy, chap. xxxii. 1, 2: "Give ear, O ye heavens, and I will speak; and hear, O earth, the words of my mouth. My doctrine shall drop as the rain, my speech shall distil as the dew, as the small rain upon the tender herb, and as the showers upon the grass." Numbers, chap. x. verse 35. And it came to pass, when the ark set forward, that Moses said, Rise up, Lord, and let thine enemies be scattered, and let them that hate thee flee before thee. And when it rested, he said, Return, O Lord, unto the many thousands of Israel." Numbers, chap. ii. verse 6. "And his host, and those that were numbered thereof, were fifty and four thousand and four hundred. All that were mustered of the camp of Ephraim were a hundred thousand, and eight thousand and a hundred throughout their armies, and they shall go forward in the third rank." Here follow several single verses from the Psalms, namely : Psalm xlvi. 46: "The God of hosts is with us; the God of Jacob is our refuge." "Lord of hosts! blessed is the man whose dependence is upon thee." "Help Lord! the King will hear us, when we call upon him." "Jehovah will give might unto his people, the Lord will bless his people in peace." Psalm xix. 14: "Let the words of my mouth, and the meditation of my heart be acceptable in thy sight, O Lord, my strength and my redeemer." And now take your fingers from your eyes, and repeat the following Psalms with devotion—Psalm cxxi.; Psalm lxvii. and Psalm xci.—combined with the last verse of the 90th Psalm, and repeat the last verse of the 91st Psalm twice. Have you strictly complied with all the instructions in the mighty protection of God, and you may proceed securely and without fear, for no evil will befall you, and neither robbers nor murderers will attack you.

IV.

Here is another mysterious means of protection for travelers furnished by this author, but in a different manner. If you should see, says Ramban, in a dangerous locality, (for example, in forest, or wilderness), heathens, robbers, or hostile troops approaching you stand suddenly still, make a circle around you, and repeat from Exodus, chap. xi. verse 8: "And all these thy servants shall come down unto me, and bow themselves unto me, saying, Get thee out, and all the people that follow thee, and after that I will go out."

ASTROLOGICAL INFLUENCE UPON MAN

—AND—

MAGICAL CURES

OF THE

OLD HEBREWS.

[From Dr. Gideon Brechee's work: "The Transcendental, Magic and Magical Healing Art in the Talmud." Vienna: 1850.]

ASTROLOGICAL INFLUENCES.

THAT the Cosmos constitutes an organic whole, whose separate parts operate upon and in opposition to each other, was well known to the ancients. Man, as the highest individuality on the earth, which served the ancients as the centre of the universe, reflects in his being as a microcosm, the macrocosm. The book of Jeziro (a division of the Talmud), accordingly parallelizes three factors of the Cosmos, namely, the earth, time and man, corresponding with the cardinal numbers and the elements of words (letters). In that place it is said: Three principal letters, Aleph, Mem, Schin, correspond in the earth with air, water and fire; in man with the breast, belly and head; in the year with mild temperature, cold and heat. The seven compound letters, Beth, Gimmel, Daleth, Khaf, Pe, Resch and Tau correspond in the earth with Saturn, Jupiter, Mars, Sun, Venus, Mercury and Moon; in man with wisdom, riches, dominion, life, amativeness, blessing of children and peace; in the year to Saturday, Thursday, Tuesday, Sunday, Friday, Wednesday and Monday. The remaining twelve simple letters correspond in the world with Aries, the Bull, the Twins, the Crab, the Lion, the Virgin, the Balance, the Scorpion, the Bowman, the Goat, the Waterman, the Fishes; in man, the organs of sight, hearing, smelling, speaking, tasting, copulating, to put things in motion (the hands), to feel anger, to laugh, and to sleep; and in the year to the twelve months. The Tali with the boundary of the earth, the book of Jeziro states further, is like unto a king upon his throne. The spheres of the years is like a king in the country; the heart of man is like unto a king in battle.

The Tali, the ecliptic, and the heart, are the points of concentration and digression of the primum mevens of the Makro and Microcosm

The Tali, already mentioned, is declared by all the ancients, and among others by Rabbi Jehuda Hallawi, to be the Dragon known in astronomy which the Arabs call Bashar. (The supposition is that it is the eccentric orbit of the moon against the orbit of the sun.) The Gymnosophists termed the distance of the moon at the point of her intersection in the ecliptic, Patona Chandera: "The offended dragon" which, however, seems impossible, for the book of Jeziro gives the Tali as the primum novens of the whole universe. It would be more reasonable to understand by it an assumed zone outside of the zodiac, on which account it appears like a king upon a throne who holds all the threads of the combined kingdom in his hands. Accordingly the Tali can be nothing else than the world serpent Seschat (Adischen Wasughl) of the ancient Hindoos, which served them as a symbol of the Divine protection and of eternity.

We have much less to do with the question how man as the Microcosm, through his spiritual powers, which he can bring into action through his will and through the mighty word operates on the whole universe, than with the physical and especially with the magical influence of the whole universe upon man as the part of nature.

Even Rabbi Jehuda Haleni calls attention to the wonderful phenomenon that even the elements and powers of nature which contribute to the maintenance of the human organism which man receives within himself, transforms and assimilates to reproduce the wasted particles of his body, and by which he preserves his corporeal integrity, that even these elements after a certain cycle of years, will exercise on their part an inimical and destructive influence upon the human organization, until man dissolves through an individual death, and he returns again unto the elements and chemistry of the general matter of nature. Admitting this constant struggle of man with surrounding nature, the book of Jeziro compares as already stated, the heart, as the fountain of life, to a king in battle, who in the beginning overpowers and subdues his enemies, but who notwithstanding, succumbs to the strife in the end.

That the whole universe, the sun, the moon, and the rest of the planets and heavenly bodies exercise a certain influence upon the earth, and consequently upon man as a part of it, and thus produce many and diversified effects, was no uncommon conclusion on the part of the ancients, for they were led to these conclusions by obvious visions and appearances, and they were compelled to discover the sidereal influences by close observation. The moon, especially, with her periods of twenty seven and twenty-eight days, made her influence upon man and his condition felt in an unmistakable manner. Among these may be classed, menstruation in women, the different phases of worm diseases according to the different phases of the moon, the increase and decrease of certain cutaneous diseases, etc., after these phases; the influence of the moon upon certain bodily diseases. Reil mentions, that the influence of the moon in causing dysentery has been recognized by many eminent physicians, who, it is said, have observed that the attacks of dysentery are more frequent in new moon and full moon than at any other periods. Others declare that pestilence is much more severe at the time of new moon. The Brahmins also give warning against the new moon. Kant says: "It is a strong argument in favor of the hypothesis, that the moon influences diseases, from the fact that the deaths from fever in Bengal were greatly multiplied during an eclipse of the sun, etc., because the attraction of the moon at this time unites with that of the sun, whose power to operate upon bodies on the earth has been established beyond a cavil." Finally, belong in this place the critical days, and the moon's power of attraction upon travelers by night.

The influence of the light of the sun and the moon upon humanity must have been evident in the earliest period, and it was soon admitted that it affected mightily both the well-being of man, and his frame of mind, as well as the exhibitions of the various temperaments. This knowledge was extended by observation of local diseases during the different seasons of the year and the changes in the weather, the beneficial effect of the rays of the sun in painful and diseased parts of the body, and the influence of daytime upon births and deaths. Acknowledging the injurious effects of the sun and moon, the Psalmist says: "The sun will not harm by day, neither the moon by night." The Talmud ascribes healing powers to the sun. Abail says: The prophet speaks of the healing sun, for the rays of the sun possess healing powers. The Talmud says: "God hung a precious stone around the neck of Abraham; all they that were sick and gazed thereon became well." But after Abraham died, God took the precious stone and hung it up in the sphere of the sun.

But the Ancients also recognized a physical influence of the rest of the planets and the whole host of stars upon man. The belief that the heavenly bodies were gifted with life, and that they with being endowed with higher powers, could exercise an influence upon man by means of mysterious magical influences could regulate his temperament, his disposition and his term of life, was spread from the Ganges to the Tiber and to the pillars of Hercules. The Talmud likewise teaches this astrological faith, with this difference, that the Israelite is placed under the immediate guidance of God, and notwithstanding the iron astrological necessity and predestination, concedes the possibility, that through the omnipotence of God good may be brought about in spite of the constellations. This is expressed in the Talmud by the words: "The Israelite has no constellation." Rabbi Joham successfully establishes this fact against Rabbi Chanina, who asserts that, "Wisdom and riches are the gifts of the constellations;" for says Rabbi Joham, it is recorded in Jeremiah x. 2: "Be not afraid of the heavenly signs as the Heathens who fear them." Rab says: Abraham spake before God: Lord of the earth! shall my servant be my heir? God said: No, thy son shall be thy heir. Abraham answered: My horoscope has shown me that I shall be childless. Then spake God and said: Get thee away from thy astrology, the Israelite is not subjected to the constellations.

On the writing table of Rabbi Jeheschna was found written, says the Talmud: "Whoever is born on Sunday will be distinguished above others." Upon this Rabbi Asche says: Both Dime bar Kakustha and I were born on a Sunday; I became the principal of a school, and he became a captain of robbers. Light and darkness were created on the Sabbath. He who is born on Monday will always be a passionate man, for on this day the waters were divided. Whoever is born on Tuesday will become

rich and given to pleasure; on this day all herbs were created. Whoever is born on Wednesday will be wise and happy : on this day the stars
of the firmament were created. He who is born on Thursday will be
constantly employed in works of love. Whoever is born on Friday will
become active in good works. Whoever is born on the Sabbath will also
die on the Sabbath, because the Sabbath was desecrated on his account.
Raba, the Rabbi Schila adds : He will be called holy. Chancna said to
his pupils : Go to the son of Levi, and say : Not the constellation of the
day has an influence but the stars of the hour of birth. He that is born
under the influence of the sun is gifted with beauty, eats and drinks of his
own possessions, but his secrets will become known ; should he become a
thief, he will be unlucky. If any one is born under the influence of Venus, he will become rich and voluptuous, because the (fire) of love is
born in him. He who is born under the influence of Mercury will become enlightened and prudent, because Mercury is the secretary of the
sun. He who is born under the influence of the moon will learn to bear
hardships. He builds and moves in, moves in and builds, eat and drinks
of the possessions of the stranger; his secrets remain hidden, and as a
thief he will be fortunate : he who is born under Mercury will find all his
plans perverted and defeated. The plans of others against him, however,
will also be defeated. Whoever is born under the influence of Jupiter
will become a just man. He who is born under the influence of Mars
will become a shedder of blood. Rabbi Asche asserts this. He will
either become a robber or a butcher. Abam adds, or a judge.

We observe that the Talmud regards the sidereal nature of man as a
hypo-tatical being of itself. This siderealism, preëxisting in the constellation of man, he denominates Masol. The most distinguished persons
were their own star, and thus, according to the Talmud, the star of the
field-general Sisra was called Meroz. Judges v. 23. The siderealism of
the proselytes was present at Sinai.

Upon the constellation, says Raba, depend—the blessing of children,
longevity, success in life. Job cursed his constellations. Since the fate
of man is fixed beforehand by the constellation, no injury can take effect
upon him, neither can an accidental death come upon him. If, therefore,
a man meet serpents or scorpions by which he is attacked, if he destroys
them, then let him be assured that they were predestined to be destroyed
by him, although he may regard the act as a miracle.

Beings who are born under the same constellation stand in close relation and magical sympathy with each other. The Talmud even sets up a
problem from these premises as to whether such persons have the same
marks, as moles, for instance.

The conjunction of the planets, eclipse of the sun and moon, exercise a
great influence upon vegetables and upon man. Samuel teaches when
the spring equinox happens upon the hour of Jupiter, the strength of the
fruit tree will be broken. Should the winter solstice fall upon the hour
of Jupiter, then the grain will wither; but with this the new moon must
also fall upon the hour of Jupiter or the moon. The first hour of Saturday
evening (between six and seven o'clock) is that of Mercury. The second
is that of the Moon. The third that of Saturn. The fourth that of Ju-

piter. The fifth that of Mars. The sixth that of the Sun. The seventh that of Venus. The eighth hour, again, is that of Mercury, etc.

The Rabbis teach: That an eclipse of the sun is an evil sign for all people. It is as if a king prepared a feast for his subjects, and placed before them a brilliant light; should he be angry with his subjects, however, he commands his servants to remove the light, in order that they might be in darkness. Rabbi Meir taught, that eclipses of the heavenly bodies were an evil sign, for the Israelites especially, because they were accustomed to misfortune. If the master enters the school with a rod in his hand, who is afraid? only he who receives daily punishment. The Rabbis teach, that an eclipse of the sun is an evil sign also for the rest of the nations; an eclipse of moon for the Israelites, for they reckon their time from the moon and other nations from the sun. If the eclipse is in the East, it is an evil omen for the inhabitants of the East; if in the western heavens, then it is an evil omen for the inhabitants of the West; if in the middle of the firmament, it is a bad sign for all the inhabitants of the earth. When the sun appears blood red it portends war. If the sun has a greyish appearance it is a sign of famine. When an eclipse occurs at sundown it is a sign that the Judgment is yet far off; if at sunrise, it is an omen of the near approach of the Judgment. According to others, these omens signify the reverse of what is stated above. A general calamity never overtakes a people in which their heavenly prince (protecting spirit) does not suffer defeat with them. If, however, Israel walks according to the will of God, it will have nothing to fear of this kind.

The Rabbis teach further: On account of sin the sun will be darkened when the presiding judge dies, and is not properly mourned; when a young woman in a city, who is engaged, cries in vain for help when violence is offered to her; and on account of the simultaneous murder of two brothers. The other heavenly lights will be darkened on account of the making of counterfeit money; on account of false witness; when forcible possession is taken of a stranger's property, or when fruit trees are unnecessarily cut down.

To this belongs the dies nefasti, in regard to which we give the following passages from the Talmud:

Samuel teaches, that the time for blessing is Sunday, Wednesday and Friday. No man should allow himself to be bled on Monday or Thursday, for Mars says: Only he who can enjoy the savings of his parents should be bled on Monday and on Thursday, because on both these days the earthly and the heavenly courts are in session. On Tuesday a man should not be bled, because on this day Mars rules the hour. Racht explains this in the following manner: Mars has the supervision over wars, pestilence and all kinds of accidents. The paired (exact) number is likewise an ominous omen, since with it the demons have power (Pessach 110), and accidents are imminent. The order of the planets is: Saturn, Jupiter, Mars, Sun, Venus, Mercury, Moon. The order of hours in which they rule, begins with the creation of the heavenly lights, namely, in the first hour Wednesday (with us between six and seven o'clock). In this hour Saturn rules, in the second Jupiter; in the third, Mars, etc., thus seven planets in seven hours. This cycle continues forever. According to this order we find that the planets rule in the first hour of each night in the following order: Mercury, Jupiter, Venus, Saturn, Sun, Moon, Mars, namely, in the first hour at the close of Sunday. Mercury, the first hour of the night on Monday; Jupiter, etc. According to this order, in the first hours of the week days are ruled further by the Sun, Moon, Mars, Mercury, Jupiter, Venus, Saturn. The first hour, on Sunday morning is ruled by the sun; the first hour on Monday by the moon, and Tuesday morning by Mars. Mars will rule again on the same day in the eighth hour, a direct hour. On other days his rule will not occur on a direct hour, but only during the night when it is not customary to be bled. Upon the remark of the Talmud that Mars rules in a direct hour on Friday, Raschi says: In the first hour on Friday Venus rules. This planet is followed in regular order by Mercury, Moon, Saturn, Jupiter and Mars. The last rules also in the sixth hour. upon follows the answer, that on Saturday many people are in the habit of being bled, and " God protects the simple."

Samuel teaches further, that he who is the fourth, fourteenth, or twenty-fourth, cannot be bled with safety, that is, on a Wednesday fourth, fourteenth and twenty fourth of the month. So likewise on a fourth, which has no four after it, that is, on a Wednesday after which no four days will intervene until new moon. At new moon, and three days thereafter, bleeding is enervating; on the third day after new moon it is known to be dangerous.

OF MAGICAL REMEDIES IN GENERAL.

As in the ancient world diseases were regarded as the work of the angry gods and malicious demons, so there were, as in the present day by nations in a state of nature, but few magical remedies employed to secure the assistance of demons or to render them harmless.

Sanchuniaton declares that the children of the Kabirists could heal the venomous bite by their songs. The Brahmins regarded diseases as a punishment for sins committed in the present life or in earlier life. The cures consisted of expiation through prayer, alms, exorcisms, but also rational means. The Vedas contain hymns and prayers, to which magical powers are ascribed, and on this account they are used, without understanding them, as forms of exorcism. All diseases, says the Brahmin, are the result of evil demons, and can only be healed by purification, through sorcery. Ormuzd awakened the great prophet Hom, from whom all the magicians originated. He healed all diseases through the word of Ormuzd and by a plant that bears his name. Many cures, it is said in the /ten books, are brought about by means of trees and herbs, others through the agency of the knife, others through the world, but perfect cures result only through the Divine Word. Even if the old Greeks cured with natural means, the common people still believed that a rapid convalescence was obtained through magical formulas, songs and incantations. The medical heroes of the Grecian primitive world were at the same time poets, lawgivers, generals and astronomers.

Of the cures of spiritual men and prophets we have already spoken. The prophets were unanimous in applying natural means, prayer and blessing. Rabbi Jitzchak said: Four things destroy the evil passions of man, namely, alms, prayer, change of name, and repentance. According to other authors, also, change of place. Josephus writes in reference to king Chiskia, God gave him the power, through fervent adjurations, to reconcile the Deity, and to cast out the evil spirits which are the cause of evil diseases; and this method of healing, continues Josephus, is the prevailing one among us at the present day. Josephus adds: I was an eye-witness to a cure which the prophet Eleazar, in the presence of the Emperor Vespasian, performed upon a man possessed of demons. He made use of a root that was recommended by King Solomon as being effectual against demoniacal disease, when the root was inserted into the nose of the patient, at the same time pronouncing the name of Solomon and the magical formula which this king taught. The Gnostics herein followed the example of the prophets. The theosophical-medical sect of the Escucans sought out the power of roots, herbs and stones for healing purposes, and at the same time attempted to heal diseases by living a devout life and by a total surrender of themselves into the idea of God, and by this means they also sought to perform wonders. The substantial word of God, which, as a mark of preference is called the Angel, the Monas, World of Light, Bread of Life, First Born of all Creatures, the Physician of all diseases, lives in the Epopts and causes them to partake of the Divine nature, so that they may heal diseases and perform wonders of all kinds. The magical Logos, who derives his analogy or origin from the exalted and holy word Oum of the Brahmins, we find again in the Book of Jeriza, where we read (i. 8): "One, the Spirit of the Living God, voice and Spirit and word." "And this is the Holy Spirit." The Divine number, the Divine Word, the Divine Scriptures, says Rabbi Jehuda Halcive, in his illustration of the Book Jezira, is one and the same with the reality. That which God thinks and wills has at the same time reality. Only man makes a distinction between the will and the act; with God these two are identical. Rabbi Jehudah Halewi continues: "We can form some conception of this when we, in thinking of and pronouncing a name, at the same time form an image of the subject named in our minds. Among the languages and writings this peculiarity may be noticed, that some specify the existence of things particularly, while others do so in a general manner. The holy language, however, with which God called the universe into being, demonstrates the prime existence of all things with the utmost definiteness. Whoever, therefore, is acquainted with the original signification of the scriptures, and grasps with pure thought the existence of the thing intended, he can, in accordance with his thoughts and his will, will the things into being. Thorough knowledge of the holy word and of the transposition of its letters may, as the Taimud says, enable man to perform wonders and even create things. Rabbi Jonathan says: "The time will come when the pious will bring the dead to life." Raha says: "If the pious desire to do so, they can create a world." It is reported of this Rabbi that he created a man, and of the Rabbis Chanina and Oschaja, that they were occupied every Friday with the book of Jezira, and that they created a fatted calf which they consumed. Gechasie caused the golden image of the bull to speak, by imprinting upon his lips a "name." Solomon gave to Benajahn ben Jehojada a chain and a seal upon both of which he engraved a "name" with which to bind the demon king Asmedi. Of Bezalel, the builder of the temple tent in the wilderness, it is said: "He understood the transposition of letters by which heaven and earth were created." Abischai uttered a holy name, and thereby suspended David between heaven and earth.

The word which expresses the being of the prototypes and the idea of the intelligentia may operate through these through the whole chain of being down to the most minute, causing changes, reverses and new creations, and may also conquer demons. "Rabbi Chanina bar Papi was required by a matron who became enamored of him, to fulfil her amorous desires. He uttered something, and his body was covered with scabs and boils. She also did something and he became whole; then he fled and concealed himself," etc.

But since there are holy words, whose literal ideas and their transpositions are countless modifications of existence, so there are also unholy words which give the prototypes of the dark side of the spirit world. And now, if the profane use of the holy name is forbidden upon pain of losing future happiness, so the use of unholy names, which Abraham transmitted to the children of his concubines is the most terrible, because they lead to the sins of idolatry, through which man acquires evil principles and becomes possessed of demons.

The Talmud, in general, forbids sorcery, heathen superstition and heathen usages. To these belong the charming of wounds and injuries, with which, notwithstanding the exorcism, a verse of the Bible was made use of; the charming of snakes and scorpions. The following usages especially, were given as being heathenish. 1. To suspend the egg of a grasshopper on the ear to cure earache. 2. To carry the tooth of a fox to promote sleep; the tooth of a dead fox was used to prevent drowsiness, and the tooth of a living fox caused sleep. 3. The bearing of the splinter from a gallows, to cure a wound caused by iron. 4. The proverb, "Good fortune! and be not weary day nor night," probably a saying to obtain good luck. "Gad" means luck, and it is the name of the idol Belus (Isaiah lxv. 11). 5. In order to obtain good luck the man assumes the name of the woman, and the woman the name of the man. 6. The saying, "Be strong, O my barrels!" to increase the wine blessing— Dan is the name of an idol. (Amos viii. 14.) 7. To have luck, people call to the male raven: "Shriek!" and to the female raven: "Croak!" and turn unto me your tail for luck. 8. If any one says: "Kill this cock, for he crows late in the evening, or kill this hen, for she crows like a cock." 9. I drink and leave some over; I drink and leave some over (so that the wine may increase). 10. Whoever dashes the shells of eggs against the wall (out of which the young chickens have already crept, so that they may not die). 11. He who stirs in a crock before the young chickens for the same purpose. 12. Whoever, for the same purpose dances before the chickens and counts seventy-one chickens. 13. Dancing during the preparation of a meal. To command silence during the boiling of the lentil. To cry out during the boiling of grain. To urinate before the pot to facilitate cooking.

Rabbi Acha says: Before bleeding we should repeat the following prayer: May it be thy will, O Lord! that this healing operation may hasten my convalescence, etc., for no one should seek the assistance of the physician, but should look for a return of health only to God. To this Aliae objects, because Rabbi Jischmael teaches, and because he deduces from the Thora (Exodus xxi. 19). The physician shall have an unconditional right to heal. The Talmud not only adopts this view of Alaie's but it forbade to dwell in a place where no physician could be met with. If again, on the other hand, we read in the Talmud that King Chiskia, suffered the Book of Healing to be destroyed, and for this act was praised by the Rabbis, then that book, as is supposed by Maimonides, contained simply superstitious astrological and idolatrous remedies, which the pious king sought to consign to oblivion, of which, however, a large portion found their way into the hands of the people, and in time also became a common benefit to the more enlightened.

OF THE MAGICAL CURES IN PARTICULAR.

1.—HEALING BY AMULETS.

The amulet Kamea was used as a remedy against diseases and especially against sorcery. This amulet was either a written parchment, properly called Pitka, or a small bundle of plants. The words written on the amulet were of a diversified character; among the contents, however, were to be found verses from the Bible. Proof *** is called an amulet, since cures have been effected through it three times, whether it was written or whether it consisted of roots. In reference to the Sabbath (whether or not it might be worn on that day or not), it must still be regarded as reliable, because it was made and perfected by a connoisseur. An amulet may prove effectual in healing a human being, while it is of no effect in the case of an animal, because in man the constellation operates in conjunction with the amulet. If it is expected to be effectual, it must have reference to the name and number of the demon. Thus, for example, the demons of the caper-tree are called spirits; of a service-tree, Schedim; in the gardens, Rispe. At the caper-tree not less than sixty Schedim congregate, and the amulet must therefore have reference to this number.

A string made of the seeds of the madder was hung upon children as a protection against certain diseases. The nurse of Abbaii taught him Three grains will check the disease, five will cure, and seven will prove effectual against sorcery. Rabbi Acha bar Jacob remarks: The last is true only when the bewitched person is not exposed to the light of the sun or moon, or to rain, and when he does not hear the ringing of iron the crowing of the cock, or the sound of footsteps. Rabbi Nachmann bar Jitzchak says that this remedy was already forgotten in his time.

2.—HEALING BY CHARMS.

The nurse of Abbaii taught him: "All numbering (naming?) shoul be done in the name of the mother (N. son of R.), and all external passages must be made on the left side of the body. Abbaii says farther: If the number is fixed it should be strictly adhered to without deviation; if the number is not fixed, it is forty-one.

As anti-heathenish customs the four following things are allowed: 1 To place the splinter of a mulberry-tree or fragments of glass into the pot, in order to make the mess boil more readily. (The Rabbis, however, forbade the fragment of glass on account of the danger of swallowing in with the food.) 2. The drinking toast: Wine and life cheer the Rabbis! Rabbi Akiba repeated this toast with every vessel of wine used at the marriage feast of his son. Against intoxication: Anoint the palms of the hand and the soles of the feet of the drunken person with a mixture of oil and salt, and say: As the ointment becomes pure, so may the senses become clean; or, lay the bung of a barrel in the water and say: As the bung becomes clean, etc.

Charm against suppuration: say for instance, Bas, Basia, Mas Masia, Kas, Kasia, Scharial and Amarlia, the angels, who came out of the land of Sodom to heal painful boils. Let the color not become redder; let it not spread further, let the seed be absorbed in the bowels. And as a mule does not propagate its species, so may this evil be not propagated in the body of N. son of R.

Charm against smallpox: For example; Drawn sword and pointed sling. His name is not Jacob, the pain rages.

Against being possessed, as follows: Cursed, crushed and banished be the demon, by name Bar Tet, Bor Tama, etc.

Charm against injury inflicted by demons of by-places: Upon the head of the lion, and in the nose of the lionesss, I found the demon Bar Schirk a Panda. I threw him into a fish-bed and slew him with the jawbone of an ass.

To make evil dreams good, three men recited certain consoling verses from the Bible. "Whosoever had a bad dream, should hasten in the morning, as soon as he awakens, to repeat a verse from the Bible, the contents of which should be favorable to him, and this must be done quickly, before a verse comes into the mind with an unfavorable meaning to him."

He that is upon the point of entering a city and fears the evil look, let him put his right thumb in his left hand, and his left thumb in his right hand, and say: I, N. N., am of the lineage of Joseph, over whom the evil eye can have no power. He makes the glance of the evil eye harmless; the tail of a fox was hung upon the horse.

3.—REMEDIES AND CHARMS AGAINST SORCERY.

Ben Asai says: Do not irritate your anus while sitting down in order to obtain a passage from the bowels, for he who does this will be attacked by sorcery, even though he were engaged in Spain. If a man, however, has done so in a mistake, after an evacuation, let him pronounce the following charm:

"Ye cannot approach, neither Tachimnor Tachtum, not all of you, not any of you, neither the enchantment of the sorcerer nor the charm of the sorceress.

Rabbi Chanina says: To drink one-eighth ounce of ass's milk, which is forty days old, is effective against the sting of a wasp; one quart against the sting of a scorpion; one-half quart against sorcery, and the drinking of fluids that have been open and exposed.

Rabbi Jochanan said: A chief among witches told me: If you meet witches you should utter the following charm: "Hot dirt, in perforated baskets, in your mouths, ye enchanting women. May your heads become bald; may the wind blow away your bread crumbs; may it scatter your spices; may the fresh saffron which ye have in your hands fly away. Witches! so long as men were gracious to me, and I was careful, I came not in your midst; now I did, and you are not agreeable to me."

The Rabbi taught: There are three things between which we should not pass, and so, also, that two persons walking side by side should not allow to come between them. These three things are—a dog, a palm, and a woman. Some add also a hog, and others, a snake. Should this happen notwithstanding, what shall a man do to escape uninjured? Rabbi Papi says: "Repeat a verse from the Bible that begins and ends with the same letters."

If women are seated facing each other on opposite sides of the street, there is no doubt that they are engaged in witchcraft. How shall a man escape them without injury? He should avoid them and go another way. If this is not possible, then he shall take some one by the hand and pass by in his company. If there is no one at hand, he must say: "The demons of sorcery have already been killed by arrows. A rat Assia, Belussia, are the names of the demons. Raschi."

The Rabbis teach: A man should not drink water in the night, either from a stream or from water that is standing still. Whoever does this, his blood be upon his own head, because by so doing he will render himself liable to become blind. How can we make drinking at night safe? If there is some one present he should be awakened and addressed as follows: "I drink water!" If you are alone, rattle with the lid of the drinking cup and say to yourself: "N., son of R., thy mother said to thee: Guard thyself against Schabriri, briri, riri, iri, ri, in a white pitcher (Raschi), this is a magical charm." As the syllables of the word Schabriri decrease, so the demon will withdraw. The Targum of blindness (Genesis xix. 11), in Schabriri.

In reference to paired numbers, of which we have already spoken, Rabbi Papa says: "Joseph, the Demon, told me that through two we kill, through four we only inflict injury. In the number two the evil will follow, whether we have done a thing in this number intentionally or accidentally. In the number four only when the thing is done intentionally. If we have accidentally partaken of a meal or drank out of a paired plate or pitcher, number, how shall we avoid the fatal consequences? We must take the thumb of the right hand into the left, and the thumb of the left into the right hand, and say: You and I make three. If answered, is returned: You and I make five. If we again hear the answer: You and I are six, we must again answer: You and I are seven. It happened that some one carried this on to the 101st time, until finally the demon burst with chagrin.

APPLICATION OF THE CHARMS AND THE REMEDIES.

We insert the passages of the Talmud which treat of the subject, on account of their coherence, in all that extent, although it may not properly belong in this place, because in several cases in the following remedies the natural cures as well as the magical charms are prescribed, and because these passages from the Talmud otherwise offer many interesting matters. They treat of proceedings against snakes and other remarkable occurrences.

He that has swallowed a snake, let him eat ivy and then walk three miles. Rabbi Sime bar Asche saw a man who had swallowed a snake. Rabbi Sime fell upon him like a warrior, gave him ivy and salt to eat, and then drove him three miles before him, when the snake came from him in pieces. Others state that Rabbi Sime himself swallowed the snake, when the prophet Eli came in the form of a wild warrior, gave him ivy and salt to eat, etc., etc.

If a man be bitten by a snake, let him take seventy-nine hairs from the tail of a white she-ass, tie them with a silken thread, and he that is bitten sit upon them. The she-ass must, however, have been free from Trefa (an organic disease). An official in Pumbedithat was bitten by a snake. Now, there were found in Pumbedithat thirteen bearing white she-asses, which were opened one after another, but all were found to have been afflicted with Trefa. It was also known that in a distant part of the city there was another she-ass, and messengers were sent to bring her. But meanwhile a lion had eaten up the she-ass. Then spoke Abaii: Perhaps the snake of the Rabbis have bitten him, against the bite of which there is no remedy. The pupils answered, Yes; so it is, master; for when Rab died, Rabbi Jitzsechak bar Bina prohibited the use of myrtle and palm leaves for a whole year. This officer, however, paid no attention to this prohibition.

If a snake should wind around a person, he should go into the water and take a basket which he should hold above the head of the snake, then lower the basket in such a manner that the rim of it shall come between him and the snake (to grasp the snake with the hands would be dangerous, because it might become enraged and wound the person). When the snake is in the basket, throw it quickly into the water and hasten away.

Should any one be pursued by an angry snake (where the snake follows the person by scenting his tracks) he should suffer himself to be carried a short distance by a person, if any one should be present (through the stranger's footsteps the snake will lose his tracks); if no one is with him he should spring across water or seat himself over a fountain. On the following night he should place himself upon four barrels, so that the snake cannot easily reach him, or let him rather sleep in the open air, so that it cannot come to him through the roof, then let him tie to the barrels and make a noise with straw or bushes, so that the the snake comes, may fall upon her and eat her up.

Should any one be pursued by a snake, let him seek safety between two beehives.

Rabbi Jochanan says: The root-drink described in the Mischna, consists of Alexandrian gum, pulverized alum and fine saffron, each of the weight of a Sus (a small coin). To cure jaundice two of them are taken in beer.

The following remedies are also recommended in cases of female weakness: Take the tops of three Persian onions, boil them in wine and let the woman drink of it, at the same time saying to her: Recover from thy sickness!

Another remedy: Take a handful of caraway, a handful of saffron, and an equal quantity of fœnugrek, boil them together in wine, and let the woman drink of it, saying: Recover from thy sickness!

Another remedy: Take sixty bungs of wine barrels, soak them in water, and give the woman of the water to drink, and say to her at the same time: Recover from thy sickness!

Or, take a quantity of the growth of tendrils, boil them in wine, and let the woman drink of it, and speak to her as above.

Or, take the plant that grows beside the thorn, and burn it to ashes. The woman should carry the ashes upon her person in a linen patch in the summer, or a woolen patch in the winter.

Or dig seven holes in the ground, and burn in each of them young grapevines not over three years' growth. Let the woman take a cup into her hands and seat herself over the first hole and drink: then rise up and seat herself upon the second hole, etc., etc. Each time speak to her: Recover, etc.

Or, anoint the lower part of her body with rose-water.

Or, take a wreath of feathers, burn them to ashes. These ashes the patient should carry in a linen bag in the summer, and in a woolen bag in the winter.

Or, open a cask of wine expressly for her. She should drink much wine.

Or, take a grain of barley that was found in the stable of a white she-ass. If she holds this one day in her hand (the right hand), the ailment will cease for two days. If she holds it during two days, it will cease for three days. If she holds it three days it will cease forever. According to others: if she takes one grain in her hand, etc.; if she takes two grains in her hand, etc.

5.—MAGICAL REMEDIES AGAINST VARIOUS DISEASES AND CONDITIONS.

ABORTUS.—The actitee (eaglestone, rattle-snake stone—stone of retaining, remaining) was worn by women as a prevention against abortion.

BLOOD-LETTING.—If you have eaten fish, you must not be bled on the following day. If you have been bled, you must not eat fish on the following day. On the third day both would be dangerous.

The Rabbis teach: After blood-letting, a man must not, on the same day, drink milk, eat cheese, onions or vegetables. If a man, however, has eaten of these things, he should mix, says Abaii, one quarter measure of vinegar, and one quarter measure of wine, and drink it. If a motion of the bowels ensues, the evacuation should take place without and on the east side of the town, for the exhalation of such is injurious.

DISEASES OF THE EYE.—The saliva of a firstborn on the male side (not of the female side) is effective in the cure of eye diseases.

RAB says: A degenerate eye is dangerous to life, for the vision-power of the eye is closely connected with the pericardium.

Rapid traveling impairs the sight of the eye; but it may be restored by uttering the blessing of consecration of the Sabbath on Friday evening.

BLINDNESS.—Against blindness at night, take a string made out of the hair of an animal; tie one end of it to the foot of the patient, and the other end to the foot of a dog, and then let the children make a noise behind the dog, and say: "Hold the dog, fool the rock." Then take seven pieces of meat from seven different houses, and let the inmates of each house hang a piece of the meat at the door-post of the patient. The dog must eat this meat in an open place. Then let the patient unbind the hair-line and let some one say; Night blindness of F., son of R., leave N., son of R., and perforate the pupil of the dog.

AGAINST DAY BLINDNESS.—Take seven pieces of spleen from seven heifers, and lay them upon the vessel used by the physician to catch the blood when bleeding a patient. The patient must be seated in a chamber. A man must be stationed on the outside, who must say: "Blind one! give to me that I may eat." The patient answers: "How can I open? Come in and eat!" After eating he must break the plate or he will himself become blind.

MIND POWER.—Rab says: The "Bird of the Vineyard" (mentioned in the Mischna) is found on the palm-tree having a single bark.

It is employed as a means to strengthen the mind. The right half of it must be eaten, and the left half of it must be preserved in a copper tube which must be sealed with sixty seals (with wax, putty, earth, etc.), and hung upon the left arm. Upon this a man obtains clearer ideas, and is enabled to comprehend matters with more ease. Afterward the other half should also be eaten, for if this be neglected, what has been learned will soon be forgotten.

THE SOFT-BOILED EGG.—Samuel says: A slave that knows how to prepare a soft-boiled egg is worth a thousand dollars. The egg must be handled thousands of times in warm as well as in cold water, until it becomes so small that it can be swallowed with a single effort. Whatever disease may be in the abdomen will be known to the physician through the decreasing egg, and he will at once know what remedy to prescibe.

FEVER.—The nurse of Samuel gave him the following remedies:

Against the Daily Fever: Take a new silver coin and a piece of salt of equal weight, and carry both over the pit of the heart, attached to a string.

Or, take a seat on a crossroad, and as soon as you observe a large ant carrying something, take her up and place her in a copper tube, close the opening with lead, and seal it with sixty seals, shake the tube and hand upon your body, and say to the ant: Thy burden upon me; and my burden upon thee.

Or, take a new earthen pipkin, go to a spring and say: Spring, Spring! lend me a pipkin full of water for the road that happens to me. Then swing the pipkin full of water seven times around your head, throw it backward and say: Spring, Spring! take the water you gave me, for the way that happened to me came in his day and departed in his day.

Rabbi Huna says: For fever recurring every three days, take seven different grapes from seven different grapevines, seven chips from seven joists, seven nails from seven bridges, seven small quantities of ashes from seven stoves, seven bits of earth from seven holes in the ground, seven pieces of pitch from seven ships, seven grains of cumin, seven hairs out of the beard of an old dog. Bind these all together and carry them with a string upon the nape of the neck.

Rabbi Jochanan says: For the burning fever, take a knife that is made entirely of iron, go to a thorn bush and tie a hair line to it. On the first day make a notch in it and say: "And there appeared unto him an angel of God in a flame of fire out of the midst of the burning bush." On the next day make another indentation and say: "Then God saw that he approached in order to see, etc." The following day make another indentation and say: "Come nigh, etc." Then cut the thorn off near the ground and say: O thornbush! O thornbush! I trust in thee!

THE END.

www.ingramcontent.com/pod-product-compliance
Lightning Source LLC
Chambersburg PA
CBHW030639150426
42813CB00050B/180